# WHAT IT MEANS TO BE HUMAN

# WHAT IT MEANS TO BE HUMAN

Essays in Philosophical Anthropology,
Political Philosophy and Social Psychology

edited by Ross Fitzgerald

Pergamon Press

Pergamon Press (Australia) Pty Ltd,
19a Boundary Street, Rushcutters Bay, N.S.W. 2011, Australia

Pergamon Press Ltd,
Headington Hill Hall, Oxford OX3 0BW, England

Pergamon Press Inc.,
Maxwell House, Fairview Park, Elmsford, N.Y. 10523, U.S.A.

Pergamon of Canada Ltd,
75 The East Mall, Toronto, Ontario M8Z 2L9, Canada

Pergamon Press GmbH,
6242 Kronberg/Taunus, Pferdstrasse 1, Federal Republic of Germany

Pergamon Press SARL,
24 rue des Ecoles, 75240 Paris, Cedex 05, France

First published 1978

© 1978 Ross Fitzgerald

Cover design by Allan Hondow
Typeset and printed in Australia by Academy Press Pty Ltd, Brisbane

National Library of Australia Cataloguing in Publication Data

What it means to be human.

   ISBN 0 08 023355 4 Paperback
   ISBN 0 08 023356 2

   1. Man. I. Fitzgerald, Ross, 1944–, ed.

128.3

'I'll tell you. It's bad to be less than human and it's bad to be more than human. What's more than human? . . . Can a god have diseases? . . . Does a statue have wax in its ears? Naturally not. It doesn't sweat, either . . . If I can talk myself into it that I never sweat and make everybody else act as if it was true, maybe I can fix it up about dying, too. We only know what it is to die because some people die and, if we make ourselves different from them, maybe we don't have to? Less than human is the other side of it . . . More than human, can you have any use for life? Less than human, you don't either. . .

' "You say less than human, more than human. Tell me, please, what is human?" . . . We study people so much now that after we look and look at human nature . . . after you look at it and weigh it and turn it over and put it under a microscope, you might say, "What is all the shouting about? A man is nothing, his life is nothing." . . . But I say, "What do you know? No, tell me, what do you know? You shut one eye and look at a thing, and it is one way to you. You shut the other one and it is different. I am as sure about greatness and beauty as you are about black and white. If a human life is a great thing to me, it is a great thing. Do you know better? I'm entitled as much as you. And why be measly? Do you have to be? Is somebody holding you by the neck? Have dignity, you understand me? Choose dignity." '

SAUL BELLOW,
*The Victim*

# Contributors

Christian Bay

Department of Political Economy,
University of Toronto,
Canada.

Hiram Caton

Brisbane,
Australia.

David E. Cooper

School of Humanities and Social
Sciences,
University of Surrey,
England.

James C. Davies

Department of Political Science,
University of Oregon,
U.S.A.

Ross Fitzgerald

School of Humanities
Griffith University,
Brisbane,
Australia.

Richard Gelwick

Department of Religion and
Philosophy,
Stephens College,
Missouri,
U.S.A.

Xavier Herbert

Redlynch,
Queensland,
Australia.

David Holbrook        Cambridge,
                      England.

H. J. McCloskey       School of Humanities,
                      La Trobe University,
                      Melbourne,
                      Australia.

John O'Neill          Department of Sociology,
                      York University,
                      Ontario,
                      Canada.

Roger Poole           English Department,
                      University of Nottingham,
                      England.

M. Brewster Smith     School of Psychology,
                      Division of Social Sciences,
                      University of California,
                      Santa Cruz,
                      U.S.A.

Fay Zwicky            English Department,
                      University of Western Australia,
                      Perth,
                      Australia.

# Acknowledgements

I would like to thank the publishers who gave their permission for reprinting the following extracts:
The epigraph: Vanguard Press Inc. (from *The Victim* by Saul Bellow, copyright © 1947 by Saul Bellow, copyright renewed 1974 by Saul Bellow). The extract on pp. 26–27: Penguin Books Ltd (from St Augustine: *Confessions*, translated by R.S. Pine-Coffin, Penguin Classics, 1961, pp. 211–212). The poem on pp. 172–174: SCM Press Ltd (from *Letters and Papers from Prison* by Dietrich Bonhoeffer, the enlarged edition, SCM Press, 1971). The extracts on pp. 171–181: Collins Publishers (from *Dietrich Bonhoeffer* by E. Bethge, Collins, London, 1970; from *The Gulag Archipelago* by A. Solzhenitsyn, Collins, London, 1974; and from *Something Beautiful for God* by Malcolm Muggeridge, Collins, London, 1972). And the poem on p. 213: Laurence Pollinger Ltd and the Estate of the late Mrs Frieda Lawrence Ravagli.

Among the many friends who have helped in the preparation of this collection, I am especially grateful to Associate Professor D.R. Burns of the School of General Studies, University of New South Wales, and Brian Reis of the Griffith University Library. In particular, I am indebted to Beverley Barnes of Pergamon Press for her extremely efficient editorial assistance. Finally, I would like to thank all contributors for their co-operation in meeting what, for many, was a very difficult deadline.

ROSS FITZGERALD

# Contents

# Introduction

Implicit in any social and political theory, indeed in any view of man and society, is an idea or a set of ideas about what it means to be human. This applies even to thinkers who reject the notion of human nature or human essence altogether. Thus Sartre's position, for example, implies a belief in the infinite malleability, for good or ill, of the human species.

To many theorists, the nature of human nature is problematic. Some believe that the forming of human nature is still unfinished, while others regard that which is essentially human as being unchanged and unchangeable. Among those who believe in a more or less fixed human nature, opinions range from the ideas of 'pessimists' like Hobbes and Calvin, representing one school of thought, to those of 'optimists' like Rousseau and the anarchist prince, Peter Kropotkin. The former hold that human beings are innately egoistic, competitive and power-seeking (or evil and depraved to use Calvin's terminology), while the latter argue that we are by nature co-operative and motivated by mutuality and concern for others, it being only pernicious institutions which have perverted our essential goodness. Clearly such views about human nature have important social and political consequences. If, for example, one holds to a Hobbesian or Calvinist position (or, for that matter, to an orthodox Freudian position), it follows that human beings need to be controlled and protected from themselves and others by law, socialization and the coercive apparatus of the State. If, on the other hand, one adopts a Rousseauist or Kropotkinist belief in

1

man's natural goodness, all sorts of scenarios for personal autonomy, increased freedom from institutional restraints and human perfectability become possible. Most underpinning beliefs about human nature are, of course, neither as extreme nor as unambiguous as the above, but they nonetheless fundamentally affect the way we all see social and political reality.

A primary aim of this collection is to make explicit these underlying ideas or assumptions about what it means to be human. Is being human merely to possess a certain anatomical and physiological structure? How are human beings to be distinguished from animals, plants, things and objects? What is the importance of language, laughter, reflexive consciousness, responsibility, volition, guilt and fallibility in defining what it means to be human? Can 'being human' be so defined? How central are the religious and artistic impulses, and ethical, moral and spiritual concerns to human nature? Are human beings intentional, purposive agents, different in kind and quality from other creatures and things, or is man to be seen simply as a mechanism? Can moral values, or a system of morality and action, be derived from propositions about human nature? These, and other issues, are dealt with in the following essays, which have all been written especially for the collection.

Editorial intrusion has been kept to a minimum. Contributors from a number of disciplines were asked to address themselves to the question 'what it means to be human' in whatever way they desired. Hopefully the result will contribute to an understanding of what human beings are like, and how we can best improve or maintain the human condition. It is not understating the situation to say that such an understanding is deeply needed in our age when the dignity of mankind is at peril.

ROSS FITZGERALD

# Essay 1

## M. Brewster Smith

The question posed to the contributors to this volume, 'What does it mean to be human?', is the oldest, most central question known to human self-consciousness, and the core of any serious attempt to answer it must be that it means being the sort of creature that can frame such a question about itself.

In the dawn of self-consciousness in individual infancy and, presumably, in the evolution of our species, self and interpreted world emerge together. Questions about human origins, human nature and human fate have always been linked indissolubly with questions about the human significance of the world in which people live their lives. Or rather, the content of human symbolic culture—the rich web of myth and ritual and folklore, then of religion and philosophy and the 'humanities' and, just very recently, of the natural, social and psychological sciences—has 'always' provided *answers* to these two kinds of questions of meaning. The questions themselves must have remained largely implicit until urbanized civilizations created the conditions for a degree of cognitive complexity to emerge in which traditional answers could no longer be taken for granted: when the culturally available answers become open to choice or doubt, the questions themselves become salient as, in our Western tradition, they did in pre-Socratic Greece, and as, with new force, they have become especially salient for us today.

Our present position is both unprecedentedly privileged and exceptionally vulnerable.

Privileged: as never before, we have ever-increasing stretches of the historical and cross-cultural record spread before us. As Malraux put it dramatically for the realm of art[1], a remarkably wide range of visions of human meaning is now available to those of us who are educated to look, a truly unprecedented situation. We are potentially at the edge of freedom from the otherwise universal human condition of being culture-bound.

But vulnerable: such freedom entails heavy costs and frightens us, as Kierkegaard put it most poignantly[2] and Erich Fromm[3] and Rollo May[4] have reminded us in more recent contexts. We—the thoughtful, analytic, mostly academic representatives of our privileged culture who are the authors of this book and the audience for it—share in the general plight, in which the plethora of meanings often seems to add up to meaninglessness. So many meanings! How is one to choose among them? By what charter can any particular answer to the perennial questions be taken as more persuasive, more valid, than the others? From this perspective, there is little to choose between the absurdism of the existentialist posture and Levi–Strauss's sometime view of his own structuralism as just another modern myth on all fours with the traditional ones. It only aggravates our predicament that the scientific view—our recent invention that is our most distinctive asset but is also (through its technological by-products) deeply implicated in our distinctive peril—has mostly been a strong corrosive of the older anthropocentric meanings cast in an appropriately human scale, but has not provided a satisfying or perhaps a satisfactory replacement. It is hard when the new answers to questions about the world dethrone humankind; it is worse when scientific accounts of human nature reduce it to terms no longer 'anthropomorphic'.

Under these circumstances, to venture to contribute to this book, to attempt any sort of answer to the big old question, requires some blend of foolhardiness and *chutzpah*. Yet we need to keep facing it, to keep talking about it as intelligently as we can. It is not good to duck problems of meaning by burying ourselves in 'value-free' specialization or technological-applied work—following the predominant American trend in psychology and the social sciences—thus

[1]  André Malraux, *The Voices of Silence*, trans. Stuart Gilbert, Doubleday, Garden City, New York, 1953.
[2]  Søren Kierkegaard, *The Concept of Dread*, trans. Walter Lowrie, Princeton University Press, Princeton, New Jersey, 1944.
[3]  Erich Fromm, *Escape from Freedom*, Farrar and Rinehart, New York, 1941.
[4]  Rollo May, *The Meaning of Anxiety* (revised edition), W.W. Norton, New York, 1977.

contributing by default (sometimes by assault[5]) to the spread of meaninglessness. It is not good to leave problems of meaning to 'countercultural' irrationalism and occultism[6] or even to philosophical specialists.

Our privileged-vulnerable position of cross-historical, cross-cultural sophistication contains at least the possibility of transcending the demoralizing relativism and attrition of meaning that it breeds. By facing the historical, cultural nature of human nature squarely, we might be able to arrive at a processual, contextual view of what it means to be human, rather than a static view that fits a particular time and place but is bound to be wrong if we take it as a timeless, universal account. (Yet we also need to worry about what it means to be human in *our* time and place!)

We have become sharply aware of the empirical fact that human beings, wherever and whenever we find them, seek meaning and create it, individually and collectively. To be human is to be engaged in a life infused with meaning. In the long eons of human prehistory spent in hunting-gathering bands and in the dozen millenia of village or pastoral life, slowly evolving systems of cultural meaning provided unquestioned frames that endowed individual lives with significance —that made them humanly livable in the face of unpredictable adversity and inevitable death. It is the shattering of these traditional frames of meaning and the transience, weak authority and human inadequacy of their successors in the brief episode of modernity which raises the problem of meaninglessness as a persisting feature of cultural crisis. Collectively, we now know about meaninglessness and we know that it is dehumanizing. So our hard-earned knowledge can provide the starting point for an attempted answer to our central question. If we take seriously the fact that people are intrinsically seekers and creators of meaning, we must regard 'the meaning of being human' as intrinsically open, an unfolding, creative human project. In Clifford Geertz's happy phrase, man is the 'unfinished animal'.[7] In culture and in history humankind participates in giving form to its human nature in a variety of ways.

The perspectives we have recently gained on human evolution make both the boundary between the prehuman animal and the truly human

[5] B.F. Skinner, *Beyond Freedom and Dignity*, Alfred A. Knopf, New York, 1971.
[6] M. Brewster Smith, 'Encounter groups and humanistic psychology' in *In Search of Community*, ed. K. Back, American Association for Advancement of Science— Westview Press, Washington, D.C., and Boulder, Colorado, 1977.
[7] Clifford Geertz, *The Interpretation of Cultures*, Basic Books, New York, 1973.

more ambiguous for us, and the distinctive features of humanness more remarkable. We have pushed our divergence from our closest primate cousins back some five million years or more. We have learned that our Pliocene ancestors could already walk bipedally and were first using, then making, crude tools long before they developed the big brains which underlie our present complexity of experience and behaviour. This greatly expanded time-frame for human evolution is a matter of fact. On it we have built the speculative construction[8] that manipulation, tool-use and tool-making—phenomena of incipient 'material culture'—gave important selective advantage to the genes that govern brain size and neural complexity. According to this now plausible view, material culture and distinctive human biology evolved in tandem and interactively.

Such speculations about the causal processes involving one feature of distinctive humanness—our technology—rest on the factual basis of dated sequences of bones and hearths and artifacts we have unearthed. The evolution of language and symbolic culture un-fortunately leaves no such traces until very late in the course of human emergence, in Neanderthal burial sites dating from about the time our own subspecies of *Homo sapiens* appeared. Burial in graves lined with flowers surely attests to well-elaborated cultural beliefs in an afterlife. But 50,000 years ago for the flower-lined graves[9] and 70,000 for other evidence of deliberate burial[10] is only yesterday in the evolutionary time span that has recently opened out behind us.

Primitive communication to co-ordinate the hunt must have been just as selectively advantageous as manipulative cleverness and tool use to those bands of proto-human hunters on the East African savannahs who excelled at it. Natural selection for communicative capacity also seems likely to be involved in the rapid increase in brain size in later Pleistocene times. What is certain is that the capacity to learn the elaborate structures of human speech is built into the human brain in intricate and fundamental ways which would seem to have required long eons to evolve—ways that differ radically from

---

[8]   See Sherwood L. Washburn, 'Speculations on the interrelations of the history of tools and biological evolution' in *The Evolution of Man's Capacity for Culture*, ed. J.N. Spuhler, Wayne State University Press, Detroit, Michigan, 1959; also S.L. Washburn, 'Human behavior and the behavior of other animals', *American Psychologist*, 1978 (in press.)

[9]   See Alexander Marshak, 'Implications of the paleolithic symbolic evidence for the origin of language', *American Scientist*, **64**, 136–145 (1976).

[10]  Karl W. Butzer, 'Environment, culture, and human evolution', *American Scientist*, **65**, 572–584 (1977).

the cerebral basis of communication in other primates. It is also clear that the universal pattern of all existing human languages has no parallel in the communication of other primates. This is a two-stage, immensely flexible coding system. First, the continuously varying sounds that are the acoustic products of vocal articulation are coded into a limited set of discrete and arbitrary 'phonemes'. Then meaning units composed of these phonemes—words—are combined creatively in open syntactical structures. Not even the fascinating apes who have recently learned under human tutelage to manipulate symbols in quasi-human ways come near this achievement; indeed the break-through in their training was to bypass the problem of articulation and therefore the entire stage of phonemic coding.[11]

Linguists are fond of emphasizing that every known human language is completely adequate to the lives of the human communities which share it. Everything 'significant' has a name, and everything that needs to be said can be said. No language is a closed system; it can accommodate and express endless novelty. We may never know just when in prehistory the slow evolution of human communicative capacity arrived at this state of affairs.

However, contemporary conjecture suggests a remarkably late date for this crucial attainment—maybe about 50,000 years ago among members of our own subspecies equipped genetically as we are today.[12] A date that recent does fit the sudden efflorescence and diversification of Late Paleolithic culture beginning about then. For more than a million years[13] the Acheulian culture, identified by its simple tool kit of crudely flaked stones, had persisted whenever early human beings were found. Something extraordinary happened around fifty millenia ago to launch a process of cultural innovation, population expansion and artistic–aesthetic objectification of human experience. Within this brief span the 'new worlds' of Australia and the Americas were colonized across formidable geographic barriers. By 19,000 years ago the Magdalenian cave paintings displayed a fully developed high art. In comparison with the cultural stability of Acheulian times, a new dynamic history began that sweeps to our own historic present in its headlong trajectory.

The late date of the 'take-off' in human cultural development is

---

[11] See *Origins and Evolution of Language and Speech*, eds Stevan R. Harnad, Horst D. Steklis and Jane Lancaster, *Annals of the New York Academy of Sciences*, **280** (1976); also Washburn (1978), *op. cit.*

[12] See *Origins and Evolution of Language and Speech*, *loc. cit.*

[13] Butzer, *op. cit.*

a matter of fact, though the link to language is conjectural. If we accept the explanation that the take-off occurred when humankind passed a critical point in the attainment of true language, we are left with extremely difficult puzzles as to how the neural bases of language could have evolved over the million years in which little change is apparent in material culture. (New puzzles continually replace old ones in the search for human origins!) However, one can imagine that the attainment of true language by a few intercommunicating bands of hunter-gatherers must have struck the speakers as a quantum leap, akin to that experienced by Helen Keller when it dawned on her that things have names—*everything* has a name and can be talked about. Whenever and however it occurred—and occur it did—humanness as we know it was essentially established.

I have begun with this account of the new perspectives on human origins because I don't think the news has spread sufficiently to psychologists, social scientists and social theorists who are more philosophically inclined. Certainly we have yet to digest its import. For the facts we must rely on our anthropological colleagues. The implication of the new facts is something for all the rest of us to work out, from many perspectives.

Let us consider the emergent situation of people newly possessed of true language. For more than a million years, the Acheulian bands of hunter-gatherers had been poised at the juncture of Nature and Culture. They had been part of Nature. Their slowly evolving culture of tools and fire and, at the boundaries of the last glaciation, of clothing and constructed shelter—also of social organization and protolinguistic communication—fed back to give a selective biological advantage to those whose bigger and more complex brains made them more adept first at using, then at inventing culture. But this insecure, partly cultural adaptation within Nature was stable. Proto-people depended more than other animals on learning, but hardly on innovation. Their tool-making culture had a universal sameness which approached the stereotyped behaviour traits of other animal species.

The attainment of language gave its speakers immense practical advantages. They could co-ordinate the activities of the band in more complex and effective ways than had hitherto been possible. They could pass on to the young a more complex heritage of skills, knowledge and belief, taking fuller advantage of the long developmental period of infancy and childhood for *socializing* the young to evolving humanness. They could build on to the biological facts of family relatedness and simple primate social organization the elaborate structures of kinship which until recently provided the universal supportive social context for human life. And, very much more effectively than before, they could *think*, thanks to the culturally transmitted symbol system of language which provided the framework and tools for thought.

Thinking mediated by language gave people new powers of 'time-binding', in Korzybski's apt phrase.[14] Forethought and afterthought became possible and a distinctive human attribute (think of the myth of Prometheus and Epimetheus)—again an immense practical advantage in the struggle for existence that assured the selective survival and propagation of language-speakers. People could now make plans, undertake commitments and recognize and correct errors—all essential adaptive ingredients of human social life as we know it.

But there were inherent consequences of becoming a speaking, thinking creature that provided no such obvious evolutionary advantage yet are central to the situation of being human and our experience of it. One is an aspect of the elaborated experience of selfhood. Though it has recently been shown that chimpanzees are capable of responding appropriately to themselves as social objects in ways not demonstrated for other mammals[15], G.H. Mead was surely right in emphasizing the *reflexiveness* of language as centrally involved in the human capacity and propensity to take the self as object, figuratively to look at the self as if through the eyes of others.[16] When we speak, we understand ourselves as if from the perspective of our hearers. We are part of our own audience, sharing meanings in terms of a common symbol system. *Self*-consciousness, the sense of *me*-ness, arises in the course of 'symbolic interaction' (the label given to the school of thought carried forward in social psychology by Mead's followers).

Mead argued persuasively that the development of reflexive selfhood is crucially 'functional', in that the implicated ability to 'take the role of the other' is essential for our participation in the co-ordinated activities of organized social life. So it surely is. Yet there are heavy costs in the side-effects. Human self-consciousness breaks the unity of Man and Nature and, when forethought and afterthought are added

---

[14]  Alfred Korzybski, *Science and Sanity: An Introduction to Non-Aristotelian Systems and General Semantics* (second edition), International Non-Aristotelian Library, New York, 1941.

[15]  See Gordon G. Gallup, Jr, 'Self-recognition in primates: A comparative approach to the bidirectional properties of consciousness', *American Psychologist*, 32, 329–338 (1977).

[16]  George Herbert Mead, *Mind, Self, and Society*, University of Chicago Press, Chicago, 1934.

as gifts of language, the ingredients of the human existential predicament emerge. As speaking self-conscious human beings, we and our forebears for more than 50,000 years have faced the cognitive puzzle of whence we came into the world, why we are here and what happens when we die. But as we all know, this is no matter of mere curiosity released by the fact that our language permits us to ask questions. (We have that too!) Primarily through language, we have become *persons*, linked to other persons whom we love and care for in a web of 'inter-subjective' meaning.[17] The inevitability of the eventual death of self and loved ones and the arbitrary unpredictability of death from famine, disease, accident, predation or human assault becomes the occasion not for momentary animal terror but for what is potentially unremitting human anguish. So the quest for meaning, for meanings compatible with a human life of self-conscious mortality, becomes a matter of life and death urgency. I don't think Ernest Becker exaggerated the importance of this theme in the history of human culture.[18]

Of course, this mainly familiar account is wrong in one obvious respect. Contrary to the old myth, our forebears cannot have been cast out of Nature's Garden of Eden in one sudden tragic event of 'birth trauma'. Perhaps, from the time perspective of the whole span of human evolution, the final full attainment of language competence worked itself out very rapidly once the basic structural-generative principles of truly human language had been hit upon. Intrinsic potentialities for organized complexity inherent in the new symbolic structures may have guided the latter stages of the process towards rapid completion. All the same, self-conscious selfhood, with its peremptory challenge to find supportive meaning in the face of creature mortality, must have been a gradual emergent.

If so, the symbolic resources of language-bearing human communities could meet the need for meaning as it arose. Thus emerged the many cultural worlds of myth, ritual and religion, which provided the traditional answers to the question of what it means to be human. They were good answers, proclaiming to each communicating tribal group its value as The People; legitimizing the group's way of life as ordained by their ancestors; giving intelligible meaning to the

---

[17]  See Alfred Schutz, *The Phenomenology of the Social World*, trans. George Walsh and Frederick Lehnert, Northwestern University Press, Evanston, Illinois, 1967; Peter L. Berger and Thomas Luckmann, *The Social Construction of Reality*, Doubleday, Garden City, New York, 1966.

[18]  Ernest Becker, *The Denial of Death*, The Free Press, New York, 1973.

exigencies of life and death; providing appropriate ways in which individual and community could participate in the encouragement of auspicious outcomes and the avoidance of ominous ones. These traditional mythic answers could not fully eliminate occasions for anguish and terror, but they could give intelligible shape to formless terror; and they could make the blows of fate more bearable to the victim and certainly more endurable to the fellow members of the victim's kindred and community. They allowed life to go on quite satisfactorily between emergencies.

Students of myth and folklore found recurrent themes and motifs wherever they turned among the world's traditional peoples. This was surely to be expected, given the universal focal events in the life cycle, in human relationships and in dealings with the natural world, and given large commonalities in the respective dramas of hunter-gatherer, pastoral or peasant life. They also found a universally applicable distinction between the commonplace objects and meanings of everyday life and *sacred* objects and meanings of transcendent power and value. The commonplace and everyday seemed to be sustained in its human meaning by its contact with and participation in a realm of the sacred and numinous. In all times and places, from the emergence of meaning-seeking humanity until the very recent immediate past, the core meaning of being human was contained in conceived relationships of human life to a more-than-human order, which was nevertheless infused with value and purpose imagined in very human terms.

I have stressed what was common among these cultural systems of meaning, but in fact we know that their accounts of the meaning of being human, and the ways of life to which they lent significance and support, were enormously various. For millenia each self-enclosed system provided a secure, unchallenged interpretation of human life. Each system was open to such novelty and change as altered circumstances of life might call for, yet was conservative of tradition —which, from our vantage point, was the source of its authority. The wide divergences among these different cultural worlds occasioned no problem. The Babel of language differentiation helped to isolate the meaning systems of tribal groups whose cultures, after all, were very locally based. And when significant contact did occur, each cultural group had the natural ethnocentric self-confidence to reject foreign conceptions and life-ways as barbarous or subhuman. (Though particular attractive cultural features were often borrowed and transmitted, and one cultural group sometimes engulfed or dominated others, with some cultural merging.)

Over the millenia what can only be described in retrospect by the unfashionable terms *progress* and *cultural evolution* manifestly occurred. As we know, a first landmark that altered the condition and meaning of being human was the invention of agriculture. First in the Middle East, then in India and China, and then again in Middle and South America, hunter-gatherers began to domesticate plants and animals and became peasant farmers, producing a surplus of food which allowed the species to multiply rapidly. In Old World and New, the parallels in the urban civilizations which soon emerged rightly continue to amaze us; and though a few continue to cling to the straws of diffusionist theories, I think we have to accommodate as part of *our* understanding of the meaning of being human the surprising fact that we are a culture-bearing species which repeatedly reinvents urban ways of life (in a word, civilizations) whenever we gain the resources to do so.

With civilizations and their attendant states and empires came the competing world religions with their now more fully elaborated conceptions of the meaning of human life. These persist until today for most of the world's people. With states and empires also came a new *political* life: first a politics of crude domination, legitimized by religious sanctions (the old myths transformed and put to new uses) and restrained mainly by the interests of what McNeill[19] has aptly called the human 'macroparasites' (the exploitative rulers) in the survival and productiveness of their peasant hosts. In our own Western tradition, the vision that eventually developed among the dominating class in ancient Attica, of a free political life as the condition in which truly human status can be fully realized, certainly does *not* describe the meaning of being human to most human beings then or now. However, the Aristotelian ideal of humankind as the political animal set forth—and the actual politics of Periclean Athens partly exemplified—a valued possibility for the meaning of human life that continues to provide us with a standard for appraising the quality of social life we have been able to attain in our urban communities. It is noteworthy that this important ideal of human social existence was formulated in the same burst of reflective inquiry that, seemingly for the first time in the proliferation of human culture, was shaking human consciousness free of purely traditional—mythic—answers to the central questions concerning humankind's being-in-the-world. It

[19]   William H. McNeill, *Plagues and Peoples*, Doubleday-Anchor, Garden City, New York, 1976.

was accompanied, as we know, by a flowering of remarkable artistic and poetic creativeness.

There *was* progress, I suggest, in the rapid and convergent invention (from our present perspective) of agriculture, urban life and civilization in the course of a quickly countable number of millenia, after the 'take-off' we speculatively attribute to our attainment of true language competence. However, the *idea* of progress[20] as a source of transcendent meaning belongs to the penultimate episode of our recent past; before that, like most of the world's peoples, our ancestors were more likely to conceive of eternal cycles of recurrence or to honour their ancestors by some version of the myth of a Golden Age.

In our mounting disillusionment following our experience of the horrors of two world wars, the human costs of totalitarian utopianism, the Holocaust, the preview of nuclear catastrophe at Hiroshima and Nagasaki, the foreshadowing of a closed, exhausted, polluted planet and the cheapening of traditional values in commercial mass society, the idea of Progress is understandably in ill repute. But if we are to formulate for ourselves a version of the 'meaning of being human' adequate to our own time and situation, we need to appreciate what, in this recent episode, compelled people to believe in Progress and how this stage in the unfolding of the nature of 'the unfinished animal' conditions, potentiates and limits the possibilities of meaning that are now open to us.

As we look back on the last half millenium of Western history— a phase of history that began parochially but came to engulf the whole human world—there was indeed dramatic progress in the standards of value shared by the people who were the major actors in the course of events. (To be sure, other peoples and their ways of life were regarded as expendable and fell disastrously by the wayside. The vanishing American Indians, the enslaved Africans, the uprooted peasants in mushrooming urban shantytowns had no good reason to speak of progress.) Knowledge increased, first in the recovery of the texts of the Ancients and in printing for the many, then in the new 'take-off' of scientific discovery—which was really a meta-discovery, a cultural mutation akin to the agricultural revolution of ten millenia ago—setting in motion a social process that (in spite of Kuhn[21]) kept leading inexorably to an ever more comprehensive grasp of the

---

[20] John B. Bury, *The Idea of Progress: An Inquiry into its Origin and Growth*, Macmillan, London, 1920.

[21] Thomas S. Kuhn, *The Structure of Scientific Revolutions*, University of Chicago Press, 1962.

workings of the world in which humankind is planted. Technology developed first in its own independent trajectory, then increasingly as a by-product and then again as an explicit goal of progress in science; it continually extended and replaced 'manpower', resulting in new and eventually frightening capacities to transform the world and affect the condition and quality of human life for better or worse. Communication and commerce expanded to include the whole globe, and the globe shrank as 'life-space' for humankind. Older ills of infancy and childhood and plagues of adulthood that in times past had checked the growth of human populations were brought under control[22] with the result that population growth leapt out of control, especially in the parts of the world that were last touched by 'modernity'. Our very success as a biological species raised doubts of impending failure.

In spite of cavernous divisions between 'haves' and 'have-nots', the era of Progress left humankind involved in a common world-wide predicament, sharing as never before a common fate. Cultures that had existed in proud and isolated independence were independent no longer; some ceased to be proud and others just ceased. The old sheltered plural worlds of cultureboundedness seemed to be fading away in every quarter; indeed, if *variety* in possible directions of human meaning is itself a value (permitting the species the adaptive advantage of a multiplicity of routes towards the realization of human potentialities), deliberate planning now seemed to be required if aspects of variety in human values were to be preserved—so strongly did the 'materialistic' values of the new world-wide technological culture corrode older sources of meaning.

But I am running ahead of our common story in noting features of the predicament with which the era of Progress has left us. While we were still caught up in its momentum and before our modern doubts arose to preoccupy reflective people, progress seemed factual; progress seemed the firmest justification of Hope. And while progress did indeed undermine the parochial, timeless certainties—the traditional mythic and religious worlds—humankind's symbolic creativeness once more provided a reconstructed and livable world which kept the human enterprise significant and satisfying.

In the era of Progress, traditional religious world views were 'progressively' secularized, a process that was by no means played out by the time modern twentieth century doubts about progress arose, so there remain enclaves of mythic conception and large sweeps of

---

[22]    McNeill, *op. cit.*

inconsistent and partly modernized popular thinking. That is, with the exceptions just noted, the old humanly universal distinction was fading between the secular and the sacred, the everyday and the numinous. People who were caught up in Progress lost touch with the Sacred. But for the time being they hardly needed it. What they needed (I tentatively suggest as a conclusion from our synoptic review of human history and prehistory) was a source of *transcendent* meaning taken for granted: a source of meaning beyond the desperate trivialities of everyday life and death and disappointment.

The sacred world traditionally provided those meanings. Worldly life gained significance through its culturally orchestrated participation in the other-worldly drama. But as Progress in its scientific-technological-skeptical guise eroded the foundations of the old and humanly satisfying mythic world view, it also provided a transcendent basis for significance in individual and social life. In this new view 'Man' is not just what is but rather, and more significantly, what is to be, and in the era of Progress whether the 'wave of the future' were interpreted grandly (as by Hegel and Marx) or more crassly (in terms of economic growth and 'the bigger the better') the Future justified the present as well as the past. We were producers of 'Whig History'—the story of 'onward and upward'—and participants in it.

At the level of individual people and their families, we could share a faith that the future would be a continually better one for our offspring and for theirs in turn. The tribulations of individual lives gained significance in this larger frame. It may not have been so satisfyingly transcendent as the religious frame that it displaced (viz. the tortured re-examinations of the human condition that abound in nineteenth century literature) but it *was* transcendent. Human life acquired meaning in terms of the greater perfection of human potentiality towards which it was understood to be tending.

We now have enough distance to see in clearly outlined perspective the drama of this recent scene in the development of what it means to be human, in the nineteenth century of our Western tradition that has now pervaded the world. The new era of Progress had been en route for quite some time, but the century of Reason and En-lightenment had been bemused by the reversible clockwork order of the Newtonian universe, and its deistic view of Cosmos did not bring change and development or history into self-conscious focus. It took the disruptions of the French and Industrial Revolutions to make the reflective denizens of the world of Progress aware of change and development as its distinctive mark. The idea of history (which of course underlies the whole approach of this essay) emerged only then as a major approach for accounting for 'what it means to be human'.

Hegel, Marx and Darwin—as we look back, the century's major intellectual lights as interpreters of the human condition—all participated in giving form to this new transcendent perspective on the meaning of human life. Early in the century, Hegel wedded the idea of Progress to deistic religion. His view of human history as the dialectical unfolding of Absolute Spirit in self-objectification included enduring insights into ways in which humankind participate in the creation of their 'unfinished' human nature; it was welcomed because it seemed to salvage the mythic, anthropomorphic sacred world as a grounding of everyday human life. The Hegelian vision incorporated the idea of Progress into the old sacred world, but in closer connection to historical human life than before. Hegel inspired the more intellectual among the romantics, who did not like the manifestations of progress in the uncontrolled, anti-human dirtiness of the early Industrial Revolution.

In the next generation Marx disavowed the mythic and 'turned Hegel on his head'. He espoused science, but borrowed from Hegel a scheme for the dynamic of Progress that was still transcendental —the dialectic of 'historical materialism'. He, too, provided a transcendent scheme of meaning in which our lives (within the limitations of 'unfinished' human nature and imperfect society) gain significance in their contribution to a progressive future. Many people today continue to nourish themselves on this meaning.

Darwin's contribution to our present understanding of the meaning of being human is the most paradoxical and interesting of all. A child of the century, the idea of development and evolution was in his bones. But Darwin was in tune, as Hegel was not—and he was certainly more closely in tune than Marx—with the spirit of the new post-Newtonian science which ripened in chemistry, thermodynamics and biology during the century: a mechanistic science in non-Newtonian domains that arrayed itself against the vitalistic, intrinsically purposive conceptions which appealed to the romantics and made contact with the old anthropomorphic world people could feel at home in.

What Darwin achieved with his principle of natural selection can be stated as a truly Hegelian synthesis, between Hegel's conception of humanity's emergent self-creation in history and the powerful physicalist conception of a colourless, unintentional world of blind cause and effect. Natural selection, through random (meaningless or mechanical) variation and selective survival and propagation of variants that happened to fit environmental specifications, provided an intelligible account of our actual biological world of manifest adaptiveness—without requiring a Designer. Subsequently elaborated by modern genetics and molecular biology, the Darwinian synthesis allows us to recognize an actual world of purposive creatures, including ourselves, without needing to believe in an exterior source of prior Purpose built into the scheme of things. Hitherto, we have always depended on such external, sacred support for our own purposes, so the 'transcendence' available in Darwinian evolution has been small comfort. Yet even as the Darwinian perspective dethroned humankind as a chosen people of special cosmic concern, it has its own glory as an account of the emergence of meaning in an otherwise meaningless universe. My attempt at a processual, historical interpretation of the meaning of being human would be inconceivable without the new way of thinking bequeathed by Darwin.

If we continue to look to our immediate past for meanings of being human—which seems almost presumptuously out of balance in the light of what we now know about the temporal scope of human history—we must also take into account the human meaning of a further step in the nineteenth century progress of the physical sciences: the Second Law of Thermodynamics. Entropy, disorder and chaos must always increase. For people who had taken progress in the physical sciences as a model and guarantee for progress in human affairs, the Second Law was shakingly paradoxical. Attending to abstract problems produced by the practical need to understand the steam-powered basis of the Industrial Revolution, physical science came forth with a principle that decreed the end of progress. Things fall apart. In the long run, progress is a perturbation within a cosmic decline.

This news threw Henry Adams into his phase of nostalgic pessimism.[23] With the harder news of the First World War, it probably predisposed Freud to propound a death instinct (Thanatos) as a second principle paralleling his conception of the libido economy. (Freud's two 'metapsychological' principles seem more closely linked to the two laws of thermodynamics as models than they are to his clinical observations.)

During the recent epoch of technological advance, Progress thus provided an evaluative frame within which people could find transcendent meaning—the only sort of meaning that makes self-conscious

[23]  Henry Adams, *The Education of Henry Adams*, Houghton Mifflin, Boston and New York, 1918.

mortal human life worth the candle. At best, Progress was never a wholly satisfactory replacement for sacred transcendence. In our own century the shock of entropy was followed by gruesome facts of current events that further undermined our faith in Progress. To satisfy existential needs which have been with us since we became self-conscious mortals, human meaning has to be transcendent of our own immediate self-interested situations. The idea of Progress, on which we relied as the older mythic meanings lost conviction, no longer gives us dependable help. Once more humankind has arrived at unprecedented and unique predicaments—in our search for meaning and in our placement in a newly vulnerable ecological niche on the small planet we have come to dominate and may be near the point of destroying.

What it means to be human has been an open venture, a developing human project. But the meaning of being human is by no means unconstrained in the present, nor was it ever in the past. The many meanings of being human that have been actualized historically have been formulated and lived by people in relation to the social and biological realities and requirements of their particular historical situations. Because, as we like to say, we now live in a 'global village' —a bad term because we have lost community, and our human setting is no longer village-like—we press one another towards common, consensual meanings of being human. We may value cultural pluralism sentimentally or politically but we know now, as we did not know before, that we live in one world, of which we embrace competing interpretations and in which we pursue competing interests. For the first time we are becoming aware of our objective involvement in a common fate, all of us constrained by the visibly fearsome consequences of letting the course of history run along present trends without our deliberate intervention. For 'unfinished animals' of our generation, the meaning of being human in our world today has to take our novel human situation sharply into account. We had better take it into account, or our fate will surely be that of just one more *finished* animal, a successor in the parade of extinction.

The core of what it has continually meant to be human, then, is processual. It lies in the endless human quest for meaning and its creation in symbolic culture. Meanings that have sustained people in the self-awareness of their mortal condition have hitherto transcended the mundane. People have attributed their sources of meaning to a sacred realm of human values and purposes read into the supposed general scheme of things. With the fading of the traditional mythic world under pressure from the enormously 'successful' strategy of science and technology (which has transformed our common sense), even the idea of Progress in its various forms has failed us as a source of hope, a secular basis for transcendence. So, with all our historical burden of symbolic sophistication and technical competence, we find ourselves back in the original position of First People contemplating their mortality, facing a new set of dangers and opportunities, to be sure, and also fortunately blessed with new resources for under-standing and coping.

In this predicament, our social scientists and humanists and prophets of popular culture would variously lead us in all possible directions, urging upon us a cacophony of competing meanings. Some, like B.F. Skinner, deify the natural sciences. According to Skinner[24] our time-honoured interpretation of our own humanness in terms of a life of intention, purpose, commitment and virtue or their lack, a drama of good and evil and human responsibility—the comedy and tragedy of life, in effect—is just as mythical as our former vision of the environing natural world in these human terms. To gird ourselves for survival, he says, we must conquer these illusions and analyze and program our own behaviour with the same dispassionate intelligence that Skinnerians apply to the training of animals. But this is extravagant and unwarranted mythocide; in calling upon us to move 'beyond freedom and dignity', Skinner would have us give up the very qualities in our self-conception that many of us have come to value most in our humanness. There is nothing in the scientific strategy, even applied to ourselves, that forces this denial of meaning upon us. To the extent that Skinner's dehumanized reinterpretation of human nature gains acceptance, this reductionist version—a non-human meaning of being human—contributes to our cultural crisis of meaninglessness rather than to its solution.

Others, especially the young and well-to-do in the aftermath of the so-called 'counterculture' of the 1960s, would pick and choose as connoisseurs in the supermarket of alternative transcendental meanings.[25] A little yoga, a workshop on primal scream, some transcendental meditation, a Zen retreat: one can experiment with many meanings in the half-world between religion and therapy,

[24]  B.F. Skinner, *op. cit.*

[25]  See Christopher Lasch, 'The narcissistic society', *New York Review of Books*, 23 (No. 15, September 30, 1976), 5-13; Peter Marin, 'The new narcissism', *Harpers*, October, 1975.

drawing upon the most disparate cultural sources, just as one can experiment with a variety of mind-altering drugs. There have been many seekers, we know, who are following that route, and there are leaders in the humanistic psychology movement who set the example and give them encouragement.[26] But such desultory experimentation with meaning is superficial and undisciplined, and rather reflects the dis-ease of meaninglessness than offers a solid cure. Meanings have to be taken more seriously if they are to matter to us.

In the recent proliferation of cults and the occult, and in the spread of Pentecostalism—the 'charismatic movement' in the established churches—we can readily see equivalents of the Ghost Dance of the Plains Indians at the end of their cultural tether or the cargo cults of the beleaguered Pacific Islanders: messianic bursts of nativistic revival, desperately reasserting traditional meanings that are rightly felt to be in mortal danger. To the non-believer, these too smack more of symptoms than of cure, though we should remember that our Christian era began with the emergent predominance of just one such messianic cult among many competitors in the faltering days of the late Classical world. We cannot exclude the possibility—indeed it fits the historical record all too well—that people's unsatisified need for transcendent meaning may be becoming so urgent that only the literalness of old-style religion will satisfy it. From the perspective of enlightenment values still cherished in the intellectual and academic community, we may indeed be at the outset of a new Dark Age. Heilbroner's grim analysis of 'the human prospect'[27] leaves this as a possibility we cannot readily dismiss.

From the standpoint of some social critics in the humanistic camp as well, not only modern technology but also the very enterprise of civilization itself has to be viewed as a disease.[28] For reasons that do not persuade me, Freud in his latter years came to see neurosis and human misery as inherent costs of civilization[29] but that did not lead him to throw in with the cause of the savage. Post-Freudian romantics have found less satisfaction in Freud's stoic posture. For many there

---

[26]  See M. Brewster Smith, *op. cit.*

[27]  Robert L. Heilbroner, *An Inquiry into the Human Prospect*, W.W. Norton, New York, 1974.

[28]  Thus, Lewis Mumford, *The Myth of the Machine*, Vol. 1 *Tecnics and Human Development*, Vol. 2 *The Pentagon of Power*, Harcourt Brace Jovanovich, New York, 1967–1970; Norman O. Brown, *Life Against Death: The Psychoanalytical Meaning of History*, Viking, New York, 1959; *Closing Time*, Random House, New York, 1973.

[29]  Sigmund Freud, *Civilization and its Discontents*, trans. James Strachey, standard edition, Hogarth Press, London, 1961.

is a strong appeal to the regressive route. Humankind is out of touch with Nature, and our life of Reason even at its best leads us towards destruction of the texture of natural life. We should retreat from the city and the machine, retreat from our delusory self-consciousness and trust the animal life of instinct. The theme has been familiar since D.H. Lawrence, and he surely had his predecessors.

But just where, in this view of the human episode, did people get off the track? The point of view developed early in this essay sees a dynamism in human transactions with Nature ever since Paleolithic times, when we began talking to each other and ourselves. The dawn of language *was* a portentous, risky break with Nature, and the myth of Original Sin does symbolize something deeply problematic about our footing in the world. However, looking through the far end of the temporal telescope we see no further Rubicon, once we crossed the boundary of language, at which humankind can be said to have gone astray. (Cogent arguments have been advanced that atomic energy and genetic engineering in our own day may constitute such Rubicons.) Our very nature as 'incomplete animals' requires culture for our viability, let alone for our fulfilment. Once we set out on our remarkable course, agriculture, villages, cities, civilization, industry and science all seem steps in a trajectory towards greater power in the world and greater understanding of our place in it. It is clear that even if we would turn back from this adventure in humanness not many of us or our offspring could survive the trip. After our recent brushes with apocalypse, apocalytic thinking has become all too understandable, but in spite of Norman O. Brown[30] I see no reason to cheer for human defeat.

If we do not let ourselves become derailed by the difficulty and complexity of our awesome problems as a species, their challenge honestly faced could provide a frame of meaning more than sufficient. The story of human life thus far reads like a long picaresque novel. Now the plot thickens, and it is hard not to believe we are moving toward a denouement. However, this time we cannot count on Progress; our fate depends, and more and more of us know it, upon our own human actions, intelligent and compassionate, or the contrary. Surely it was such a reading that led the biophysicist—and polymath and prophet—John Platt to call the title essay of a recent book 'The Step to Man'.[31] He argues that *if* we manage to solve the interrelated ecological and human problems defined by exponential trends that

30  Norman O. Brown, *op. cit.*
31  John R. Platt, *The Step to Man*, Wiley, New York, 1966.

seem to be carrying us to catastrophe, we will have transformed our human nature as we know it in the process. He seeks to engage our transcendent commitment to this high task—not in fulfilment of a fated Progress, but in response to a momentous challenge in which the stakes are very high. To meet the challenge would indeed be a giant step toward the adult, responsible conduct of our lives in the world.

My understanding of the open-ended meaning of what it is to be human is in good accord with Platt's rallying cry. Human beings *have* formed their own human nature very substantially in the course of coping symbolically, as well as technically, with their world and with themselves and their fellows as increasingly salient components of that world. Though we are seriously at risk in new ways by the very success of the strategy our unique species hit upon, the forming of human nature is not finished—nor would it be should we accomplish Platt's devoutly-to-be-hoped-for Step to Man. The meanings of being human that served us so long and so well—the mythic and religious ones handed down to us by tradition—formulate important emergent truths of human life, but they no longer give us good guidance or dependable support in the world we must deal with today. The problems of the real world should now yield sufficient high drama to engage and make meaningful the lives of those whose imaginations can be aroused by them.

If we are to give ourselves a chance to respond adequately to this challenge, however, we need to conserve and re-form our *human* resources, and deploy our scientific resources with all the intelligence and wisdom we can muster. Our ways of life shape who we are; and our self-conceptions of what it means to be human participate in constituting our actual human nature. We need to re-knit our ravelled human relationships in family and community life: part of the enduring meaning of what it has been to be human is our mutual support in loving care of one another, which has suffered in a time of exaggerated individualism. We need also to re-knit our connection to historical continuity, badly strained everywhere by the headlong rapidity of culture change. We need to practice caring more deeply than has become customary about our posterity and the future, if we are to become capable of doing the hard things that preserving a human future now requires of us. We need to take nourishment in our 'natural' joy in the world's beauties and in our kinship with all living things. We need to raise our sights in the standards of our political discourse and controversy, because it is in the political world that we can take steps towards coping with our species-wide problems

—and it is in the political world that we can pursue our narrow interests until it is too late.

In the social, psychological or behavioural sciences, we need to find or restore a language caring and respectful of people, and a formulation of our enterprises that feeds information and insight back to people to increase their competence and satisfaction in relating to one another and dealing co-operatively with their common problems. The last thing we need from the sciences of people is the mistaken and self-diminishing message that people are just programmable mechanisms, not really people after all.

In this new challenge to critical self-conscious social and personal reconstruction, we should take heart in some remarkable recent changes in how we conceive of our humanness that are still in an early stage of being worked out in actual social life: gains in the recognized humanness of women, minorities and Third World peoples, both in the humanity they claim and espouse for themselves and in the humanity they are accorded by others in what had been the mainstream of Progress. We must remember that the project of being human traditionally left women in a limited, secondary position[32], and that the other face of Progress for the dominant classes of the industrialized West was imperialism, colonialism and exploitation— the white man's privilege that was implicit in the 'white man's burden'. We are far from having earned the right to complacency about actual results of the struggle for justice towards women, minorities and 'have-not' peoples: the actual gap between 'haves' and 'have-nots' is even increasing. But we have certainly gained the basis for *hope* in the remarkable advance in our conception of what justice requires.

I say 'our' conception, but to understand the real basis for our new hope—in turn the basis for commitment and action that can redefine what it means to be human in the relations of our daily life—requires us to penetrate the ambiguity of 'our'. In times past 'we' were the more or less enlightened passengers on the train of Progress, who sometimes exhorted one another towards more inclusive definitions of fellow humanity. But today 'we' also include those who were formerly 'others', who are now making their own claims and, in gaining their own self-respect, are earning the respect of the rest of us.

A profound revision of the meaning of being human would seem to be in progress. We have become the people we are by a long hard road which in the reconstructed 'scientific' account is just as miraculous

[32]   Simone de Beauvoir, *The Second Sex*, trans. H.M. Parshley, Alfred A. Knopf, New York, 1953.

and awe-inspiring as the accounts of Creation in religious myth. The tragedy and comedy, the pathos and glory of our earthly life includes the fact that our common human project of self-understanding is also one of collective self-development and social creation and reconstruction. The meaning of being human is not a given, not a stable constant. We have encountered many reasons for believing our own time to be a critical one in which to have a part in re-creating it. Let us get on with this important agenda!

# Essay 2

# John O'Neill

It is only in the life of a human being that the question about the meaning of being human can be asked. This is not to say that each of us asks this question. Rather, it is more likely that we dwell in the midst of the answers others have given to this question, without much imagining there will ever come a time when we shall have to ask for ourselves what it means to be human in order to go on living, or to bring our lives to a close. Of course, in a daily way we provide for our lives to be sufficient. We trust to family, community and religion or to our own selfishness, prejudices and ideologies to defend ourselves from the ultimate question underlying the gift of this life, its brief trust and certain loss.

Here we shall explore with Montaigne the experiment, or essay, of being human.* In this exploration Montaigne is a friendly guide, careful of the concerns that others have expressed for their lives, while testing their practices in himself as he finds himself in the person of the essayist. Montaigne seeks the particulars of living that nevertheless tie us to the general condition of mankind. Yet Montaigne is neither a philosopher, nor a theologian, and is quite outside any school. Like Socrates, Montaigne begins with no received version of our humanity. He requires of us that we essay the problem of meaning

---

* This is part of a forthcoming larger study, *Essaying Montaigne, a study of the arts of reading and writing.* All references to Montaigne are from *The Complete Essays of Montaigne*, translated by Donald M. Frame, Stanford University Press, 1965.

in a manner faithful only to the diversity of life's moods and historical patterns, trusting no center but what we truly find in ourselves. Thus any exploration guided by Montaigne is simultaneously an essay in sharing our humanity with one who, like Socrates, was never more himself than in the company of others but who shaped his own life by never leaving hold of the question it offered him.

We might seek who we are in that infinite difference between ourselves and God, of which the lack in ourselves is the merest, though most positive, reverberation. For we are earth-born and we borrow briefly the seasons of the earth on our way to death:

> But what do I love when I love my God? Not material beauty or beauty of a temporal order; not the brilliance of earthly light, so welcome to our eyes; not the sweet melody of harmony and song; not the fragrance of flowers, perfumes, and spices; not manna or honey; not limbs such as the body delights to embrace. It is not these that I love when I love my God. And yet, when I love him, it is true that I love a light of a certain kind, a voice, a perfume, a food, an embrace; but they are of the kind that I love in my inner self, when my soul is bathed in light that is not bound by space; when it listens to sound that never dies away; when it breathes fragrance that is not borne away on the wind; when it tastes food that is never consumed by the eating; when it clings to an embrace from which it is not severed by fulfilment of desire. This is what I love when I love my God.
>
> But what is my God? I put my question to the earth. It answered, 'I am not God,' and all things on earth declared the same. I asked the sea and the chasms of the deep and the living things that creep in them, but they answered, 'We are not your God. Seek what is above us.' I spoke to the winds that blow, and the whole air and all that lives in it replied, 'Anaximenes is wrong. I am not God.' I asked the sky, the sun, the moon, and the stars, but they told me, 'Neither are we the God whom you seek.' I spoke to all the things that are about me, all that can be admitted by the door of the senses, and I said, 'Since you are not my God, tell me about him. Tell me something of my God.' Clear and loud they answered, 'God is he who made us.' I asked these questions simply by gazing at these things, and their beauty was all the answer they gave.
>
> Then I turned to myself and asked, 'Who are you?' 'A man,' I replied. But it is clear that I have both body and soul, the one the outer, the other the inner part of me. Which of these two ought I to have asked to help me find my God? With my bodily powers I had already tried to find him in earth and sky, as far as the sight of my eyes could reach, like an envoy sent upon a search. But my inner self is the better of the two, for it was to the inner part of me that my bodily senses brought their messages. They delivered to their arbiter and judge the replies which they carried back from the sky and the earth and all that they contain, those replies which stated 'We are not God' and 'God is he who made us.' The inner part of man knows these things through the agency of the outer part. I, the

inner man, know these things; I, the soul, know them through the senses
of my body. I asked the whole mass of the universe about my God, and
it replied, 'I am not God. God is he who made me.' (Saint Augustine)[1]

What we are, we are for others and yet the question of who we
are remains for ourselves. We cannot borrow ourselves from others,
or not entirely; nor can we keep ourselves to ourselves without what
others bring to us of ourselves. This is the riddle of our public and
private lives. We cannot come to the end of ourselves and we cannot
keep that distance upon ourselves that others observe towards us.
We must, however, observe their standpoint in order to make
ourselves known to those around us. At the same time, we must
withhold that source within us from which we launch our life, its
dreams and its freedom. We never possess ourselves, yet we need
to call ourselves our own. Despite the abiding difference between
who we are and what we are, we must nevertheless seek self-
knowledge and place ourselves in the trust of others. For we cannot
suspend our living in the mystery that a man is to himself and that
others are to him.

Thus we take upon our own humanity as an experiment. We need
to place ourselves in a natural light, to show ourselves neither more
nor less than we are. In this, vanity and self-abasement are equal
traps. For we can always exceed ourselves in fortune, or in misery,
and in either one never come upon ourselves, though we may well
surpass others whom we call to witness our masques. The problem,
then, is to find some measure between endless self-questioning and
the answers upon which we build our lives and self-assurance. No
man can withhold himself from others, or from himself, in order to
make his life an open question without any underlying form, unless
he is blind to the repetitions and encroachments of living, from which
none of us is separable and from which each of us draws an original
bearing and habit. At the same time, we cannot surrender ourselves
to the circumstances of our birth and family; nor can we remain slaves
to custom and fashion. We owe something to ourselves, as well as
to our land; something to conscience, as well as to the law. How,
then, are we to keep alive the meaning of the question we are, while
remaining wise enough to live as others do, holding ourselves neither
above them nor beneath them?

We encounter our own living only through the way others live.
It is in their families, in their villages and in their customs that we

---

[1] *Confessions*, Book X, 6, pp. 211-212.

behold our own. Here too, however, the meaning of our lives is no more settled by the findings of anthropology than it is by the facts of anatomy and biology. For the knowledge we accumulate through the comparison of men's beliefs and practices serves only to deepen the inquiry concerning the possibility of the universal ideal of humanity that might be entertained by all men whatever the circumstances of their living. *Ethical anthropology* is therefore not an idle accumulation of the differences between men. Rather, it informs itself of these differences in order to avoid embracing an abstract unity of mankind. But to do this, an ethical anthropologist must essay the differences he finds between men, just as he must abide with the differences he finds in himself over the course of his life's journey.

The meaning of our humanity cannot be raised as a question that puts us outside the practices of men around us living today, or in earliest times, in our own country or in far-off places. The pursuit of this question leads us to ourselves only through other men. We have no certain mark upon ourselves given to us in our animal nature. We can count less upon our instincts than our habitat and the sublime accommodations of our language and culture:

> I do not want to forget this, that I never rebel so much against France as not to regard Paris with a friendly eye; she has had my heart since childhood. And it has happened to me in this as happens with excellent things: the more other beautiful cities I have seen since, the more the beauty of Paris has power over me and wins my affection. I love her for herself, and more in her own essence than overloaded with foreign pomp. I love her tenderly even to her warts and her spots. I am a Frenchman only by this great city: great in population, great in the felicity of her situation, but above all great and uncomparable in variety and diversity of the good things of life; the glory of France, and one of the noblest ornaments of the world. (III:9, 743)

At first sight, humanism would seem to be the easiest of all attachments. After all, how is it possible that man should not value himself most; at least among living creatures? However he might belittle himself before God, having nevertheless been made in the image of God, man is surely lord of the rest of creation. Since God has made all men in his image, and placed man so far above other creatures in the hierarchy of creation, the value that man has for man ought to go without saying. Rather, humanism is at best a prayer of thanksgiving and not an argument essential to the condition of man. On the lips of a Christian, humanism, then, would sound like Pico della Mirandola's exultation upon the dignity of man:

It is truly divine possession of all these natures at the same time flowing into one, so that it pleases us to exclaim with Hermes, 'A great miracle, O Asclepius, is man.' The human condition can especially be glorified for this reason, through which it happens that no created substance disdains to serve him. To him the earth and the elements, to him the animals are ready for service, for him the heavens fight, for him the angelic minds procure safety and goodness, if indeed it is true as Paul wrote that all ministering spirits are sent in ministry on account of those who are destined to be heirs of salvation. No wonder that he is loved by all in whom all recognize something of their own, indeed their whole selves and all their possessions.[2]

However inspirational the Christian hierarchy of being might be for humanist meditation, it is not at all tempting to Montaigne. It represents a form of excess that Montaigne wished to avoid. Moreover, it is easily jeopardized by an equally Christian practice of meditation upon the emptiness of man in contrast with the plenitude of his divine maker. Montaigne himself had inscribed upon the ceiling of his study these reminders of man's vanity:

Holy Writ declares those of us wretches who think well of ourselves: 'Dust and ashes,' it says to them, 'what has thou to glory in?' And elsewhere: 'God has made man like the shadow, of which who shall judge when, with the passing of the light, it shall have vanished away. In truth we are nothing. (II:12, 368)

It is Montaigne's opinion that nothing in human reason permits us to ground its reasoning outside itself, or to reason upon things outside man's own experience. The task of a humanist, as understood by Montaigne, is to work in the middle ground between the excesses of Christian optimism and despair. The ground of this humanism is its *learned ignorance*; that is to say, socratic ignorance, which knows itself, tests itself and is thus never a complete ignorance:

The wisest man that ever was, when they asked him what he knew, answered that he knew this much, that he knew nothing. He was verifying what they say, that the greatest part of what we know is the least of those parts that we do not know; that is to say that the very thing we think we know is a part, and a very small part, of our ignorance. (II:12, 370)

It is essential that we do not separate Montaigne's reliance upon the doctrine of learned ignorance from his reflections upon the limitations of the human mind in relation to *man's bodily estate*. Thus Montaigne's humanism is essentially tied to man's condition as a living

---

[2]  Giovanni Pico della Mirandola, *De hominis dignitate, Heptaplus, De Ente et uno, e scritti vari*, ed. Eugenio Garin, Florence, 1942, pp. 302-304.

being, in whom reason and the senses are inseparable and thereby impose a limit to the excesses of philosophy and Christianity alike. Thus it is impossible to confine Montaigne's thought within the forced alternatives of the Skeptics, Stoics and Epicureans, or between Christian hope and despair. In every case, the excesses in these positions are betrayed by the living tie between our minds and our bodies that makes our life the ultimate ground of goodness. It is possible for us to suspend belief in the finest of philosophical arguments, yet Socrates himself could not resist the good in scratching himself once they released his chains. To be sure, there is nothing about the human body, considered in itself, that cannot be surpassed for strength, agility, vision, health and longevity in animals. Indeed, there are many human qualities that are modelled upon those of animals to whom they are natural, yet to man valued achievements. In fact, men and animals have always had a certain fascination for each other, even to the point of love. (II:12. 347) Yet we are far below the animals in our willingness to maim and slaughter one another, and quite unlike them in the ingenuity we exercise in subjecting one another to pain. Although all men have the same bodies, and are subject to the same bodily necessities of birth, hunger, sex, pleasure, pain and death, just as their souls are cast in the same divine mould, they are nevertheless engaged in infinitely varied adaptations to their circumstances, which create among men differences of reason and sensation far beyond the differences between men and animals. In the face of the fantastic variation between men and women, kings and cobblers, Frenchmen and Italians, Catholics and Protestants, Stoics and Skeptics, not to mention every variation in custom and belief regarding dress, food, virtue and vice, the humanist is hard-pressed to remind man of himself. No creature in the world is as capable as man of creating distinctions between himself and his fellow men. Above all, man's ability to separate himself from himself, to engage in cruel and deadly controversies, and generally to submit his fellow men to his whims, is abetted by the belief that his soul or reason is somehow higher than his body. Thus men have subjected their own bodies, as well as the bodies of others, to incredible fates in the pursuit of reasoned glories. In fact, they have so convinced themselves that they are destined through these pursuits to achieve 'fanciful goods, goods future and absent' like reason, knowledge and honour, that they have been content to assign to the animals 'essential, tangible, and palpable goods: peace, repose, security, innocence, and health'. (II:12, 357)

In this regard, Montaigne cites two stories and proceeds to weigh them in a comment which, I think, contains the very fundament of his humanist conviction as I have tried to convey it. In the first, he reports that even the Stoics dared to say that if Heraclitus and Pherecydes could have exchanged their wisdom for their health, in order to be rid of the dropsy in one case and lice in the other, they would have done well. They preferred, however, to set wisdom above health. But the Stoics have another story about Ulysses and Circe, in which they say that if Ulysses had been forced by Circe to choose between two potions, one to make a fool a wise man, the other a wise man a fool, he ought to have chosen the cup of folly rather than allow her to change his human figure into that of a beast. They argued in this way because they believed that Wisdom herself preferred the figure of man to that of an ass. From this confession of the Stoics, Montaigne concludes in the strongest terms that all things, even God, are proportionate to man, provided he accepts his properly mixed condition of embodied soul.

> What? So our philosophers abandon this great and divine wisdom for this corporeal and terrestrial veil? Then it is no longer by our reason, our intelligence, and our soul that we are superior to the beasts; it is by our beauty, our fair complexion, and the fine symmetry of our limbs, for which we should abandon our intelligence, our wisdom, and all the rest.
>
> Well, I accept this naive, frank confession. Indeed, they knew that those qualities about which we make so much ado are but idle fancy. Even if the beasts, then, had all the virtue, knowledge, wisdom and capability of the Stoics, they would still be beasts; nor would they for all that be comparable to a wretched, wicked, senseless man. In short, whatever is not as we are is worth nothing. And God himself, to make himself appreciated, must resemble us. . . (II:12, 358)

Montaigne speaks frankly to us and yet his method is hardly direct. How is this possible? In particular, Montaigne's method is by and large launched upon paradoxes. At first sight, these might seem to be designed to knock heads together, a method of gaining attention, to be sure, yet one that we would ultimately find tiresome. The use of paradox must be artful if it is not to anger us with its suspension of belief and its irresolution. It does not occur to us, however, to condemn Montaigne's practice in this way. How, then, does Montaigne ground his use of paradox? Of course, he was trained like any educated man of his time in the use of argument by paradox, the formulation of an opinion together with an equally well formulated contrary opinion. Thus, if it were a question of technique, Montaigne would not be unusual, and might well have had contemporaries who exceeded him in this skill. One immediately thinks of Erasmus' *The Praise of Folly*. By the same token, the contrast in favour of Montaigne begins to emerge. It is difficult to find in Erasmus' essay anything like the presence of an author engaged in self-essaying. The observer's stance is transcendent; it is never undermined by the author's exploration of his own bodily commitments to folly. By contrast, Montaigne's *Essays* mine, from beginning to end, the human reversibility of truth and falsity, pleasure and pain, virtue and vice. Above all, they never stray far from contemplation of the central Delphic paradox of the command of self-knowledge laid upon the one creature in this world most given to self-ignorance, fantasy and aberration.

It is possible to argue that Montaigne loved paradox for its intellectual and aesthetic properties. But this would be as true of any other good mind in his day. Rather, Montaigne was attached to the use of paradox because it displays the *ethical tension* of living which cannot proceed without an intelligent and sensible capacity for dwelling within the limits of relationships that resist fantasies of omnipotence. Thus a man may learn from living, but he will never learn to live nor learn to die. This is not an irrationalist argument. We could hardly understand the *Essays* if we were tempted by such a reaction. Montaigne's paradoxes are distributed between life and reason. The thinker who abstracts from the limits of embodiment is no better than a dreamer. His fine arguments on the immortality of the soul and the essentially transitory nature of pleasure will not prevent him from howling at a knock he receives. But this is, admittedly, the kind of objection that is telling only in the moment. For we may still place all our hope in reason, since our bodies hardly promise us anything beyond the grave. If we oppose mind and body in this way, the wager might well go to the side of reason. On the other hand, if we take death seriously, the fate of our bodies instructs us to make better use of our reason this side of the grave, and to ignore its fantastic deployments in military or magical and omnipotent or theological pursuits. In practice, Montaigne's own reflections on life and death moved beyond the rhetorical opposition of the mind and body, towards a simple affirmation of the value of life to a living being without further confession.

So much of the *Essays* turn upon the paradoxical relationships between Life and Death, or between Knowledge and Ignorance, that we cannot avoid a closer examination of Montaigne's use of these themes. For many people philosophy and religion are recognizable as commitments to reflection upon the paradox that Life is Death, and the reversed truth that Death is Life, or that Knowledge is Ignorance, and only Ignorance is Knowledge. The religious paradox turns upon acceptance of a life after death. In the Platonic tradition, the philosophical paradox turns upon a mind/body dualism that denies the status of knowledge to the senses, on the ground that they are merely the instruments of opinion. The mind, inasmuch as it separates itself from the senses, whether in this life or the next—and here philosophy and religion overlap—is capable of true contemplation of the eternal ideas of Truth, Justice and Beauty. Montaigne, of course, was quite familiar with the classical and Christian tradition of reflection upon the double paradox of Life and Death, Reason and Ignorance and their permutations. Thus the Christian may prefer to remain ignorant in this life, at least from the standpoint of philosophical knowledge, in order to know God in the next life. Indeed, a philosopher like Socrates will prefer ignorance as a mark even of the philosophical life rather than pursue the vanities of Reason. At bottom, however, both the believer and the philosopher are caught in the *paradox of ignorance*, namely of how it is they know that they cannot know truly either God or the eternal ideas. This problem is more pervasive than the problem of that professional pride in scholars and medical men that Montaigne was at pains to ridicule. It is a question of where we stand once we refuse the excesses of philosophy and religion. And, of course, the religious and civil war that surrounded him made Montaigne a man sick of such excesses. Thus his attachment to the use of paradox cannot be understood as yet another instance of the general passion for argument and contradiction. Montaigne's use of paradox is ruled by the ethical purpose of subjecting men to a sense of limit and tolerance. It is intended to restore the community of thought and speech by making it clear that there is no principle from which they can be subdued monologically. In this sense, Montaigne's paradoxes are the instruments of civil reform.

Everything in the human record shows that man is at once the poorest of creatures and yet the most given to excess. We cannot escape this paradox as long as we continue to separate ourselves from ourselves in the service of philosophical and religious arguments about the relationship between life and death, or between the mind and the body. The excess of man over himself is unparalleled. There is no practice among men that is not contradicted by the practice of other men. What creature, other than man, can treat life as death, poverty as wealth, pleasure as pain? What other creature can be so divided over the meaning given to his food, dress, housing, wealth, health, illness, power, weakness? How is it possible that however a man conceives of himself, or whatever it is he thinks right or wrong, some other men will find it is constituted in quite a different fashion, so that there is more difference—that is, absolute excess—between men than there is between men and animals? How can the human condition be so at odds with itself, while at the same time nothing that obtains of man can be truly said to be alien to man? It is on this *anthropological question*, rather than upon any epistemological or theological question, that the *Essays* dwell. Moreover, they never leave this anthropological ground, so it is quite useless to try to find in Montaigne any trope of philosophical development whereby he came to terms with the anthropological question.

Like Socrates, Montaigne had no other interest than man. Every topic of the *Essays* serves only to further his study of man. In search of man he overlooks nothing, and therefore anything can serve his purpose, giving to the *Essays* an incredible variety of topics and discourse. History, philosophy, poetry and theology, education, war, food, dress, love, friendship and death are only a few of the themes to which Montaigne addresses himself in his search for man. At first sight it is possible to see in the variety of the *Essays* nothing but that *busy indolence* in Montaigne which allowed him to pick here and there, without anywhere achieving any depth or certainty in his inquiry. The result of many years of work in this way offers us a rich pastime, but deserves to be read only by a similarly *nonchalant reader*, happy to while away his time in the labyrinth of the *Essays*. Indeed, much of what Montaigne himself says about the method of their composition, his use of books, his generally poor memory and disinterest in specialized knowledge favours the conclusion that the *Essays* are hardly a profound anthropological treatise. From what he tells us of himself, Montaigne lacked the stamina for any serious moral treatise:

> As for the natural faculties that are in me, of which this book is the essay, I feel them bending under the load. My conceptions and my judgment move only by groping, staggering, stumbling and blundering; and when I have gone ahead as far as I can, still I am not at all satisfied: I can still see the country beyond, so that I cannot clearly distinguish it. And when I undertake to speak indiscriminately of everything that comes to my fancy without using any but my own natural resources, if I happen, as I often do, to come across in the good authors those same subjects I have attempted to treat—as in Plutarch I have just come across his discourse on the power of the imagination—seeing myself so weak and puny, so heavy and sluggish, in comparison with those men, I hold myself in pity and disdain. (I:26, 107)

Yet even in such a confession we see the strength of Montaigne's *anthropological method*. Just as he sets himself aside as a thinker of any importance, even diminishing his contribution as an author, so he fills the *Essays* with observations upon the ambitions of men, only in order to marginalize their significance. But, then, it is from this very margin of intimate self-observation that he is able to reaffirm the abiding achievements of some great men and women of history, as well as the ordinary accomplishments of those like himself who have learned how to live with a limited ignorance. Thus Montaigne is not content to indulge the tropes of Christian humility, disparaging the puffed-up attempts of man to raise himself in the world. Of course, he is critical of reason and custom, of vanity and glory—nothing human escapes his watchful eye. But there is no transcendental standpoint, no divine alienation underlying Montaigne's observations. This is because Montaigne's anthropology is ruled by the ethical task of *self-essaying*. The *Essays* therefore are not content to record human ignorance or humiliate man in God's favour. Montaigne is resolutely on the side of man, and nothing attaches him more to man than truly human ignorance, rather than those flights of fantasy and excesses of reason whereby men hope to find themselves on the side of the gods. To him who exclaims 'O what a vile and abject thing is man if he does not raise himself above humanity!' Montaigne makes the following reply:

> That is a good statement and a useful desire, but equally absurd. For to make the handful bigger than the hand, the armful bigger than the arm, and to hope to straddle more than the reach of our legs, is impossible and unnatural. Nor can man raise himself above himself and humanity; for he can see only with his own eyes, and seize only with his own grasp. (II:12, 457)

Here, as elsewhere, we see Montaigne's anthropological method tied resolutely to *the human frame*, to the body's reach and to the lessons of its plain living. Nothing of the body as the vehicle of sin, the veil of ignorance or the dark soil of the passions! And for all his admiration of the death of Socrates, Montaigne is not inclined to consider the body a prison from which the soul is happy to escape. On the contrary, he believes that men are far too anxious to escape this life, urged on by philosophical fantasies no better than the religious quarrels and military exploits which so readily cost them their lives and limbs. Montaigne is not concerned so much to humiliate man, as to confound the excesses of his reason which lead him to make claims about everything in the universe, constructing magnificent schemes of thought upon the most remote matters, while with respect to himself man is ruled by nothing so uncertain as the opinions, customs and laws of that small corner of the universe in which he happens to live:

> Those people who perch astride the epicycle of Mercury, who see so far into the heavens, yank out my teeth. For in the study I am making, the subject of which is man, when I find such an extreme variety of judgments, so deep a labyrinth of difficulties one on top of the other, so much diversity and uncertainty in the very school of wisdom, you may well wonder— since these people have not been able to come to an agreement in the knowledge of themselves and their own state, which is ever present before their own eyes, which is in them; since they do not know the motion of what they move themselves, or how to depict and decipher to us the springs that they hold and manage themselves—how should I believe them about the cause of the ebb and flow of the river Nile. 'The curiosity to know things was given to men as a scourge',[3] says the Holy Scripture.
> (II:17, 481)

It serves man just as little to have his eye on heaven as upon the stars. Montaigne is above all opposed to the Platonic and Christian separation of man's body and soul in order to improve heaven at the expense of this earth. After all, things were faulted from the beginning and, for all its splendor, the project of going to heaven hardly seems to improve our time on earth, and is certainly not free from contributing to our present miseries. Witness the cruelty of the wars of religion, in particular over the bodily presence of Christ in the sacrament of communion. In view of all the terrible bodily mutilations that men have made a part of religion (II:12, 388), including Christ's own passion and crucifixion, there might well be some merit in the Protestant argument for a purely abstract conception of God, quite free from magical images. Yet while rejecting any other image of God, Montaigne believes there are necessary arguments for those corporeal images through which man represents God to himself. The first argument is a conservative one, in the purely political sense, and the second is an argument from Montaigne's fundamental anthropology:

> Pythagoras adumbrated truth more closely in judging that the knowledge of this first cause, being of beings, must be undefined, unprescribed, undeclared: that it was nothing else but the utmost effort of our imagination toward perfection, each man amplifying the idea of it according to his capacity. But if Numa undertook to make the piety of his people conform to this plan, to attach it to a purely intellectual religion, without any predetermined object or material admixture, he undertook something unusable. The human spirit cannot keep floating in this infinity of formless

---

[3] Ecclesiastes I, 12, written on a beam of the ceiling in Montaigne's study: *Cognoscendi studium homini dedit Deus, ejus torquendi gratia.*

ideas; they must be complied for it into a definite picture after its own pattern.

The divine majesty has thus let itself be somewhat circumscribed within the corporeal limits on our behalf; his supernatural and heavenly sacraments show signs of our earthly condition; his worship is expressed by perceptible rituals and words; for it is man that believes and prays. (II:12, 381)

Society holds together best when men remember their own limits. To this end the imagery of the *body politic* no less than that of the body of Christ is a saving reminder. There is no limit to argument, and no length to which men will not go on behalf of abstract principles. The civil war that surrounded Montaigne was a testament to the way language bewitches men. Thus civil order is best served through rituals that give bodily and sensory shape to the concerns of men and society so that they are not diminished through abstraction and interminable controversy:

> The senses act as the proper and primary judges for us, and they perceive things only by their external accidents; thus it is no wonder that in all the functions that serve the welfare of society there is always such a universal admixture of ceremony and outward show that the best and most effective part of a government consists in these externals. It is still man we are dealing with, and it is a wonder how physical (*merveilleusement corporelle*) his nature is. (III:8, 710)

The model of humanity which attracted Montaigne most was the life and death of Socrates. It is significant that we never speak of Socrates' life except in the light of his death. Socrates died under the laws of the city in which he was the most free and ordinary citizen. His freedom lay not in any superior position, politically or philosophically speaking, but in his patient apprenticeship to self-knowledge. Socrates recognized his need of the city and the conversation of ordinary men as the proper resource of inquiry. That Socrates was not welcome to his fellow citizens was not due to his neglect of civic duties. At the same time, Socrates was not ruled by the letter of the law. If Socrates knew his limits, it was not because they were given to him by religion and the State. It was rather because his own self-examination had taught him that the city and the laws were true to the limited nature of man, so long as they serve men in the everyday affairs and do not try to make them heroes in the abstract name of the State. It is harder to live each day unknown than to die celebrated as a hero. It is even harder to live each day without alienating our undertaking in favour of priests and professional philosophers, let alone soothsayers of every kind who exploit the misery of ordinary lives.

Montaigne examines the Socratic model from his earliest essays to his last. Indeed, the first extensive reference (I:11, 29-30) already shows how sane Montaigne can be, once he shifts inside his ostensible topic —'Of Prognostications'—to self-observation. On this ground, he can compare his own experience of an inner voice of reason, moved more by intuition than logic, with that of Socrates. Here Socrates is not appealed to as an authority, but rather comes to mind from a similar quest into self-knowledge. Indeed, in reflecting upon the way ordinary people, without much benefit of philosophy, meet quite awful deaths with equanimity, (I:14, 34) he again thinks of Socrates, remarking that there is nothing to choose in his favour. Of course, it is because Socrates, too, ignored philosophy that he faced death in his calm fashion—and even with good humour:

> To the man who told Socrates, 'The thirty tyrants have condemned you to death,' he replied: 'And nature, them. (I:20, 64)

Here we can see Montaigne's appreciation of Socrates already searching for that middle ground of constancy and plain speech that avoids the excesses of man's self-wrought vanity and misery. Thus, in contemplating the hold that custom and habit have upon us, despite our flights of fantasy and philosophy, Montaigne nevertheless weighs our local attachments on the scale of what we owe to human society, to which we cannot be indifferent; and here again the example of Socrates comes to mind:

> Society in general can do without our thoughts; but the rest—our actions, our work, our fortunes, and our very life—we must lend and abandon to its service and to the common opinions, just as the great and good Socrates refused to save his life by disobedience to the magistrate, even to a very unjust and very iniquitous magistrate. (I:23, 86)

Of course, the knowledge that society can do without us is, as Socrates shows to the Hippias, the kind of knowledge that feeds upon divisions and competitiveness, which has no place in a well ordered State. (I:25, 105-106) Such knowledge may give a man local importance, for it is not much different from the attachments and prejudices whereby men judge everything in the light of their own circumstance, imagining what they see and believe to hold good for everyone and anyone elsewhere in the world. What is remarkable in Socrates is that he could be loyal to his community without absolutizing its values. Montaigne admired Socrates as a citizen of the world because he understood the world to contain all differences without any possibility of a single dominant perspective:

Wonderful brilliance may be gained for human judgment by getting to know men. We are all huddled and concentrated in ourselves, and our vision is reduced to the length of our nose. Socrates was asked where he was from. He replied not 'Athens' but 'the world'. He, whose imagination was fuller and more extensive, embraced the universe as his city, and distributed his knowledge, his company, and his affections to all mankind, unlike us who look only at what is underfoot. (I:26, 116)

At the same time, when Athens was under the plague, Socrates never left it to save his skin and seems never to have been the worse for it—something which Montaigne was quite unable to emulate under similar circumstances as mayor of Bordeaux! And, again, it seems that Socrates and Montaigne were divided over the use of travel, but not so far as to prevent Montaigne's appreciation of Socrates' humour:

Someone said to Socrates that a certain man had grown no better by his travels. 'I should think not,' he said, 'he took himself along with him.' (I:39, 176)

Montaigne, of course, loved travel because like Socrates he understood the difference between escapism and the kind of journey that employs its shifting circumstances as occasions for the practice of self-inquiry.

Montaigne's relation to Socrates is from the very beginning close but not servile. Certainly, there is no need to see in the cumulative references to Socrates the underlying ideal of the *Essays*. In the essay 'Of Solitude', Montaigne repeats Socrates' comment upon the activities best suited to one's state in life: the young should learn, grown men practice doing good, and old men retire from office. (I:39, 178) Montaigne straightaway modifies Socrates' advice in the light of his own more-studied experience of the relation between man's natural temperament and his beliefs and ideas. In Montaigne's view, there is no virtue in fighting our nature, and a great deal in trying to follow it, especially when it leads us away from the acts of an 'excessive virtue'. The more Montaigne relates to Socrates, not simply as the exponent of learned ignorance and the art of dialogical self-questioning, but as man subject to the bodily limits of birth, illness, death and marriage, the more Montaigne shapes Socrates in his own image. Indeed, Montaigne twice came very close to rejecting the Socratic ideal of humanity, when he considered the possibility that in Socrates' view virtue experiences no internal opposition, and that this assurance of victory really emptied Socrates' equanimity in the face of death. (II:11, 308) It is essential to Montaigne's view of Socrates that his bodily experience was similar to that of any other person and thus he places far more belief in Socrates' equanimity in the face of death upon noticing how Socrates could not resist scratching himself when released from chains. In this small detail, Socrates, unlike the noble Cato, provided for any person to identify with his otherwise matchless calm:

> And who that has a mind however little tinctured with true philosophy can be satisfied with imagining Socrates as merely free from fear and passion in the incident of his imprisonment, his fetters, and his condemnation? And who does not recognize in him not only firmness and constancy (that was his ordinary attitude), but also I know not what new contentment, and a blithe cheerfulness in his last words and actions.
>
> By that quiver of pleasure that he feels in scratching his leg after the irons were off, does he not betray a like sweetness and joy in his soul at being unfettered by past discomforts and prepared to enter into the knowledge of things to come? Cato will pardon me, if he please; his death is more tragic and tense, but this one is still, I know not how, more beautiful. (II:11, 310)

Montaigne cannot admire Socrates as a paragon of virtue. It is essential to his admiration that Socrates display a tendency to vice (II:11, 313) and an ultimate subjection to the limits of embodiment. Socrates would be of no significance to us had he not been a person like the rest of us, and of this his bodily experience is the ultimate testimony that we have of his truly human achievement:

> The saliva of a wretched mastiff, spilled on Socrates' hand, could shake all his wisdom and all his great and well regulated ideas, and annihilate them in such a way that no trace would remain of his former knowledge:
> > The power of the soul
> > Is troubled . . . and, asunder cleft,
> > Is all dispelled, by that same poison reft.
> > > Lucretius
> And this venom would find no more resistance in this soul than in that of a child of four; a venom capable of making all philosophy, if it were incarnate, raving mad. (II:12, 412)

It cannot be denied that Montaigne had a profound respect for Socrates. Yet it is clear from the very beginning that what interests Montaigne is the evidence of Socrates' humanity, his humour and irritability, as much as anything in his teaching. Above all, Montaigne rejects any interpretation of Socrates that makes him a monster of reason and self-control, if only because virtue unmixed with vice could be a lesser virtue—or else unheard of among people and of no relevance to their affairs. Indeed, it does not tarnish his image of Socrates to consider that his equanimity in the face of death was as much due to his preference for death rather than see his mind collapse with old age. (III:2, 620) For the lesson he saw in Socrates and himself was that one must live in relation to one's capacities and circumstance —a thing harder to accomplish than the conquests of Alexander:

> Therefore retired lives, whatever people may say, accomplish duties as harsh and strenuous as other lives, or more so. And private persons, says Aristotle, render higher and more difficult service to virtue than those who are in authority. We prepare ourselves for eminent occasions more for glory than for conscience. The shortest way to attain glory would be to do for conscience what we do for glory. And Alexander's virtue seems to me to represent much less vigor in his theater than does that of Socrates in his lowly and obscure activity. I can easily imagine Socrates in Alexander's place; Alexander in that of Socrates, I cannot. If you ask the former what he knows how to do, he will answer 'Subdue the world'; if you ask the latter, he will say, 'Lead the life of man in conformity with its natural condition'; a knowledge much more general, more weighty, and more legitimate. (III:2, 614)

Man is quick to glory and the world is full of the marvels he has left as monuments to his own name, his family, state and religion. There is nothing so strange that it cannot be pressed into the service of this glory. So long as men are mortal, we can expect them to continue in the pursuit of being remembered. What makes Socrates remarkable is that he knew there is no external mark of our success in self-understanding and nowhere else to look for it than within ourselves, on the very spot where all our flights of vainglory are fuelled. That Socrates could stay at home does not mean that he was afraid or tired of the world. It means that he had mastered the art of not straying from himself and the daily care of his soul. Thus Montaigne, too, could stay at home, attendant to the daily care of the *Essays*. But he confesses he could never bring himself to prefer death to exile, as Socrates did. Though he can admire him for it, he cannot love him for that decision. (III:9, 743) Still, he would have chosen with Socrates to drink the hemlock, rather than with Cato to have stabbed himself to death. (III:9, 752) Montaigne needs only an imperfect ideal—another man—however exceptional, but not a god. Socrates married and could not count. He spoke of nothing but carters, joiners, cobblers and masons, using words and similes from life that anyone can understand:

> There is nothing borrowed from art and the sciences; even the simplest can recognize in him their means and their strength; it is impossible to go back further and lower. He did a great favor to human nature by showing how much it can do by itself. (III:12, 794)

Yet in the very last pages of the *Essays* (III:13, 856) Montaigne decidedly rejects that side of Socrates which had to do with his daemon. It is essential to the contemplation of the death of Socrates that his last words were those of an ordinary man speaking in his own voice and not the instrument of either the gods or their poetry—though he might have been better looking (III:12, 810) as befits the beauty of his soul! The death of Socrates remains a glorious example for us, not because his soul was immortal but for the very reason that he was mortal. Therefore Socrates lives only in those who have learned from him to live in themselves.

Montaigne is adamant that there can be no first principles of reasoning regarding man. Every line of thought and feeling is subject to the overlap of mind and body. What is difficult in man, as opposed to the animals, is that his nature is not given to him apart from his own efforts to find it out and to ascertain its limits. This is the humanist enterprise and the *Essays* are a fundamental innovation in the humanist method of self-inquiry, just as Montaigne's lived experience is their origin and resource:

> My behavior is natural; I have not called in the help of any teaching to build it. But feeble as it is, when the desire to tell it seized me, and when, to make it appear in public a little more decently, I set myself to support it with reasons and examples, it was a marvel to myself to find it, simply by chance, in conformity with so many philosophical examples and reasons. What rule my life belonged to, I did not learn until after it was completed and spent. A new figure: an unpremeditated and accidental philosopher! (II:12, 409)

Thus, Montaigne is quite free of any constructive or principled inquiry into the nature of man because such an enterprise already presupposes what it pretends to be in search of with respect to reason. The humanist enterprise cannot be grounded transcendentally, any more than it can rest for very long upon an alienated and ironic comparison between types of men or the varieties of folly. The *Essays* are therefore a genuine methodological innovation, the discovery of an unpremeditated and accidental inquiry into the nature of a being without any intrinsic nature, apart from this very inquiry. In short, Montaigne comes upon the discovery that *the self is a form of writing*, an improvisation of nature and culture that not even Wisdom herself is willing to separate against man. Writing is the moving trace of our temporality, holding in being what comes to be through its withholding. Writing is the event within that fold of being created by a man bent upon himself in the evocation of his life through which he sounds out the truth and goodness of his own sense and reason as exemplars of his kind. Writing is the unfinished creation of man because man is never ahead of himself, but always there at work upon himself, proportioned to his abilities and circumstances, strengthened by the traditions and community which previous writings continue to resound. *Writing, then, resounds man's being.* But not in the sense that it engages in any literal transcription; nor even that it saves the first sounds of speech. It resounds because it is an intersensory and bodily accumulation of man's experience that has always to be taken up in telling, or listening, or in writing and reading, in pain and in pleasure.

# Essay 3

## Ross Fitzgerald

So many today, especially among the 'educated', are still determined to be determinists. The aim of this essay is to argue (against those who undermine the dignity of the human personality) that individual choice, volition, intentionality and personal responsibility are the cluster of characteristics that make human beings uniquely human. From this perspective, the central reality of the human condition is the fact that human beings can choose. Also implied is an imperative that if we are to be, or to become, authentically human we ought to exercise and extend our distinctly human capacity for freedom of choice and for purposive action. Being human in this sense is only a potentiality, not a given. It does not come automatically with the chromosomes or with the physiological make-up of the species *Homo sapiens*. The capacity to be human is something to be attained or striven towards, and which can be either helped or hindered by the actions and attitudes of the self, and of others.[1]

The last century has witnessed a pronounced tendency, from within the Academy and from without, to diminish or deny the domain of human freedom. According to the dominant intellectual paradigm, human beings are driven or conditioned creatures, determined by forces outside our control. It is often held we are not responsible for our actions and are incapable of choice. If human freedom is not denied entirely, then fewer and fewer of our everyday actions are regarded

[1] See Bernard Zuger, 'Understanding Human Freedom', *American Journal of Psychotherapy*, Vol. 26, April 1972, p. 263.

as being free. More and more forms of human behaviour (and especially compulsions, which allegedly absolve human beings of moral responsibility) are attributed to unconscious psychological processes or to external social pressures which are beyond individual control.[2] In tune with this regnant view, notions of purpose, goal, intent and autonomy are regarded as being illusory.

Those, especially among our educators, who deny or diminish the reality of personal choice and purposive action are, in a precise sense, aiding and abetting the dehumanization of man. The propagation and acceptance of deterministic theories of human action lead like a self-fulfilling prophecy to a sense of individual powerlessness among human beings, which in turn undermines our sense of personal responsibility and our perceived capacity for choice. No one can stand the belief in one's powerlessness for long without degenerating into apathy, meaninglessness and despair, or breaking out into violently destructive or self-destructive activities. Apart from the denial of the massive human fact of reflective consciousness, because deterministic theories have such critical consequences it is vital to defend and maintain the reality of human freedom and the perception of being free. Even those like Herbert M. Lefcourt, who hold that 'freedom and control are both illusions, inventions of man to make sense of his experience', emphasize that the 'illusion' that one can exercise personal choice has a definite and positive role in sustaining human life. Indeed, Lefcourt concludes, the alleged illusion of choice 'may be the bedrock on which life flourishes'.[3] Lefcourt and his like are profoundly mistaken in denying the reality of personal choice. But he is certainly right in implying that it matters enormously which stand we take on the fundamental issue of whether human beings are seen to be determined or seen to be free to decide for ourselves —or a mixture of both. In fact there is no more important task for educators and for the human sciences than to decide by which image of humanity we are to be led and which concept of humanity we are to adopt.

Denial of the possibility of human freedom and of the reality of individual choice is often tied to the philosophical position that we are never morally responsible for *any* of our actions because all of

---

[2]  See Robert Audi, 'Moral Responsibility, Freedom and Compulsion', *American Philosophical Quarterly*, Vol. 11, No. 1, January 1974, pp. 1–14.

[3]  See Herbert M. Lefcourt, 'The Function of the Illusions of Control and Freedom', *American Psychologist*, Vol. 28, 1973, pp. 417–26. See also Ivan D. Steiner, 'Perceived Freedom', *Advances in Experimental Social Psychology*, Vol. 5, 1971, pp. 187–248, esp. pp. 188 and 240.

our actions are causally determined. To hold someone morally responsible for an action, the bare minimum condition is that the act in question must be voluntary. That is, we presuppose that the person could have chosen to act otherwise on the relevant occasion, which in turn presupposes indeterminacy. To deny choice makes it meaningless to talk of moral responsibility. And we cannot speak of 'choice' without implying that human alternatives are present.[4] Notions of personal choice and the freedom of human beings to act (within the limits we shall later discuss) are, of course, intimately related to each other. The reality of both is denied by the dominant determinist paradigm.

Contemporary philosophical determinism is itself often, if not always, connected to an outmoded positivistic view of science which in turn is based on a mechanistic Newtonian-Galilean model of the universe. Applying the Newtonian model of cause and effect to human beings results in man being viewed solely as a mechanism. The effect of using the 'objective' mechanical-causal model of explanation (that is, human beings as mere matter in motion) has been to reduce the intentionalist vocabulary of desire, goal and purpose to something resembling the 'hard' technical language of mechanics, for example, drives, impulses, inputs, output, conditioning. In the 'scientific' study of human action we have seen the attempt to convert human beings into things; in other words to dehumanize human beings by adopting a reductionist, mechanistic and materialist model of what it means to be human. Especially in the social sciences, the Newtonian view of man and the universe still holds sway. This is despite the fact that the very foundations of that 'objective' view (that is, the absolute reality of space, time and matter, and the notion of causality) have long been dissolved by quantum physics, Einstein's theory of relativity and Heinsenberg's uncertainty principle.[5]

Of all the attempts to undermine personal responsibility and choice in our age, the impact especially of Freudian theory, stressing the primacy of drives and instincts, and of behaviourism, employing the model of stimulus–reinforcement–response, has been to vastly increase the sphere of determinism. (Marxist theory, via the notion of

[4] See Robert Young, 'Moral Responsibility', *The Journal of Value Inquiry*, Vol. VIII, Spring 1974, pp. 57-68, and Gerald W. Smith, 'Determinism, Freedom and Responsibility', *Issues in Criminology*, Vol. 3, No. 2, Spring 1968, pp. 183-194, especially pp. 186-7.

[5] See, for example, Floyd W. Matson, *The Broken Image—Man, Science and Society*, George Braziller, New York, 1964, pp. 129-155, and Ludwig von Bertalanffy, *Problems of Life*, Harper Torchbooks, New York, 1960.

Historical Materialism, is the other most important determinist attempt.) The upshot of the acceptance of a deterministic definition of man, especially in philosophy and the psychological sciences, has led many to the conclusion that human freedom or volition are absurdities, and has produced the belief that the more we know about people's past history, the less they seem responsible for their present behaviour. The acceptance of determinism thus threatens to produce a revolution in moral theory by denying the notion of human responsibility altogether.[6]

Despite all their obvious differences, both behaviourist psychology and Freudian theory have promoted a conception of people as driven and determined beings—as creatures either conditioned by external stimuli or at the mercy of their 'instincts'. The same applies to Marxist theory (where the possibility of individual choice and volition is, by definition, strenuously denied) although here the driving force is class conflict and changes in the mode of production.

Behaviourism, employing the mechanistic model of stimulus and response, reduces the human being to the level of a conditioned animal and regards all mental phenomena as physical events. All human responses are held to be determined by discoverable physical occurrences, namely external stimuli. Choice, will, decision, purpose and personal intention—indeed the whole mental life—are seen to be illusions. Behaviourism thus views the human being as one thing among other things. This view of the human being as a stimulus–response machine involves the reduction of human existence to nothing but physical happenings and converts intentional human phenomena into mere epiphenomena.[7] But things, like rocks, clouds and mushrooms, make no decisions, have no purposes and do not *act*. An essential attribute of human experience is lacking in things which are not agents, which no strict behaviourism can capture, precisely because behaviourism views the human being as a thing to which things *happen*.[8]

Behaviour(al)ist psychology thus treats the human subject as a

[6]  See Sidney Hook ed., *Determinism and Freedom in the Age of Modern Science*, Collier, New York, 1961, pp. 8–9.
[7]  See Viktor Frankl, 'Reductionism and Nihilism' in *Beyond Reductionism—New Perspectives in the Life Sciences*, ed. A. Koestler and J.R. Smythies, Hutchison, London, 1969, pp. 396–416, and David Holbrook, 'Politics and the Need for Meaning' in *Human Needs and Politics*, ed. R. Fitzgerald, Pergamon Press, Sydney, 1977, pp. 174–194.
[8]  See Stephen David Ross, *The Nature of Moral Responsibility*, Wayne State University Press, Detroit, 1975, pp. 44–45.

dehumanized object and, in the name of positivistic objective science, demeans the 'object' further by fragmenting it into drives, traits, reflexes, etc.[9] This approach makes meaningless any notion of moral responsibility. In his novel *Walden Two* and later in his book *Beyond Freedom and Dignity*, B.F. Skinner in fact drew the logical behavioural conclusion of determinism by maintaining that people are entirely incapable of controlling their own conduct by choice and personal decision, and that only by disposing of autonomous intentional man can we turn to the real causes of behaviour.[10] Skinner further held that by employing behavioural conditioning one could manipulate human beings—who were seen to be totally malleable—for the good of society. This view of using behaviouralist psychology as an instrument of social manipulation (in Skinner's case for the ill-defined goal of cultural survival) follows directly on from the ideas of John B. Watson, the father of behaviourism. If one accepts their model of the human being as a stimulus–response machine, then all human behaviour, by definition, is determined entirely by environmental stimuli, and the possibility of manipulation by controlling the external environment is almost limitless. There are several logical paradoxes involved in Skinner's statement of the behaviourist position, for example regarding all thinking and speech acts, including his own, as purely conditioned non-intentional behaviour (an attack ably mounted by Noam Chomsky in his review of *Verbal Behaviour*[11] and never answered by Skinner). Apart from Chomsky's objections, Skinner's view, and that of all other behaviouralists, is of course neither 'objective' nor value-free.

Freudian theory agrees with behaviourism in the fundamental image of the human being as a stimulus–response machine, although from the Freudian point of view the stimuli that work their will upon human beings come from within rather than from without. Freud's determinism was not environmental, like Watson's or Skinner's, but psychogenic. It was a theory of *instinctual* determinism which left little, if any, room for rationality, autonomy or responsibility. Whereas behaviourism placed all its stress upon stimuli from the external environment as the controlling factor in behaviour, psychoanalytical

[9]   See Floyd W. Matson, 'Humanist Theory: The Third Revolution in Psychology', *The Humanist*, Vol. 31, March/April 1971, pp. 7–11.
[10]  See Joseph H. Fichter, 'The Concept of Man in Social Science: Freedom, Values and Second Nature', *Journal for the Scientific Study of Religion*, March 1972, Vol. 11, No. 1, pp. 109–121.
[11]  *Language*, Vol. 35, No. 1, 1959, pp. 26–58. See also Tabor Machen, *The Pseudo-Science of B.F. Skinner*, Arlington House, New York, 1974.

theory placed its emphasis upon drives and instincts operating from within.[12]

Freudian psychology, because of its basis in instinct theory and its attempt to explicate human action in terms of determinate psychogenetic causes, radically undermines human autonomy and personal responsibility. This is because when people are viewed as creatures subject to unconscious impulses and drives which determine their behaviour they cannot at the same time be held to be moral agents who can make genuine choices.[13] In terms of its consequences, Freudian theory is therefore equally as catastrophic for personal freedom and responsibility as is behaviourism.

There is a clear contradiction between Freudian *theory* and its practical *therapy*. Freudian theory stresses the powerful role of irrational forces that press their claims from 'below' (the instinctual id) and from 'above' (the introjected superego) allowing the individual ego little room for autonomous manoeuvre. Psychoanalytical therapy, paradoxically, places great faith in consciousness ('The truth will set you free') and in practice depends on encouraging and enabling the patient to be free enough to choose between two or more courses of action. It is important to stress that psychoanalytic therapy is in many ways at radical variance with the theoretical foundations upon which that therapy is based. In fact, the aim of much psychotherapy (be it of a Freudian, Adlerian or Jungian nature) is to enable human beings to move from the realm of determined necessity (for example, compulsions, obsessions) to that of freedom of choice.

In terms of our current concern, what matters is that in his theory Freud aimed to establish a deterministic science, based on the image of nineteenth-century natural science. That is, Freudian theory was based on a mechanical, hydraulic cause and effect system. The nineteenth century view of mechanism, and Ernst Brücke's theory of instinct on which Freud drew, has now been repudiated in its entirety.[14]

Consistent with his psychic determinism, Freud attempted to view the human being as a libidinal energy system obeying mechanistic

[12]  See especially Floyd W. Matson, *The Broken Image, op. cit.*, pp. 194–205, and 'Humanistic Theory, The Third Revolution in Psychology', *op. cit., infra.*
[13]  *Ibid.* See also Rollo May, *Love and Will*, Norton, New York, 1969, pp. 182–183, and William Horosz, *The Crisis of Responsibility: Man as the Source of Accountability*, University of Oklahoma Press, Norman, 1974, pp. 287–8.
[14]  See, for example, Sir John Eccles' work in brain physiology, especially *Neurophysical Basis of Mind, the principles of neurophysiology*, Clarendon, Oxford, 1953, and *The Understanding of the Brain*, McGraw-Hill, New York, 1973. See also Ludwig von Bertalanffy, *Robots, Men and Minds*, George Braziller, New York, 1967.

material laws not essentially different from those that regulated the movement of the planets. In his early work particularly, he described mental operations with terminology borrowed from mechanics, hydraulics, electricity and physical chemistry—'displacement', 'conversion', 'repression', 'regression' and 'catharsis'. (On close inspection Freud's 'mechanism' is really nothing more than a mixture of mechanistic metaphors for which no physical description whatever has been given, or ever will be.) This mechanistic, reductionist vocabulary and imagery carried over into his later work, as did his mechanistic conception of the human personality. Freud's basic theory is that all human conduct is determined by 'unconscious forces' which are themselves the product of early experiences and more fundamentally of the primary instinctual drives, Eros and Thanatos, which by their nature were in perpetual conflict. As Matson points out, the crucial similarity between Marxism and classical psychoanalytical theory lies in the selection of a single type of antecedent cause as a sufficient explanation of virtually all subsequent human events: in Marxism, the 'causes' are economic conditions; in psychoanalysis they are psychogenetic and family–historical.[15] Again, as with the contradiction between Freudian theory and Freudian therapy, one also sees the variance between Marxist, or Marxist-Leninist, theory stressing the determining character of the material substructure and communist practice where *individual* choice has been of paramount importance. Lenin's decision (disputed by most of the Bolsheviks) not to wait for the electoral results before mounting the October Revolution and Mao's celebration of the revolutionary potential of the Chinese peasantry (in violation of the orthodox line of urban insurrection and the centrality of the proletariat) are two prime examples.

The dominance of determinism has not gone unchallenged. Especially in the last quarter of a century there have been many reactions against behaviourism, Freudian theory and Marxism. Humanistic psychology, the 'third force', reacted against both behaviourism and orthodox Freudian psychoanalysis. With the former it rejected the notion of determinate conditioning, and against the latter it argued that the human being was not a creature ridden and ruled by instincts, but a person capable of choice and responsibility.[16] What this produced

---

[15]   'Humanistic Theory: The Third Revolution in Psychology', *op. cit.*, pp. 8–9.

[16]   For a 'typical' statement of the position of its advocates vis a vis behaviourism and psychoanalysis, see J.F.T. Bugental ed., *Challenges of Humanistic Psychology*, McGraw-Hill, New York, 1967; c.f. the neo-Freudian critique, summarized by Karen Horney, 'Tenth Anniversary', *American Journal of Psychoanalysis*, 11, 1951, p. 7.

in theory, and what this involved in practice, was a much greater reliance upon volitional consciousness than was the case with behavioural therapy, or could be the case given the premises of psychoanalytical theory. Humanistic psychology implied an enhanced respect for personal powers of will and of reason, and of the capacity of human beings to choose and understand. Likewise, many political radicals who acknowledge a lineage from Marxism have attempted to slough off or play down deterministic aspects (as do those who emphasize the Marx of the 1844 manuscripts) and have lain great stress on personal engagement and individual decision-making. However, what must be stressed is that despite the above, the determinist image of the human being and of the explanation of human behaviour is still very much with us in the West, and especially in the Academy. This image is crucially connected with (and dependent upon) the positivistic conception of objective science outlined earlier.

A determinist view of human action, be it of behaviourist, Freudian or Marxist derivation, demeans human beings. Among all the objects and creatures in the world, we are the only ones whose behaviour is not solely determined by antecedent events, be they environmental stimuli, psychogenetic causes or economic circumstances. Human behaviour can be chosen in accordance with our conception of ourselves, our intentions and the goals we seek to attain. We alone have the capacity to choose how to act (and therefore in my sense the possibility of being or becoming 'human'). This is why we are acutely aware when this capacity is denied, or markedly diminished, as in the case of a person's physical imprisonment and coercion, or in the case of compulsive-obsessional behaviour. And this is precisely the reason we recognize the obsessive neurotic, whose ability to *act* is rendered impotent by an inability to choose, as being in some clear manner a stunted human being.

The most obvious character of obsessional-neurotic behaviour is its compulsive or 'driven' and therefore its predictable mechanical quality. In such cases (two prime examples being alcoholism and drug addiction) knowledge itself is not enough to change or remedy the situation. The classic psychoanalytical fallacy is that once alcoholics or addicts (or compulsive gamblers) know *why* they act in such a self-sabotaging manner they will cease so to act.[17] Most of us now understand that human beings may know the quality of their deeds

[17]   Similarly, behavioural conditioning therapy that allegedly teaches, for example, compulsive alcoholics to become social drinkers has been a total failure, despite some press reports to the contrary.

and yet be driven by compulsions too strong for them to withstand. That is what the word obsession literally means—'to be pushed from the wings'. People who are blocked or in conflict, whose perception is drained and distorted by neurotic obsessional drives are clearly not free enough to see even available choices, let alone be capable of making an objective, life-enhancing choice.[18] In such cases human beings are not responsible for their actions, if what they do can be termed actions at all. (Freedom of choice, it seems, can occur only when such people are released from obsession by fundamental personality shifts or transformations.)

Undoubtedly people free from external constraints may still be at the mercy of compulsions beyond their control. Personal autonomy is freedom from *control* by inner forces (not, it must be stressed, by their existence) as well as from control by external events and circumstances. All personal autonomy, of course, is constrained by *human limits*, that is, age, death, bodily requirements and the contingencies of the space-time universe. Ross argues that autonomy is more properly a property of actions than of persons, because human beings may act autonomously at some times and compulsively at others.[19] But it is the person who acts, not the act itself. A person's ability to make uncoerced choices and decisions is contingent on his or her internal and external conditions. Our biological and psychic make-up, and our physical and social environment—for example, the capabilities of our mind and body, and the climate, culture, laws and technology of our society—stimulate us to act in some ways and restrain us from acting in others. These conditions shape and define the extent and quality of our options. There are many limitations and many forms of necessity operating upon us. As Aristotle said, we are in many ways enslaved. Our condition may be 'necessitous' in a number of ways but this does not constitute determinism; for example, intelligence sets a limit on what we can hope to do or think, but leaves the content open. Unlike animals, objects or things, we are distinguished by the capacity to *know* we are limited and to choose our relationship to necessity. We alone can and must, unless we deny our consciousness, choose how we will relate to death, old age, limitations of motor skills and intelligence and, above all, how we will relate to the factors that have operated upon our upbringing and

18  See J. Schnee, 'Freedom of Choice', *American Journal of Psychoanalysis*, Vol. 32, No. 2, 1972, pp. 206–9.
19  S.D. Ross, *The Nature of Moral Responsibility*, Wayne State University Press, Detroit, 1975, p. 214.

personality, and the social forces that continue so to operate. Human *response* is the basic question here, volitional to the core; will we accept these necessities, deny them, rebel against them, shape them, mould them? The acceptance of necessity and limitation does not involve the abdication of personal responsibility. On the contrary, the response to necessity and human limitation places choice and volition in the forefront. The basis of human freedom in this sense is our relationship and response to necessity.[20]

Bearing in mind all these aspects of necessity and limitation, it is important that we choose between two radically different approaches towards human activity and the conduct of inquiry.

The first approach is to regard human activity as an event essentially similar to non-human events, like eclipses or thunderstorms. This approach involves classifying human activity as *happening* (that is, as behaviour determined by causes) rather than as *action*, which is directed towards the attainment of goals and which therefore has ethical implications. By so doing, this 'objective' approach commits the investigator to treating human beings essentially as no different from things. The type of explanation involved is reductionist and materialist.

The second approach involves a totally different paradigm and provides quite a different type of explanation. In this approach human action is regarded as a unique achievement of which only we are capable. From this perspective, the fact that human beings are free to *act*—are capable of choosing among alternative courses of action —is what distinguishes us from objects and animals. It is this potentiality which enables people to become moral agents. All human action, in contrast to things that happen to people, involves choice and takes place in a context of value. Hence no human action is devoid of moral implications.[21] Human action in this sense involves reasons and meanings, rather than mechanistic causes. The type of explanation involved is thus intentionalist and purposive.

The above, of course, are only models. Thus explanation in the natural sciences is not uniformly deterministic, and cannot be if Newton is outmoded, as indeed is the case. In practice 'scientific' explanation is diverse—for example, statistical, teleological, hierarchical, volitional and subjective, as well as mechanistic. But the mechanistic *model* predominates and provides the paradigm for

[20]   See Rollo May, *Love and Will*, Norton, New York, 1969, p. 269.
[21]   See R.S. Peters, *The Concept of Motivation*, Routledge and Kegan Paul, 1958, especially pp. 12–25.

'objective' explanation. Such a paradigm not only provides no basis for understanding what it means to be human, but also militates actively against it. The intentional explanation of human action is fundamentally at variance with the mechanistic explanation of natural phenomena, and even here the mechanistic approach faces grave difficulties.

Let us take a specific example. The differences between the mechanistic and intentional approaches, and their practical implications, are clearly seen in psychotherapy where a person may be viewed either as a patient (from the first perspective) or as an agent (from the second).

That the dominance of determinism has taken hold of common language is clearly to be seen in our understanding of 'mental illness'. In Websters Dictionary, for example, the psychiatrist's concern is defined as being with behaviour 'originating in endogenous causes or resulting from faulty interpersonal relationships'. As Thomas Szasz argues, we should focus our attention on the words 'causes' and 'resulting'. By assigning endogenous causes to human behaviour, such behaviour, he points out, is classified as happening rather than as action. Szasz continues:

> Diabetes mellitus is a disease caused by an endogenous lack of enzymes necessary to metabolize carbohydrates. In this frame of reference, the endogenous cause of a depression must be either a metabolic defect (that is, an antecedent physiological event) or a defect in 'interpersonal relationships' (that is, an antecedent historical event).[22]

But what, he asks, is the status of human action in this scheme? The answer is: None. There is no such thing as action to attain a goal —only behaviour determined by causes.

In direct opposition to the determinist model, Szasz has made the notions of Freedom and Choice central to his work.[23] Szasz's approach to psychiatry as essentially a moral and political enterprise involves him in trying to show on the one hand, that by seeking relief from the burden of their moral responsibilities, human beings mystify and technologize their problems in living; and on the other hand, that the

---

[22]   See Thomas S. Szasz, *The Myth of Mental Illness: Foundations of a Theory of Personal Conduct*, Hoeber-Harper, New York, 1961. Real clinical explanations, it must be granted, are rarely this simple. The assertion made here falls to the ground when it is found that there are those with diabetes mellitus who are *not* depressed and, conversely, those who are depressed who have no (discernable) organic defect.

[23]   See especially Szasz's Introduction to his *Ideology and Insanity: Essays on the Psychiatric Dehumanization of Man*, Penguin Books, Middlesex, 1973.

demand for 'help' thus generated is met today by a behavioural or psychotherapeutic technology ready and willing to free human beings of their moral burdens by treating them as sick patients (rather than as moral agents).[24] Despite stridently, and falsely, denying the reality of *any* mental illness (as did many of the other anti-psychiatrists in the late 1960s),[25] Szasz rightly argues that the bases of modern psychiatry dehumanize and diminish human beings by denying the existence, or even the possibility, of personal responsibility.

Certainly behavioural or psychic determinism (or economic determinism for that matter) undermines the concept of the human being as a moral agent. If human dignity is to be restored to the 'mentally ill' (central to that much maligned notion precisely being an inability to choose) or is to flourish in the psychically healthy (in whom the capacity for goal-directed behaviour and autonomy of motive is by definition both more actual and apparent) we must revive and reinforce notions of human purpose and intention.

The ideas of Rollo May and Soren Kierkegaard are particularly pertinent in this regard. May's *Love and Will*, published in 1969, is one of the most important books to appear in the last two decades. Like most of psychology's 'third force' and those who are influenced by phenomenology, May makes freedom, will and intentionality central to his work.

While rightly arguing that one of Freud's great contributions lay in cutting through the futility and self-deceit of the Victorian conception of will power, May believes that Freud's view of the will has undermined our sense of personal responsibility:

> In describing how 'wish' and 'drive' move us rather than 'will', Freud formulated a new image of man that shook to the very foundations Western man's emotional, moral, and intellectual self-image.[26]

The same image of the human being as a determined creature—not *driving* any more, but *driven*—also applies to behaviourism and Marxism, as we have seen.

In rejecting the determinist model of man, May, like Szasz,

---

[24] See for example *Ibid*, p. 11, and *The Myth of Mental Illness, op. cit.*, p. 22.
[25] Apart from Szasz, see the writings of Laing and Liefer.
[26] Rollo May, *Love and Will*, Norton, New York, 1969, pp. 182–83. See also William Horosz, *The Crisis of Responsibility: Man as the Source of Accountability*, University of Oklahoma Press, Norman, 1975, pp. 287–8. On one level May's statement implies a crude knowledge of 'Western man's' self-understanding. There have been *many* determinists among the greats, for example, the Epicureans, the Stoics, Spinoza, Hobbes, Calvin and Nietzche, but most of these have also been 'free-willers' of some stripe.

emphasizes the peculiarly human property of *intentionality* which is assumed in, and underlies, the notion of meaningful human action.[27] By intentionality May means that structure that gives meaning to experience: 'It is not to be identified with intentions, but is the dimension which underlies them, it is man's capacity to have intentions . . . Intentionality is at the heart of consciousness'.[28] Intentionality implies goal-directedness. As May argues 'Each act of consciousness *tends toward* something, is a turning of the person toward something, and has within it, no matter how latent, some push toward a direction for action.'[29]

In *Love and Will* May makes a crucial distinction between explanation (for behaviour) in terms of 'reason why' and explanation (for action) in terms of 'purpose'. This distinction is slightly different from that made earlier between mechanistic causes on one hand and reasons and purposes on the other. In terms of denying the determinist model of man, however, his intention is the same. May argues that 'reason why' explanation (in my language, mechanical causal explanation) is particularly relevant to problems of neurosis in which past events *do* exercise a compulsive, repetitive, chain-like, predictable effect upon the person's actions.[30] (In my language, what is referred to here is behaviour and not action.) May maintains that *'Freud was right in the respect that rigid, deterministic causality does work in neurosis and sickness.'*[31] But, May argues, Freud was wrong in trying to apply this to all human experience, especially to those areas of life that include purposive action. The aspect of purpose that emerges when individuals can become conscious of what they are doing, May argues, opens them to new and different possibilities in the future, and introduces the elements of personal responsibility and freedom.[32]

On the basis of our knowledge of many forms of neurosis, May's claim for the working of rigid, deterministic causality in such cases can be doubted. Not even sexual fixations and deep habits like smoking are that rigid. Contrary to May's stance here, the notion of mechanism must be *entirely* abandoned in the explanation of life phenomena, and

---

[27] See especially *Love and Will*, and *The Meaning of Anxiety*, Ronald, New York, 1950.
[28] *Love and Will*, *op. cit.*, p. 223-24. See also Horosz, *The Crisis of Responsibility*, *op. cit.*, pp. 291-2.
[29] *Love and Will*, p. 200. His emphasis.
[30] *Ibid*, p. 93.
[31] *Ibid*, my emphasis.
[32] *Ibid*, p. 94.

especially of the activity of human beings. The causal–mechanistic framework cannot explain and account for human action that is motivated by purpose and intentionality. Moreover, it is instructive to realize that no one has ever *completely* described a single human action, just as no one has ever observed a single instance of evolution. Amazing, but true, given dominant objectivist intellectual paradigms. Certainly the two types of explanation—intentional and mechanistic —generate very different consequences and very different models of man.

Apart from the fact that 'mechanism' is inadequate even for the explanation of bodily movements and natural phenomena, the domi-nance of the causal–mechanical model is to the detriment of human dignity and to an understanding of the distinctive meaning of being human. As we have seen, human beings are distinguished by their capacity to choose their relationship to necessity and limitation. But, as May eloquently argues:

> Man does not simply 'stand outside' in his subjectivity, like a critic at the theater, and look at necessity and decide what he thinks of it. *His intentionality is already one element in the necessity in which he finds himself* . . . Intentionality not only makes it possible for us to take a stand vis-a-vis necessity, but requires us to take this stand. This is illustrated ad infinitum in psychotherapy, when the patient argues rigid determinism, generally when he is discouraged or wishes to escape the meaning of his intentions.[33]

May concludes that the more such people argue that they have nothing whatever to do with the fate bearing down upon them (itself an example of intentionality) the more they are making themselves determined. Here is a clear example of how the actions and attitude of the self can hinder the possibility of freedom of choice and of personal autonomy. Such people are choosing to make themselves determined. If therapists conspire to reinforce the determinist self-image they too are part of a destructive and dehumanizing process. If, on the contrary, they are able to help people to understand the mechanisms of defence and fear and to take up responsibility for their lives, then therapists are part of the process of liberation. (Granted, there is another radically different side to 'being fated', namely its energizing and vitalizing capacity—for example, seeing oneself as an instrument of God or destiny bound to triumph in righteousness. However, all this shows is that 'being determined' is an *intentional* structure. And so is freedom.)

[33] *Love and Will, op. cit.*, pp. 269–70. My emphasis.

May's stance towards freedom and determinism is very similar to the suggestions of Soren Kierkegaard.

Kierkegaard argues that failure to take responsibility for oneself, for what one is and for what one has been, is to lose the possibility of being a person or, in my terms, to forfeit the possibility of becoming human. Despite the fact that he considered human beings to be in many ways determined and conditioned, Kierkegaard suggests there is nothing so fearful as getting to know how enormously much one is capable of doing and becoming. Central to becoming human, for Kierkegaard, is choice and especially the fundamental choice of 'choosing oneself'.[34]

As George J. Stack expresses it:

> For Kierkegaard, in order to become the self I ought to be, I must first understand and accept the self I have been. This is what he means by the admonition (which is often misunderstood or dismissed as mere rhetoric): choose oneself. To choose oneself, for Kierkegaard, means to choose oneself as responsible for what one has been and to take up responsibility for one's life.[35]

Implicit in Kierkegaard's position is the notion of a 'good' or 'real' self able to be actualised.

Stack continues:

> One may yield passively to causal factors which have influenced one's moral development and renounce responsibility for what one is, or one can take up his being as his own responsibility. Not to choose or, in Freudian terminology, to allow the unconscious aspects of the self to 'choose' for one . . . lead(s) to the loss of freedom and, hence, the loss of freedom for possibility. The self is, as it were, a 'product' of inherited dispositions or traits (physical and psychic) and our own choices, decisions, and actions. Our freedom, which is by no means absolute, is realized in and through choice.[36]

Kierkegaard maintains that the necessity which dominates one's natural being can be overcome by resolute and deliberate choice, by choosing to accept responsibility for what one has been and for what one now is. Only a being who possesses the freedom to choose or

---

[34] *Soren Kierkegaard's Journals and Papers*, trans. and ed. E. Hong and H. Hong, Bloomington, London, 1967, I. p. 440.

[35] 'Kierkegaard: The Self as Ethical Possibility', *Southwestern Journal of Philosophy*, Winter 1972, Vol. 3, pp. 35–61. This article appears in a slightly revised form under the title 'Kierkegaard: The Self and Ethical Existence', *Ethics*, January 1973, Vol. 83, pp. 108–25. All references here are to the 1972 article. The quotation above is from p. 37.

[36] Stack, *op. cit.*, p. 37.

not to choose is a being who has possibilities. Paradoxically, to unlock our possibilities we must first of all accept those personal characteristics which have been acquired independent of our own (deliberate) choices. Kierkegaard suggests that one ought to take responsibility for what one is, even though one is not, strictly speaking, responsible for many aspects of what one has been. Not to choose to be responsible for one's life is, for Kierkegaard, not a choice but a passive yielding of one's life to necessity.[37] As Kierkegaard says 'There comes at last an instant when there is no question of an either/or, not because he has chosen but because he has neglected to choose, which is equivalent to saying, because others have chosen for him, because he has lost his (true) self.'[38]

For Kierkegaard there are some options one encounters that are momentous. Examples are: Should I keep my promise or not? Should I serve in combat or not? Should I believe in the existence of God or not? A choice, for Kierkegaard, is truly significant when it concerns ethical or religious commitments. Here the important thing, for Kierkegaard, is to choose, because choice is an affirmation of one's self. Irresolution is either an incapacity or unwillingness to choose. As Stack argues, it does make sense to say that certain choices are momentous for the pattern or direction of one's life and are extremely difficult to make. Thus there are many who postpone such choices—who do not choose to choose—indefinitely. And from an existential point of view, it does make sense to say that one may never choose to make an authentic choice, as Kierkegaard has described it.[39]

When Kierkegaard argues that the important thing is to choose as an affirmation of one's self, one might well ask is the point to choose or to choose well? And what if my 'self' is a monster? Do I (ought I) choose to be a monster? Once more we are faced with the problem of good and evil, to which Kierkegaard does have an answer, but one he never makes explicit. Connected with the notion of a 'good' or 'real' self, implicit in Kierkegaard's position, is also the assumption that those who choose authentically *will* choose well, in the sense of making species-enchancing, life-affirming choices.

Kierkegaard asserts that the decisive choice, to choose oneself, from which all other choices stem is a voluntary intentional act which is

---

[37] *Ibid*, p. 39.
[38] *Either/Or*, trans. W. Lowrie, New York, 1959, Vol. 11, p. 16. See also p. 170.
[39] Stack, *op. cit.*, pp. 41–42.

within the power of every individual.[40] In this he is clearly wrong. A psychopath, for example, is precisely the kind of being who is incapable of choice (and self-acceptance) as Kierkegaard understands it. How many others of our species, apart from grossly pathological cases, are unable so to choose is a question he ignores.

An individual who chooses himself, Kierkegaard maintains, chooses himself as this concrete individual who exists here and now and whose present existence has been shaped by causal factors which he appropriates. That is,

> The individual . . . becomes conscious of himself as this definite individual, with these talents, these dispositions, these instincts, these passions, influenced by those definite surroundings, as this definite product of a definite environment. But being conscious of himself in this way, he assumes responsibility for all this.[41]

As Stack explains, having freely chosen what has been imposed upon them, as it were, individuals are now able to bear responsibility for what they do with these inherited dispositions, these psychological tendencies or characteristics.[42] For Kierkegaard human freedom is not limitless, as it is for Sartre. Rather, it is a finite freedom of a being shaped and influenced by a number of circumstances which are outside the individual's power. Kierkegaard suggests, paradoxically, that individuals can choose to accept responsibility (through self-knowledge) for what they are not responsible for, to attain a freedom for their own unique possibilities. To Kierkegaard, one of the many paradoxes of human existence is that individuals are determined in their being, but determining in their becoming.[43] My own position, clearly, denies that individuals are *determined* in either being or becoming.

Individuals' release from neurosis often begins when they are able to accept the historical and psychosocial necessity that 'made' them

---

[40]    Stack, *op. cit.*, p. 42. Sartre expresses an even stronger version of this position, (M)an is what he wills . . . (W)hat we usually understand by wishing or willing is a conscious decision taken—much more often than not—after *we have made ourselves what we are.* I may wish to join a party, to write a book or to marry —but in such a case what is usually called my will is probably a manifestation of a prior and more spontaneous decision. If, however, it is true that existence is prior to essence, *man is responsible for what he is.* Thus, the first effect of existentialism is that it puts every man in possession of himself as he is, *and places the entire responsibility for his existence squarely on his own shoulders. Existentialism and Humanism*, trans. P. Mairet, Methuen, New York, 1948, pp. 19-20. My emphases.

[41]    *Either/Or*, II, p. 255.

[42]    *Op. cit.*, p. 45.

[43]    *Ibid*, p. 46.

what they are. The process of personal autonomy begins to occur only when individuals accept the fact that they are, to a greater or a lesser extent, products of the social psychological world into which they were so involuntarily placed and in which they were nurtured and formed.[44] In a similar vein, Morris Isenberg, the analyst, maintains that:

> Although no person, neurotic or not, is entirely responsible for his acts, it behooves him to live as if he is fully responsible for himself. Although freedom of choice is minimal in the neurotic person, that person did respond to the adverse circumstances of his childhood with his own specific neurosis. *If he assumes responsibility for this choice, he will be better able to tackle his neurosis. Furthermore, by assuming he has full responsibility for his acts, he may find he has more power than he believed and may be able to tap hidden potential.* He may become more aware of his real assets and limitations, of his body and his actual identity. He may be in a better position to resist any exorbitant demands others make upon him.[45]

As a personal or psychotherapeutic tactic, this stance makes enormous sense, often opening hidden reservoirs of intentionality and volition.[46]

To stress freedom of choice is not, of course, to deny that some human beings are often controlled by internal and external forces (in ancient language, by their passions and by their circumstances) and that perhaps most human beings are at some times so controlled. However, it is to point to the possibility of increased autonomy—of becoming human. In terms of this schema, the more human beings can choose their relationship to internal and external circumstances the more free and human they become. (It must be stated clearly that this is on the assumption that those who choose authentically will choose well—an assumption which cannot by its nature be rendered unambiguously empirical.) However, if people fail to gain such freedom of choice, they remain enslaved and in some ways less than human. If having gained it, they lose or relinquish it, they again

---

[44] See Ronald Fernandez, 'Toward a Social Psychology of Freedom', *Journal of Human Relations*, Vol. 19, No. 1, 1971, pp. 57–67. My emphasis.

[45] 'Responsibility and the Neurotic Patient', *American Journal of Psychoanalysis*, Vol. 34, No. 1, 1974, pp. 43–50. The quotation is from p. 46. See also B. Zuger, 'Understanding Human Freedom', *op. cit., infra.*

[46] Many empirical studies have demonstrated how important is the ability of human beings to gain, and sustain, a sense of personal control (see, for example, Richard de Charms, *Personal Causation: The Internal Affective Determinants of Behavior,* Academic Press, New York, 1969, and M. Brewster Smith, 'Metapsychology, Politics and Human Needs', in R. Fitzgerald ed., *Human Needs and Politics, op. cit.,* p. 139). An important recent study in this regard (among the institutionalized elderly) is that by Ellen J. Langer and Judith Rodin, 'The Effects of Choice and Enhanced Personal Responsibility for the Aged: A Field Experiment in an Institutional Setting' in *Journal of Personality and Social Psychology*, Vol. 34, No. 2, 1976, p. 191–198.

become enslaved and less than human. Becoming human then is a process in which personal choice and intentionality is at the forefront.

Partly because people in the grip of obsessional-neurotic patterns of behaviour are less than human, compulsions *do* absolve human beings of responsibility, in as much as at that time they are incapable of choice. But while this is true, it is of paramount importance to emphasize the possibility of shifting from the realm of necessity to that of determining freedom. Expressed another way, this is to say that becoming human involves the possibility of moving from the domain of involuntary behaviour to that of voluntary action. Despite all the ontological problems involved, increased personal autonomy is *not* an illusion, and no one who has practiced psychotherapy or been released from compulsive obsessions can doubt the reality and immense human significance of unfolding personal freedom and acquisition of responsibility. Here, as elsewhere, which model of man one adopts is crucial.

Given the reality of necessity and human limitation, people are essentially confronted with two choices. (The same applies to those who study them.) As May and Kierkegaard make crystal-clear, either individuals can lament what they are by appealing to a universal determinism which 'made' them what they are, or they can take up their own beings, their past and present selves, as their own responsibility. One can begin to become autonomous (or human, in my sense) only when one can accept responsibility for what one is. Making this crucial human choice does not negate—on the contrary it emphasizes—that such choice occurs in the context of limitation and necessity. It also points to the fact that knowing and accepting the self, let alone rejoicing in it, very often requires the help of significant others.

The aim of this essay has been to argue that as persons or professionals we ought not escape our human responsibilities by taking refuge in simple determinism, by claiming that we are driven by 'instincts' which overpower us or that we have been conditioned by family–historical or socio–economic forces outside ourselves to be as we unfortunately are. The 'advantage' of determinism is precisely that it lays the blame on someone or something else. And in one sense it *is* advantageous if those who are ugly and abject, poor and powerless, can attribute their condition to Fate, economic forces or the will of God. But the 'advantage' thus gained is at the price of reducing human beings to the status of things or objects.

While we can choose not to be responsible, becoming human is also a choice. Despite all the necessities of the world, there remains the possibility that we can choose ourselves, and take responsibility for our lives and for our actions. It is true that many are unwilling or unable to confront the existential risk of freedom of choice, which is the basis of personal responsibility. How many of our species are unable is indeed a moot point. Confronting and accepting responsibility for one's self is often, if not always, accompanied by much fear and trembling. But it is only by so doing that we can be or become human. Those who deny this possibility, in the name of deterministic theories, render human dignity a grave disservice.

# Essay 4

## James Chowning Davies

### Existence, living, and I

Existence would be simple, easy and durable, if I were a proton. Once I established a relationship with an electron, I could maintain it, not for a transitory life but forever—unless of course some cosmic force decided to split my electron from me or some humans found how to split us and, without thinking, blew everything apart. Even then, I would continue to exist. Momentarily separated from my electron, I would naturally be attracted to another one. In some minuscule orgasm we would be united and again it would be 'forever'. If in a universal winding down of energy there developed in the universe some kind of cold, entropic, total uniformity, my electron and I might still be together 'forever'. We could hibernate, retaining our elemental power, our potential, that defines us as amounting to something. We could wait for the next renaissance or resubstantiation or activation of matter. I would never cease to exist, if I were a proton.

In saying this, I am not feeling oceanically, because atomic particles don't feel. But I do exist. On the other hand, wrapped up in and alone with my electron, I would never really be alive.

Living would surely be simple, easy and probably forever, if I were a one-celled organism. My conspecifics and I could forever spend our time gathering our substance from the environment, in an orderly manner controlled by our ribonucleic and deoxyribonucleic acids which enable us to create and procreate ourselves. Life would be simple but far more challenging and interactive than the mere existence of atomic particles. And we would live 'forever' unless some higher cosmic order destroyed all life, or some human intelligence found out how to destroy me and all my conspecifics—found out how to destroy all life—and did so. But given the right circumstances, we would return, even if it took eons to rediscover our genetic program. It is determined that life shall exist and so we shall exist, alive, 'forever'.

In saying this, I am not feeling oceanically, because one-celled life is not supposed to feel. But I do live. On the other hand, I could not much control circumstances or even myself.

Living would be more complex, varied, uncertain and less surely forever, if I were a multicelled organism like an insect, a worm or a crustacean, like a clam, or a vertebrate, like a snake, a salamander or a shark. My own life would be terminal but, with cosmic and human sufferance, my own wit and my own will, I could quite confidently guarantee that my species would live forever. Existence would be better for me than for one-celled organisms and for inorganic matter, because existence for me would be a larger challenge to my ability to control circumstances and myself. To effect such control, I would need all the neurones and hormones my DNA had genetically programmed into my nature and caused my nature to mature, but it would be worth it. I could seek food, shelter and a transitory mate, and try to avoid becoming food for some more advanced and mobile creature. I could fulfill my purposes and live and procreate and control my environment a little.

In saying this, I am not feeling oceanically, because such relatively simple forms of life are not supposed to feel. But my life would be as varied as I could stand. I could control myself and my actions, a little, probably not in the pursuit of happiness but surely in the pursuit of self- and species-survival. On the other hand, I would remain controllable and controlled by external forces, including intelligences superior to my own.

Living woud be even more complex, variegated, and challenging if I were a higher vertebrate having more than a rudimentary cortex, like a mouse, a cat or a dog. My own life would be terminal but, by storing experience in my memory neurones, I could learn and even pass on to my off-spring some of the benefit of my own experience that helps make my species survive. I could teach them to distinguish food from poison, prey from predators, mates from rivals for mates, and friends from enemies. The same forces that threaten the life of lower creatures would affect me: flood, drought, disease, predators and the carelessness of my own hunger, illness and old age that sometimes makes killers out of even my own conspecifics.

But, having learned from my parents and other parts of the environment, I could meet the challenges of survival with some optimism. And I could live with some happiness, in the pursuit not simply of survival but also of the enjoyment of association, of mutual regard and of just plain fun. I could play with objects and fellow creatures and leap and chase, just for the fun of it.

Life for me would be far more of a challenge than for an insect or a snake, because I would be more capable of adapting to circumstances and of changing my circumstances. As a mouse, I could learn where other creatures store food and could steal it. As a cat or a dog, I could even learn how to live openly with the most advanced creatures—human beings—and, even more exciting, how to work and play with them.

In saying this I am probably not feeling oceanically, because it is not supposed that such vertebrates experience such feeling. But I am capable of other feelings and do have an intelligence and memory that make some complex learning possible and transmissible from one generation to the next. On the other hand, I would be more controlled than controllable, in comparison with human beings, who don't always consistently command me to do what they want me to do and who play with me when they want to, not when I want to.

### Conscious identification and the oceanic feeling

This anthropomorphizing of simpler forms of matter and of life is both fantasy and reality. It is fantasy in that it attributes such human characteristics as observation and introspection to these simpler forms. It is reality in that it distinguishes the kinds of interaction with environment that successively higher forms of life experience. But in no event can this verbalized, written, conscious kind of identification be regarded as the oceanic feeling on my part, as a human being.

It is clear that there are common characteristics of interaction, even as between atomic particles and their environment and human beings and theirs. Both interact with high specificity and predictability to particular aspects of their environment. Both are subject to forces arising from within and from outside themselves: they manifest their own nature and interact with other aspects of nature. And both operate in accordance with discoverable but not yet very much discovered natural law—that is, with basic principles of interaction. The laws governing the interaction of atomic particles of complex, and we are just entering a new and deeper level of analysis, of subatomic particles: quarks, whose quirks are not yet well understood. The laws governing the interactions of humans with their environment are almost infinitely more complex and much less well known than those pertaining to quarks.

Anthropomorphizing here serves two purposes, in addition to indicating that all matter interacts in accordance with its discovered and undiscovered natural characteristics on the one side and its environment on the other. It serves the purpose of showing that there is an interdependence between all matter and that this interdependence, this mutual determination, works in accordance with the laws of their interactions.

Electrons and protons do not behave in accordance with one set of principles in outer space and with another when they pass from molecule to molecule in copper wire or from neurone to neurone in the brain. The circumstances in which electrons move limit their natural velocity. If the signal velocity of electricity is approximately the speed of light (roughly 300,000 kilometres or 186,000 miles per second) in a copper wire and only about 100 metres or 328 feet per second maximum in the nervous system,[1] it is the characteristics of the copper wire and the nervous system which make for the different electrical velocities. And when electricity in the nervous system behaves differently (for example, travelling at different speeds), again it is the circumstances (for example, number of synapses between the points measured) which elicit different behaviours of electricity.

We suppose at least some of the basic principles of storage of information, of experience, in the brains of goldfish[2] are like those that govern information storage in the brains of human beings. The pheromones that attract some male insects to females are not the same as the scents that attract male to female dogs, but the neurochemical processes in all such cases are presumed to obey the same principles of organic chemistry. In short, there is a supposedly coherent unity to all matter and life which is not perhaps a total unity but is one which nevertheless establishes a common base, both for orderly interactions among all entities (organic and inorganic) and also for orderly, scientific analysis of these interactions.

[1]  Mary A.B. Brazier, 'The Electrical Activity of the Nervous System', *Science*, 146, 1423–1428 (11 December 1964).
[2]  See, for example, B.W. Agranoff, 'Agents That Block Memory', in G.C. Quarton *et al.*, eds, *The Neurosciences: A Study Program*, The Rockefeller University Press, New York, 1967, pp. 756–764; and B.W. Agranoff, 'Memory and Protein Synthesis', *Scientific American*, 216(6), 115–122 (June 1967).

A second purpose of such anthropomorphizing is to indicate the cumulative element as one moves from atomic to human entities. That is, not only are there orderly interaction patterns between various forms of life. There are also stored in the genes of more complex forms of life interaction patterns which summate some of the interaction patterns of simpler forms. The human central nervous system passes signals from one neurone to another in accordance with basic principles of organic chemistry, notably the transport of ions of potassium and sodium across the synapse.[3] But the human organism also, in somatic (that is, non-nervous) tissue, uses methods of cell division like those functioning in single-celled organisms.

Human reproduction is in complex ways akin to that of other vertebrates, even to creatures that are rather low on the phylogenetic scale. Like some insects, human beings are sexually attracted by odours. Like fish, they fertilize eggs. Like amphibians, they copulate. Like some other vertebrates, they form transitory or enduring sexual and nuclear family ties with one other individual. But in addition to copulating, humans also make love.

In short, human existence and human behaviour are, in one of their most basic and universal characteristics, summative of a host of laws governing all matter and in part governing much if not all lower forms of life. The laws governing human behaviour are thus not only consistent with those governing other forms of matter and life; they are also inclusive. The laws spell out basic principles first grandly enunciated by Darwin and ever since examined in deeper understanding and growing detail by natural scientists.

The identification process as anthropomorphically outlined above differs from the oceanic feeling Freud described.[4] The basic difference is that identification, which may start and continue as an unconscious process, can also become conscious and self-conscious. The oceanic feeling, on the other hand, which may start in exhausted or bored consciousness, becomes an unutterable, unconscious process.[5] Identification is emergent; the oceanic feeling is submergent. The

[3]  For the excitement of early work (including philosophical dialogues with Karl Popper) on the synapse, see John C. Eccles, 'Under the Spell of the Synapse', in F.G. Worden et al., eds, The Neurosciences: Paths of Discovery, The MIT Press, Cambridge, Massachusetts, 1975, pp. 158-179.

[4]  Sigmund Freud, Civilization and Its Discontents, The Hogarth Press, London, 1930, pp. 12-14, 21. See also J.C. Davies, Human Nature in Politics, John Wiley, New York, 1963, pp. 81-82.

[5]  For a summary of the experiments with stimulus deprivation, which often precedes the oceanic feeling, see J.C. Davies, op. cit., pp. 105-108.

identifier becomes and remains aware that (s)he is not an electron, an atom, an amoeba, an insect, a snake or a primate, but remains human. And it is precisely because (s)he is human that (s)he is able to 'objectify' and 'symbolize' the very real relationship between discrete objects in nature and components of human self.

The oceanic feeling, on the other hand, involves a merging with the environment, but one in which an individual loses consciousness of self and becomes in his own mind indistinct, indistinguishable from any aspect of the environment. It is a necessarily transitory phenomenon. One cannot maintain the oceanic feeling forever, any more than one can forever be falling asleep or waking up. Even more critically, the oceanic feeling dissolves an individual so that the contact and the interaction with other objects is lost, because there is no longer anything distinct to establish contact with. The oceanic feeling in that aspect is like a drop of water that falls into the sea, rather than like a human, a dolphin or even a rock or a particle of dust that jumps out of or falls into the sea without losing its distinctness.

The oceanic feeling, being transitory, can be a real feeling only in some purely mental sense, one that is dissociated from distinct objects in the environment. It does not represent an object in the environment but rather the enveloping and mental dissolution of a person in the total and undifferentiated environment, from which the individual is no longer capable of distinguishing self. This de-differentiation occurs in the mind, even though the individual in an objective sense and as seen by other human beings does remain distinct and does regain a sense of distinctness—unless (s)he dies in the hunger or cold or solitude or other intrusion or normal interaction with environment that can induce the oceanic feeling. Its etiology may be objectively various, but its objective environmental references become dissolved in the feeling, the sensation, that merges into nonfeeling, nonsensation, unconsciousness.

The distinction between objectifiable human identification with hundreds of discrete aspects of reality and the oceanic feeling is a crucial one, because without the distinction here described it is impossible to denote objects with which one can or does identify. When one does so identify, one is denoting, recognizing, distinguishing those objects. Without a human observer, objects could not be aspects of the interaction, in which the other necessary part is a human being. (S)he not only senses the interaction but also becomes aware of it, conscious of it and can describe it symbolically. A person experiencing the oceanic feeling, so to speak, dissolves into incoherent, inarticulate unconsciousness. A person identifying with atomic particles, amoebae, birds or other human beings is at the same time aware of her or his separateness, distinctness and identity. (S)he never loses a sense of self, but gains a sense of dynamic, interactive ties with other objects; and is able to express the sense of identity established between objects and the distinct relationship between objects.

One cannot stand apart from the universe or any object in it without being a part of it. The paradox of distinctness necessarily includes a relationship and identity with other objects. This relationship to and identification with some aspects of the environment in some ways makes an individual part of these aspects. As an electron related to a proton is part of an atom, so an individual is part of a community, of nature and of matter. Individuals are not definable, not identifiable, except as defined in such contexts. Both the existence of the relationship and the awareness of it distinguish identification as a process from the oceanic feeling as a process.

### Natural harmony and human identity

With respect to these interactions, these interdependencies with the natural world, what does it mean to be human? Two things are critical, and it is hard to say which is more so. One is that we are ultimately derived from nature. The natural harmony between human nature and the natural environment has made humankind more a product than a producer of the world around human beings. Nature has made us what we are organically, even in the fundamental sense that our enormous ability to learn and to do things to the environment is a natural characteristic. We need therefore have no fear of any *naturally* established or imposed alienation from nature. We are made from it and remain part of it. If we human beings function contrary to natural laws, the probabilities of destroying environment (natural, social and cultural) and ourselves rise rapidly. On the other hand, if we human beings function in accordance with these laws, the probabilities are very high of some good outcomes. What this means can be examined more specifically later.

The second critical thing is that to be able to function harmoniously and creatively with natural laws—including neurophysiological and genetic laws that constitute human nature—human beings have to understand them. Crucially, many such laws remain to be discovered and not all will ever be known. But until recent centuries this did not make much difference because the ignorance was so vast and the knowledge so minuscule. There is some kind of unconscious interaction that has governed and continues to govern virtually all natural processes, including the evolution of life from its simplest viral and cellular forms to its most complex. An atom of hydrogen does not need to know that it is composed of one electron and one proton to be so composed. Water need know nothing of laws of gravity or of Boyle to flow down as a liquid and to expand (upwards) as a gas. And the evolution of life forms has involved no human intelligence, even though it took that intelligence billions of years to get where it is now in *Homo sapiens*; and a Darwin—only a century ago—to understand the principles of the very varied but orderly processes of evolution.

However, for human beings to exercise even a modicum of the control they are capable of, they cannot interact with or try to act upon their environment altogether unconsciously. If they do interact unconsciously, their interaction is in kind indistinguishable from that of unconscious atoms, viruses and cells—or from the more voluntary 'willed' actions and interactions of vertebrate life forms which have complex brains, that is, central control systems.

Human beings remain controlled by natural laws, even when they are conscious of them, but by understanding these laws they are able to act and interact not just more harmoniously but also more creatively. Human beings have very often regarded themselves as being not only above and apart from nature but also able to control it with a power that is nearly total, nearly divine. This is the fantasy of omnipotence of which King Canute reminded his followers. People do control nature, a little, but only to the extent that they are conscious of its laws. That is, human beings can make changes on their natural (including their human) environment, but can make creative changes only when they consciously act in accordance with natural laws. By creative, I mean changes that more nearly fulfil the total human potential—that is, the potential not only for more healthy survival of self and species but also for more happy, simple and intricate interactions with the natural and human environment. The consequence of acting in accordance with our nature is to make possible the fulfilment of its innate potential.

Creative changes are not the only ones human beings are capable of making consciously: they can also destroy, returning themselves and other forms of life to lower forms and even to elemental matter—all in accordance with accidentally applied physical principles that have been governing the interactions of atomic particles since the beginning of time and matter. One way to distinguish creative from destructive actions by human beings is to say that the latter are made in ignorance of natural laws and the former in some knowledge of such laws. That is, the degree of consciousness, of awareness, correlates positively with the degree of constructiveness. And so the degree of unconsciousness, of ignorance, correlates positively with the degree of destructiveness. In either event, the natural laws prevail.

### Identification and consciousness

Discussing what it means to be human requires consideration of the natural environment. In a sense, that covers it all; but the part of the natural environment that is human requires special consideration. It includes the most intimate part of the environment that is called the self, as it is seen by each individual looking inwards. With respect to consciousness or awareness, the self is the node that composes the individual organism and the total environment; in being aware of self, one is perceiving simultaneously subjectively and objectively. One is seeing both one's self and its environment, simultaneously as both observer and participant interactor. Awareness of this nodular identity, of the self as an outgrowth of its uterine and postnatal environment, distinguishes the self from all else, the subject from the object, the subjective from the objective—in the very limited and relational way in which these 'opposites' are distinguishable. Consciousness so conceived is the paradox that both separates and defines individuals at the same time as it unites them to each other and to the other parts of their environment.

However, consciousness and identification are not the same thing; understanding the process is not the same as the process itself. The genetic relationship between a fertilized human ovum and a fully developed human being is intimate and continuous. Although awareness of the process of development modifies development, awareness is not the basic component of development. Fortunately and unfortunately, awareness of either the genetic potential or the role of the environment (uterine and postnatal) which nurtures this potential is not necessary for humans to develop.

These assertions need to be amplified a bit. A human gamete, a fertilized human egg—actually, as distinguished from potentially—amounts to no more than any other fertilized ovum, including the kind contained in the eggs hens produce and humans eat. Until its uterine environment has nurtured it for nine months and it emerges as a baby, the first human diploid cell remains at the common starting point of cellular life, viz., a single cell. Yet there is a natural tendency for parents, even at the earliest stages of their prospective infant's uterine development, to identify with it. The tendency does not always appear, and probably never appears at the time of conception if the parents are unaware of conception, but when the mother (and usually the father) become aware, the awareness adds the dimension of identification. Again, there is a unification of the objective quality of apartness with the subjective quality of togetherness, when the parents realize that this potential human being is a part of themselves as individuals.

This identification between parents and fetus is a starting point for a long journey towards more inclusive, stable and enduring identifications between human beings. Unfortunately people often detour en route, and they sometimes (whether as parents, children or mere conspecifics) passionately insist on their uniqueness and lack of identity with each other and with other parts of the natural and human environment. People see themselves thus as being only apart from, rather than also a part of, the rest of the human race.

Why people dissociate being apart from being a part is one of the major concerns of psychiatrists, and of social scientists, philosophers and moralists. The dissociation is a major concern of politicians seeking to compose conflicts of interest among citizens. All I can suggest at this point is that the problems relate to the same subject-object split; the same overweening sense of superiority, of greater power versus lesser power, of omnipotence versus total impotence; and the same desire to be *only* separate from (and not together with) nature that I have discussed in analyzing the identity between human beings and the natural universe.

As a first step, then, what it means to be human involves establishing identifications both with the natural world, organic and inorganic, and with the human part of the natural world, with human beings at all stages of their development, from womb to maturity and from primitive human being to the most advanced human culture.

It is one thing to read, write or think 'dispassionately' about identifying with the natural world, with other human beings, and with oneself. It is altogether another thing to identify. The ways it is done successfully are perhaps as numerous as the number of individuals who do so. Scientists in laboratories develop an intense interaction with the object of their experiment. Even scientists developing a theory with pencil and paper will identify with the object of their theorizing. At one point when Linus Pauling was developing his theory on the structure of long chain molecules, he said to himself: if I were such a molecule, how would I arrange myself?

Identification of the sort just described is the product of the *interaction* between person and object, rather than just the contemplation or abstraction of an object by a person. And, willy-nilly, such (subjective) interaction occurs much more often than the observer may realize. Not all identification is conscious or acknowledged. However much they protest that they are being altogether objective in their interactions with what are loosely labelled 'the things out there'— that is, outside their heads—these identifiers with atoms, molecules, laboratory rats, chimpanzees or their own children are also subjectively identifying with them. In their minds, the phenomena under investigation and the organism being observed have become part of the observer. This observer–observed interaction is consistent with the reality of the universe—if I am not altogether mistaken in asserting earlier that all human beings are not simply acting in accordance with natural laws that everywhere regulate interaction between objects, but are also in some very elemental ways part of the same interacting objects. Human beings don't make natural laws or objects, but their interaction incorporates both laws and objects.

Identification with nature, with other human beings and with self is a gradual and developmental process. The same must be said of the handmaiden of identification, consciousness; it too is gradual and developmental. The process is therefore cumulative, both with the individual human being, and within the culture that is both the *un*written and the written product of the interaction between human beings and their natural (including human) environment. Human interaction is qualitatively much the same as other interaction: in many fundamental ways, identifications with 'nature' and other human beings differ only in (often very great) degree. Because of its enormously greater complexity, the process of identification of one human being with other individual human beings and with the species at large, is in its quantitative aspects far more intricate and intense than the identification process between human beings and nonhuman aspects of the environment.

With each individual human being, the interactive processes of identification and consciousness begin at birth, or not much later. Indeed, the mental process of identification requires initially some awareness of the fact of separation. The infant has to sense that (s)he is separated from the uterine and postuterine environment of the mother before (s)he can identify with the mother and other human beings. These joint processes—growing apart and becoming a part— require organic growth and environmental nurturance, both to commence and to continue throughout life. In the individual human being, identification and consciousness increase up to maturity, and maturity itself is a gradual process that optimally continues throughout life.

To reiterate, identification and consciousness are partly organic processes: they require the natural capacity—the potential—of the cortex of the brain to increase in the subtlety and complexity of its comprehension of others and self. But identification and consciousness are also environmental processes. The brain of each individual human being requires an environment that nurtures its growth, and therefore the individual's growth.

## Environmental gaps and gaps in fulfilment

The natural, the human, and the cultural environments play a crucial part in producing human beings, who require *constant* nurturance (physical and mental) to approach their full potential. Human beings living during the epoch when the species first became distinct, hundreds of thousands of years ago, must have been much closer to other primates and vertebrates in their daily behaviour and concerns than to human beings in the twentieth century, particularly in complex, highly integrated societies. That is, the early human beings could survive, and little else. With the same innate characteristics of body and brain—the same innate potential—they had less chance to develop their bodies, because of primitive circumstances, than people do now and much, much less chance to develop their minds. That is, they had much less chance to become human.

The same primitive environment prevails in shocking degree for most individual human beings on earth in the late twentieth century. That is, the natural and cultural environment for most human beings today inhibits rather than facilitates the realization of their innate human potential. They are compelled to concern themselves merely with the lower animal preoccupations: staying alive and together, in rudimentary interaction with others with whom they share the survival preoccupation.

This enormous gap between the degree of their potential that is ever actually fulfilled and their full potential is one of which such deprived individuals are only dimly aware—though more clearly now than in earlier centuries because of radio and television. The gap between their actual circumstances and those of people in the most advanced cultures is one of which fulfilled individuals in the most advanced cultures are only dimly aware—though more clearly now that in earlier centuries because of radio and television.

### To become more human, regress a little

Many, perhaps most, of the individuals who are most advanced and live in most advanced societies have detached themselves from those in their own cultures and everywhere else in the world. In lives not just of getting and spending but also of fulfilment as artists, writers, psychiatrists, physicians, lawyers, politicians, statesmen, these people have abandoned their contact with humanity and thereby with themselves as human beings. They have established a symbolic interaction which has led them inhumanly to separate symbol from reality and humanity from human beings. They have become encapsulated, contained, imprisoned by their sophisticated world of symbols and their abstracted relationships with other people, just as primitive human beings were and are by their world of magical forces.

To become more human thus means regressing, to the point where an individual re-establishes directly sensing, sensitive contact with other human beings as individuals and with the rest of the natural world. I commenced this essay with an imaginary identification with a proton, to stress the need for this regression, this re-establishment of contact.

The separation of human beings from their own past and present environment has produced an overweening arrogance. The separation has caused human beings in earlier eras to punish and even to destroy those who denied the earth was the centre of the universe; and to assert that human beings are apart from other life forms, and not part of life processes which have developed in accordance with the same or similar principles. Some men (and women) have asserted that men are not only different from but also superior to women. Some women (and men) have asserted that women are not only different from but also superior to men. The separation of human beings from their individual and collective past and present natural and cultural environment has caused some people to imagine that human beings are totally in control of the socio-economic systems which they create; and that human beings are totally conscious of the causes of their actions because there are no unconscious causes, because human beings have no unconscious.

Many of these innocent arrogances are like those of small children. They are the product of development which is quite incomplete, and is at once hypertrophic and dystrophic. It has accentuated apartness at the expense not only of identification, conscious identification, but also of self-fulfilment. In separating themselves from the rest of the species, modern human beings have caused to atrophy a continuously natural and therefore necessary part of their own selves: their direct contact and identification with other human beings. In one of its worst forms, it has become the frantic perusal and pursuit of depersonalized sex, as though copulation and togetherness were the same thing. The very frenzy of the pursuit has often reflected not so much a desire for sex as for achieving togetherness through sex. Sex becomes sublimated love in such circumstances, reversing the posited Freudian relationship.

Regression to establish another kind of identification is also necessary to become human. This is the experience of the nonhuman natural world, in any one of a variety of ways that can re-establish contact with the natural world from which humankind emerged. Such experience can take the form of travelling through nature—along mountain trails, across fields, on rivers, lakes and oceans. The American naturalist John Muir, after whom a long trail cresting the High Sierra mountains in California is named, once climbed a tall tree during a storm to find out what it was like for a tree to experience such an event. More universally, the simple pleasure in hearing the sounds of water has caused people to seek the experience of high waves, rushing streams and the gentle uncomplicated sounds of the fountains people have erected to bring nature to their cities.

It is a little upsetting, at first, for people who live in circumstances protecting them from raw nature to spend a night in the mountains, to swim, to fly in a small aircraft which diminishes the isolation from air and sky and earth when one is carried in a huge aircraft from airport to airport. But when people overcome the rather mild anxiety about becoming controlled by forces outside themselves, they seem to enjoy establishing contact with these forces in the wild.

It is very upsetting, at first, for people who live in circumstances that protect them from other people who are less advanced, less civilized, to establish real contact with such people. The circumstances that are so different can vary from a newborn child's helplessness—which can produce rather intense anxiety in its parents—to the vagrant, arrant lifestyle of people living in poverty, whether in urban ghettos in advanced nations or in rural villages in Third World nations.

Fascinated and anxious about such elemental contacts, people in advanced circumstances watch on television the life of poor people in another part of their own country, or another part of the world, as though such life were on another planet. Their fascination comes from the kinship that people watching television sense with the images on the screen. Their anxiety comes from a desire to maintain the alienation that different circumstances have produced for people—people who are in fact members of the same species and inhabitants of the same planet.

The gap is mainly cultural, not natural; it consists of the difference in circumstances. The bridge is mainly natural, not cultural; it consists of the likeness in human responses to the same circumstances. At the same time as people are fascinated by others' responses to the processes of modernization, people who have become modern are anxious about what they don't want to see—that their own ancestors in centuries past (even in millennia past) went through the same process of development, from pre-literate beginnings to the most intricate complexities of modern living.

There is another form of contact with nature, seemingly very different: the excitement that occasionally overtakes biologists, geologists, astronomers, chemists and physicists in their research and theoretical endeavours. They have come in contact with some hitherto-baffling phenomenon, and understand how it occurs in accordance with concepts themselves derived from observations of nature. Scientists on such occasions bridge the gap between the world inside their heads and the world outside. The subjective and objective are conjoined.

The process of identifying and re-identifying with the natural (including the human) environment is one in which abstractions that human beings have generated in their minds are conjoined with complexities of reality. The fruitful product of abstraction is to see through superficial observations to more fundamental, universal aspects and principles of reality. The barren product of abstraction is to dissociate the abstraction from reality.

What I have said to this point relates to the need to establish and re-establish contact with our own origins, as these are to be found by examining not only nature as seen by physicists and biologists but also our own past as individuals and the cultural past of *Homo sapiens* back to our—not its, but our—prehistoric beginnings. This contacting is a process that can be undertaken quite simply, because it is natural for the human brain to be able to absorb experience of the most complex, subtle and real sorts. If it is also natural for the human brain to fear the unknown, then it is natural to lose fear when the unknown becomes known.

The anxiety and the oversight that cause people to forget or turn away from their individual and cultural past, reflect a fear that if that past is examined it will somehow overpower us and we will have to return to it. The reality about the past is that not only can anxiety be reduced by establishing contact with it but also, in understanding how we got here from there, we will understand the origins and thus the causes of development, of modernization, of civilization.

## Lost emotion

It is the emotional elements in this process—the involvement with and commitment to others, to self and to the future—that modernized human beings are in danger of losing. If they lose these, they lose the ability to develop further as human beings. They destroy the future by turning away from the past, in some kind of blind and false egocentricity that takes people out of temporal, developmental contexts. The anxious, fearful denial of emotion alienates people from themselves, as it cuts off contact with others. This implosive process generating within individuals in the most advanced cultures is a far greater threat to the future of humankind than any explosive nuclear weapon produced by human technology.

Establishing identifications across the long-established but crumbling barriers of time and space is a necessary (though not sufficient) condition of the humanizing process. Such emotional ties are necessary because it is part of human nature to get and keep real ties, real identities, with other people. The innate needs for such ties, while not quite so strong as the needs for physical nutrition and health, are stronger than anything else beyond the physical needs. And the tendency to identify with people dimly seen on bright television screens, also natural, has to be strengthened because failure to do so can become a threat to the survival needs themselves.

When people in other and less developed circumstances sense the indifference of people in more developed circumstances, the former are inclined to develop hostility generically the same as that between physically and emotionally bereft children and the societies in which they become juvenile delinquents. Indifferences of the more advanced to the less advanced is repaid with hostility.

While it is a mistaken view that only emotional ties are needed to become human—that love is enough—the need demands emphasis in our era because of the speed and intensity with which societies and cultures are mechanically and technically developing and integrating. The velocity and pervasiveness of development seriously threaten to divorce people not just from nature but also from each other and from themselves. And this alienation threatens the fulfilment of human beings just because love is a prior condition, in the same sense that good health is a prior condition.

## Beyond survival and identification

What then are beyond survival and identification, beyond the physical and affectional needs? People totally preoccupied with the sometimes devastating emotional consequences of separation find it hard to imagine there is anything else. They note the consequences of neglect of small children, by upper-middle class professional parents too busy with their own careers to establish a solid affectional base for their children's future. They note the consequences of neglect of small children in poor and often single-parent families, in producing children who as adolescents turn to anomic violence. And many observers do not see that there is anything else to becoming or being human than mutual love and mutual aid.

But ultimately people have an organic, genetically based desire to fulfill their own unique individuality, in perhaps as many ways as there are individual human beings on earth. In possibly all times, there have been some people whose individuality has been more fulfilled than others. They are the people who are part of recorded history and culture, who have fashioned statues and statutes, estates and states, sonatas and sonnets, philosophy and science. Phidias and Hammurabi and Moses. Croesus and the Benedictine monks and Henry Ford; Charlemagne and Queen Elizabeth I and Washington and Jefferson and Mao. Beethoven and Shakespeare. Kant and Darwin and Marx and Einstein. All these distinctive individuals have come far closer to fulfilling the human potential than was average in their time.

Such events as the lives of these individuals have tended to make us abstract their self-actualization, both from their own childhoods and from the historic context in which they lived. Their lustre has tended to make us forget the antecedents of their fulfilment, from their birth to their explosively blossoming maturity. We do not note the stage of culture—artistic, scientific, economic, political—in which they grew up. And so we do not see that those origins were necessary preconditions for their blossoming. We (and sometimes these gigantic individuals) divorce their achievements from the physical and emotional nurturance, and the personal recognition and esteem, that fostered them as they grew. When asked whether a teacher in one of his early years of school had understood mathematics, Einstein is reported to have said: she didn't understand mathematics, but she understood me.

## The alienation of the fulfilled

It is this forgetting of the origins and the contexts of development that impedes the full development of all human beings. People who are fulfilling themselves in some scale comparable to that of the most distinguished often, very often, divorce themselves from others—not only others with whom they have day-to-day contact, but also others beyond their families and friends. These others become and remain digits in statistical tables, images on television screens that can be turned off or an abstraction like 'Suffering Humanity', complete not with dried blood but with the word 'blood'. In sum, such hypertrophied, atrophied people divorce themselves from their spouses and children, actually if not formally. They divorce themselves from their family origins. They divorce themselves from the society and culture that fashioned them, their parents, grandparents and ancestors, back to the indistinct earliest ones—the society and culture that made possible the cumulative interaction process, that in turn made possible their own fulfilment.

This alienation from the origins, the roots, of fulfilment among people who are at least somewhat widely known in their cultures is bad enough. What is worse is a comparable alienation of some of the most advanced peoples—the most advanced nations—from some of the least advanced. That is, people in nations like Great Britain, Switzerland, Sweden, Germany and the United States tend to suppose they are miraculous products, sprung fully developed from history and culture, as Athena did from the brow of Zeus. They regard themselves not as a part of but apart from their own and humanity's cultural, technological and scientific development. They assume that some kind of genetic, supermanly superiority has magically produced their fulfilment—with no help from any people, anywhere, at any time.

By miraculously examining themselves out of context in time and space, they weaken and threaten destruction of the very foundations on which their own self-fulfilment is based. They do this in at least two ways: they cut off their roots in their own environment; and, just as perniciously, they ignore less developed peoples. The latter threatens to arouse people in less advanced nations who naturally have the same aspirations (which culminate in self-fulfilment) as people in advanced nations and who do sense their kinship to people in the most advanced nations. These two alienations are synergically destructive. The divorcement of some of the most distinguished individuals from the societies that nurtured and recognized their great innate potential threatens to become the divorcement of entire peoples who separate themselves from the rest of the human race. This alienation is an action which, as Newton noted in the natural world, is likely to produce an equal and opposite reaction. If more advanced peoples do not concern themselves with less advanced peoples, then why, say the latter, should they be concerned for those who are more advanced? Double and redouble and quadruple the price of oil!

An improperly fulfilled individual is one who is fulfilled at the cost of others' equal desire and right to become fulfilled. (S)he is alive, vital, in motion, excited by life more in the manner of a child taking its first steps than of a fully mature adult taking a big step for mankind. Charlie Chaplin is quoted as saying: 'One cannot do humor without great sympathy for one's fellow man. As the tramp I think I endeared myself through his terrific humility—the humility which I am sure is a universal thing—of somebody without money. As a youth, I was very unhappy, soulfully unhappy, not so much from being deprived or hungry . . . There was always plenty of bread and butter around. It is the humiliation of poverty which is so distressing.'[6] In portraying his own humility as he padded across the movie screen, Chaplin took a giant step for mankind.

A society that by present-day standards maximizes opportunities only for its own members to fulfill themselves is also showing the hubris of a child taking its first steps—stumbling in the process. When a child makes missteps along with its first steps, the parents help. When adults make the same childish missteps, they are likely to fall down and back to the first stages of mankind. Then everyone hewed his or her own wood, drew his or her own water, and for a time said: let the devil take the ones who are farther from wood and fire and water than I.

The hypertrophy and dystrophy of the most advanced people threatens their own atrophy. People in the least advanced societies continue to develop and advance, and they are not much threatened, at least by atrophy. They are learning from the most advanced societies, particularly from people who have advanced farthest in those societies. And the latter seem to suppose that almost all other people are fulfilling themselves, in societies at all stages of development. The most advanced people bleed a little, perfunctorily and bathetically, for the 'few' who are not; then they go on to fulfill themselves and ignore the rest.

---

[6]   Quoted in Associated Press story, *The Oregonian*, Portland, Oregon, 26 December 1977.

# Essay 5

## David E. Cooper

Saul Bellow's hero, Herzog, urges that a moratorium be put on definitions of man and his essence. Among those who have ignored this advice, a favourite definition has been the one which focuses on human possession of language. One has, to be sure, encountered *Homo faber*, *Homo ridens*, and *Homo civilis*; but a show of hands would reveal *Homo loquens* as the preferred candidate for the role of true, essential man. (Here, as throughout, the masculine gender carries no semantic weight.) It is this familiar idea of man as linguistic man which I want to explore in this essay—so let us give it a name, 'Loquentialism'. Having made some initial remarks of a methodological nature, I shall explore the idea first, by sketching it and a line of argument to support it; next, by considering some contrasting ideas; and last, by examining and warding off a challenge. So you can see already that I count myself among the ranks of the Loquentialists.

Herzog's ban on searches for human essence needs to be taken seriously. At the very least, it should prompt us to enquire just what kind of questions are being asked by 'What is human essence?' or 'What is it to be human?'. Forging ahead in search of an answer will be fruitless until we have some glimmer of what would count as a possible answer, and why. Hence the following somewhat skeletal remarks of a methodological sort.

One way to take the question about human essence is as a request for some characteristic which is both necessary and sufficient for a creature to count as a human being; for a feature which is common to all, and only, human beings. There are plenty of good reasons, however, for *not* taking the question this way. To begin with, one would immediately feel daunted by the remarkable philosophical obscurity surrounding the notions of necessity and sufficiency. Opinions, after all, have ranged from Leibniz's, to the effect that every characteristic of a thing is necessary for its being what it is, to the view that no feature is necessary in this way. So cowardice alone might prompt us to take the question differently.

Secondly, and more importantly, I am tempted to think that any characteristic discovered to belong to all, and only, human beings, is going to be at once dull and irrelevant to the motives which prompted the search in the first place. This is because any such characteristic is going to be pretty recondite, and available only to the specialist —the physiologist, for example—after detailed research. Certainly the most popular candidates for human essence would fail the test. Some people never laugh; others are bone idle; some are hermits; others cannot speak. Nor would one suggest that the tiger in the zoo was human were it suddenly to display a typically human talent for laughing or tool-making. Precisely because the common, unique feature is going to be recondite, and discoverable only through specialist research, it is bound (for most of us) to have the appearance of being accidental. Suppose we are presented with this feature which distinguishes each human being from all else in nature. Given the way it was discovered, we shall not feel illuminated as to *what* it is—*man*—that is being thus distinguished. That is why I said that any such characteristic would seem dull. Further, it would surely fail to satisfy the curiosity which motivated the search from the start. Certainly there is the occasional puzzle whether to count a certain creature—*australopithacus*, for example—as human. But most people with a concern in what it is to be human are not asking for an identikit, by reference to which one could decide in these marginal cases. The aim is not to draw an exact line between the human and non-human, but to reflect upon the nature of what is quite *definitely* human. Someone with this aim is no more aided by the discovery of an *outré* characteristic which belongs to all, and only, human beings than someone concerned with the nature of Woman is helped by the kind of test Olympic doctors employ for banning Russian athletes from women's field-events. When Professor Higgins regrets that his fair lady is not more like a man, he is not ruing a slight hormonal deficiency on Eliza's part.

A third reason for not interpreting the search for essence as a search for a characteristic common to all, and only, human beings is that it allows one to escape the grim threat of having to say much about alleged animal language. I think it is fairly clear that no animal species in its natural environment possesses anything sufficiently like human language for the word 'language' to apply univocally. I say this despite considerable suspicion of the arguments it is fashionable nowadays to adduce in support. It is frequently stressed, for instance, that animal systems are insufficiently complex in their structure; or that animals lack that power that is 'crucial to true language', of 'producing new combinations . . . to describe a completely unusual event'.[1] Such arguments merely raise questions. What is the measure of complexity here? By what criterion is an average human sentence more complex than an average bee-dance? What is a 'new' combination of signs? Would aboriginals' difficulty in describing the 'unusual event' of a visit from a nuclear submarine show they did not have a language? Moreover, such arguments miss the true point, which is not the structural complexity or novelty of linguistic combinations, but the appropriateness of certain combinations for performing a crucial role —that of asserting or stating how things are. Strings of animal signs can be as complex or as new as you please; but there will be no pressing reason to regard them as belonging to a language unless we recognize assertions or statements among them. As far as I can see, we simply do not have to recognize this. (I shall not argue this point here. I think most of the obvious objections can be handled by stressing there is all the difference between asserting that, for example, one is in pain and making sounds from which others (including animals) could infer one was in pain.[2])

What I have said applies only to animals in their natural or relatively natural states. For there is certainly a growing body of evidence which tempts one to say of certain talented monkeys, brought up in highly non-simian ways, that they possess a rudimentary language. If we succumb to the temptation (perhaps wisely) and *also* insist that what is essentially human must be unique to human beings, we face a dilemma. Either the talented monkeys are human or *Homo loquens* is not the essential *Homo*. Clearly the monkeys are not human; but to opt for the second alternative is surely too brusque a way with

---

[1]    C. & W.M.S. Russell, 'Language and animal signals', in *Linguistics at Large*, edited by N. Minnis, Paladin, 1973. p. 173.

[2]    For the distinction in question, see H.P. Grice, 'Meaning', *Philosophical Review*, 66, 1957.

Loquentialism. We should surely not want to dismiss that thesis, simply because of some strangely educated monkeys. What must be wrong is the way the question about human essence has been interpreted—a way that forced us into the unpleasant dilemma just mentioned.

So let me simply assert how *I* am going to take the question, with the hope that it corresponds to how many human beings have felt, albeit vaguely, the nature of their enquiry into human essence. There are many salient, obvious features of human life which plainly distinguish the lives of normal human beings from those of normal non-human beings. ('Normal' plays an important role here, allowing us, for example, to ignore the over-achieving monkeys.) To search for human essence is to search for some single characteristic of human beings which, above any other, best explains these salient, distinguishing features. In fact, I prefer 'illuminates' or, perhaps 'throws into perspective', to 'explains'. For we are not, at any rate, looking for a *causal* explanation. If we were, it would be impossible to understand the dissatisfaction felt towards an answer that appeals to the diencephalon or the enlarged cerebral cortex. When one is told that human essence resides in, say, human rationality, the point is not that reason causes social existence to have the features it does (whatever that would mean) but that it is illuminating to see these outstanding features as belonging first and foremost to the life of *rational* beings. The features are significantly grouped together, so to speak, and thrown into relief through being seen in this way. Talk of 'illumination' and 'perspective' is vague, of course. I can only hope that the sense in which, for a Loquentialist, it is human possession of language which explains, illuminates or throws into perspective the salient features of social existence, will emerge as we proceed.

Before proceeding it is surely wise to concede at once that when the question is taken as I am taking it, any answer will, to a degree, be stipulative. There will be little sense in insisting that all but one answer must be *mistaken*. In part, this is because of the degree of freedom enjoyed in initially picking out the salient features of social existence which it is the task to explain or illuminate. And it is also because the success of an answer will depend on how much illumination people actually feel it provides. The goal is not a causal explanation whose correctness is independent of whether anyone actually accepts it; it is more akin to the critic's explanation of a painting's merits or the historian's attempt to portray the character and tenor of an epoch. How successful such explanations are must depend, in part, upon the variegated interests, backgrounds, perspectives and attitudes of audiences. This is not to say there are no holds barred. No one, for example, can seriously regard *laughter* as the essential human characteristic; as the one that best illuminates the salient, distinguishing features of social existence. (Not at present, at least. Perhaps one should not rule out the possibility of a psychologist of genius doing for jokes what Freud did for sex.) The point is, simply, to admit that any answer may fail to persuade sections of people because of the way these people are—their interests and their personalities. And in this murky, abstract area of debate, it is unclear to what higher court—having failed to carry people with one —appeal could be made.

What now follows is a derivation of Loquentialism; a case for seeing human social life in its most salient features as—*au fond*—the life of language-users. But what are these features to which I have been referring? At least the following, I suggest: the life of human beings together is typically both highly organized and co-operative; we live and move in a world largely constituted by our own sophisticated artefacts; we engage in a remarkably wide range of activities during a single, relatively short period of time—switching smoothly from one to another and back again, or carrying on several concurrently. I say these features are salient and distinguishing for they are, surely, among those by which one's favourite Martian would quickly be impressed as characterizing human, but not animal, life. It would be boring, incidentally, to ask if such features distinguish us in kind or only in degree from animals. That depends on how they are described. In terms of molecular density, chalk differs from cheese only in degree; nevertheless they remain as different as chalk from cheese.

What most obviously unites these features, perhaps, is their *complexity*. Indeed, it is the complexity of human life which our Martian might detect as its distinctive flavour. So let us raise the question of what makes possible the complexity which characterizes our degree of social organization, our world of artefacts and the like. A crucial precondition, surely, is the capacity for forming and co-operating upon relatively long-term projects; to focus upon and pursue relatively distant goals. It is the variety and distance of these goals which demand the high degree of social organization that is absent from animal life. A world of sophisticated artefacts requires artisans who can set themselves and unite upon long-term projects—the construction of a skyscraper or a precision watch. This same distance of human goals is presupposed also by human ability to do so many things during a short space of time. Animals are notable for their single-mindedness, their intense concentration on the single job at hand —such as eating the bone or getting the ball of dung back to the colony. This single-mindedness is not so much a sign of animal virtue as a symptom of their inability to put off, or place in the background, achievement of an aim. Human beings, with their longer-term goals, can afford to be more leisurely and more spasmodic; hence they can pursue more aims at the same time.

The pursuit of distant goals and projects presupposes, in turn, the *rationality* of the agents—in a sense of 'rational' that is stronger than that of 'intelligent'. To pursue and co-operate on such goals requires not merely that human beings can adjust to contingencies—the hallmark of intelligence, perhaps—but that they can infer, hypothesize, test the general against the particular and recognize inconsistencies. For to engage on a variety of long-term projects with any success requires not only that I recognize what each entails for the shorter term, but that I am able to infer what is possible from my past successes and failures, and that I am able to judge the consistency or otherwise of the various projects with one another.

I hope that nothing in the last few paragraphs has been especially controversial; but I hope, too, that what now follows is less banal. Rationality—in a sense which requires recognition of entailments, inconsistencies and the like—presupposes, it seems to me, a special concern with the truth of thoughts or beliefs.[3] A dog may certainly be concerned with whether its bone is buried at the foot of the tree. But it is not concerned with the truth of the belief that the bone is buried there. Or rather to say that it is can only be another and more pretentious way of saying that it is concerned with the bone's being buried there. Dogs, if you like, worry about bones but not about beliefs about bones. In the case of a man, however, attributing to him the thought that a belief is true is by no means another way, simply, of attributing the belief to him. For I am attributing to him a grasp both of what a belief is and of what truth is. Merely to say of a creature that it has beliefs is not to say of it that it grasps the *concepts* of belief and truth. That human beings must be credited with a grasp of these concepts is presupposed by crediting them with rationality.

[3]   Neither word, 'thought' nor 'belief', has quite the generality I require. 'Supposition', 'judgement', 'hypothesis' or many others might often be more appropriate. Philosophers sometimes use the term 'proposition' for whatever can be regarded as true or false. But this is to give the term a technical meaning different from that of 'assertoric sentence', which is how it is meant later in this essay.

This is because the currency, so to speak, of entailments, contradictions and so on, are beliefs about bones or whatever, not bones themselves. Logical relations—which we are crediting human beings with recognizing—hold not between bones-buried-under-trees but between beliefs.[4] To recognize an entailment is to recognize that one belief's truth is guaranteed by another's. To recognise an inconsistency is to see that one belief is true if, and only if, another is false. If we are right to see human goal-directed behaviour as involving rationality in the sense described, we must see it also as the behaviour of creatures endowed with the concepts of belief and truth.

Is it possible to end the derivation here? To rest with characterizing human social life as the life of human beings endowed, first and foremost, with the concepts of belief and truth? If it is, then Loquentialism has not left the ground—for, there has so far been no mention of language at all.

But we cannot rest here—and this is because the conceptual grasp with which we are crediting rational human beings presupposes their grasp of a language in its barest essentials. Perhaps it is possible to explain what belief is without any reference to language. It is not likewise possible to explain what it is to hold a belief to be true or what it is to hold that one belief entails or contradicts another. In short, the notions of the truth of a belief and of logical relations among beliefs require explanation in terms of linguistic notions.

For a belief to be true, it is required that the elements of the belief be so structured that the belief corresponds to how the world actually is. Logical relations among beliefs equally depend on how the elements in the beliefs are structured. What the Loquentialist holds is that our only insight into what the elements and structures of beliefs might be is through our understanding of the elements and structures of *sentences* in a language. It is only through this latter understanding, therefore, that we can grasp what it is for beliefs to be true or logically related.

Fortunately—and thanks to the work of Frege, Tarski and other logicians—we do have a very reasonable understanding of how, in virtue of the structuring of elements, sentences can be true or false.[5]

---

[4]  Though see the previous note. The idea that logical relations hold, not between things in the world, but between thoughts or propositions (in the technical sense) is, incidentally, a central claim in Wittgenstein's *Tractatus Logico-Philosophicus*.

[5]  The fact that I mention some logicians rather than linguists is significant. For the elements and structures in question are not those of traditional grammar (nouns, participles, word-ordering, etc.) but ones identified in terms of their logical roles (referential expressions, predication, etc.). To use fashionable terminology, the elements are those of 'underlying semantic structure' rather than of 'surface' or 'superficial' grammar.

That is, we have a *theory* that enables us to determine the conditions under which arbitrarily taken sentences are true or false. The theory does this, first, by specifying semantic information concerning the most basic elements in a sentence (for example, the references of names) and, secondly, by displaying the effects of applying various operations (such as conjunction or quantification) upon these elements. What such a theory achieves, if you like, is an account of that elusive relation *correspondence*, which must hold between a sentence and the world if the sentence is to be true. Such a theory of truth, based on an account of sentential elements and structures, provides us with a theory of logic as well. For by being able to determine the conditions under which any two sentences are true, we are able to determine if the one entails the other. (It does if the conditions for *its* truth include those for the latter's truth.)[6]

To be sure, we speak of beliefs and not just sentences being true; we speak of 'elements' of beliefs and call them 'concepts' or 'ideas'; and we speak of these concepts or ideas being combined to produce beliefs or thoughts. The fact is, however, that we have no inkling of how elements in a belief can be combined that is not derived from our understanding of how sentential elements can be structured. And we have no account of how conceptual elements in beliefs relate to things in the world that is not derived from our account of how sentential elements (names, etc.) relate to things. Hence, our grasp of what it is for a belief to be true is thoroughly parasitic on our theory of linguistic truth. Roughly speaking, to understand what it is for a certain belief to be true is to understand what is is for certain sentences—those said to 'express' the belief—to be true.

The point of view I am urging does not, incidentally, require the extreme claim that belief-elements (concepts, ideas or whatever) are identical to linguistic elements; or that beliefs are merely sentences held to be true. Nor are we forced to agree with Shelley in *Prometheus Unbound* that 'speech created thought'. All that is insisted upon is that our understanding of belief-elements and of the truth of beliefs is derived from our understanding of linguistic matters. It follows that if we are to conceive, as we have been conceiving, of human beings as creatures with a reflective concern for the truth of beliefs, we are thinking of them as creatures whose understanding derives from their understanding of their language—their system for producing and structuring sentences.

---

[6]   Actually, I am being idealistic in this paragraph. There are many kinds of sentences about whose truth-conditions we do not as yet have an adequate theory.

Let me rehearse how this position, Loquentialism, has been reached. The search for essence was construed as the search for a human attribute that would best illuminate the salient, distinctive features of human life. Such features—social organization, sophisticated artefacts and the like—were characterized by their complexity; a complexity, I suggested, that reflects a capacity for setting and pursuing relatively distant goals. That pursuit, in turn, presupposed that human beings reason—in the strong sense of recognizing entailments, contradictions and the like. Such rationality, in its turn, required a distinctive capacity for reflecting upon the truth of beliefs. And this capacity, it was finally urged, must be derivative from a grasp of what it is for linguistic entities—sentences—to be true; for we have no theory of what it is for a belief to be true that is not generated from a theory of linguistic truth. Even if there is a 'mental museum', in W.V. Quine's happy phrase, containing concepts, ideas or whatever, people's only entrance to it is the pretty well-travelled road of their public language. The Loquentialist invites you, then, to see human life as primarily the life of creatures with an understanding of this public language.

In this part of the essay I want, first, to contrast Loquentialism with a much tamer thesis and, secondly, to compare it with another famous approach to the question of essence—the 'Marxist'. Both the contrast and the comparison are, I hope, of some intrinsic interest; and each will provide an opportunity for adding some flesh to the admittedly skeletal body of Loquentialism so far depicted.

It would commit a serious error and at the same time emasculate Loquentialism to confuse it with a rather dull, unobjectionable thesis of a sociological kind. Many readers might, quite rightly, have arrived at the linguistic factor in human life at an earlier stage of my derivation than at the final stage I myself located it. They would have stressed, quite correctly, the immense role language plays in the communicative process required by co-operation on complex, distant goals. But some of them would then have stopped—leaving us with the unobjectionable thesis that language has been a powerful instrument in moulding history and society. This is not the Loquentialist thesis.

The sociological claim is compatible with—and left by itself actually encourages—the idea that had human beings been more empathetic or telepathic and less reliant on a physical means of conveying beliefs and intentions, human life could still have been much as it has been. Language is seen as dispensable in principle, if not in practice. The claim is also compatible with viewing the relation between belief and language as like that between content and label, as an inner-outer relation. Loquentialism, though, is compatible with neither of these ideas.

The Loquentialist claim is not an empirical one about the historical, contingent connection between language and the conduct of social life, but a conceptual thesis concerning the presuppositions of that life. If complex social life is to be described as the life of goal-seeking creatures, then it is the life of rational, logical human beings who not only have beliefs but understand what it is for beliefs to be true. They must, if the Loquentialist is right, be language users. Or—to put matters in reverse—unless human beings spoke they could have no conception of what it is for beliefs to be true and logically related. In that event, we could not ascribe to them the distinctive rationality that belongs to the pursuit of distant goals. But unless we can ascribe this to human beings, it is unclear how much of the apparatus we employ in describing complex social life can any longer be made to fit. The welter of concepts employed in describing this life fit, I suggest, only if one ascribes the distinctive rationality. I have in mind such concepts as *institution, family, tool, property*. For example, there is all the difference between a property and a wooden or stone structure in which creatures happen to spend a lot of time eating, sleeping or mating. Once such a structure is given the title of 'property', we see it as having a place in a system of rights, expectations and plans. And this is to see it as having a place in the life of rational creatures pursuing distant goals.

This is a natural point at which to proceed to the comparison I mentioned, between Loquentialism and a broadly Marxist account of essence, for some of the considerations just raised will be relevant. The Marxist account of human essence—that essence from which, famously, we are supposed to be 'alienated' in class society—does not have to be but can easily become incompatible with the Loquentialist view. In *The German Ideology* Marx and Engels write that men's 'mode of production . . . is a definite form of expressing their life, a definite *mode of life* . . . As individuals express their life, so they are. What they are, therefore, coincides with their production . . . The nature of individuals thus depends on the material conditions determining their production.'[7] For Marx, man's essence consists in his being a producer—of a complex, creative kind that distinguishes him from any animal. True, human nature varies with how human beings

---

[7]    International Publishers Co., 1963, p. 7.

produce; but it is *always* how they produce which determines how they *are*. In that sense, creative production is of the essence.

Whether this claim is incompatible with Loquentialism depends on how it is interpreted. It might be taken as a *causal* theory to the effect that the major areas of human life including 'politics, laws, morality, religion, metaphysics' are primarily shaped by the nature of material production. 'Life is not determined by consciousness but consciousness by life.'[8] To this the Loquentialist need take no objection, even when language itself is included as one of the phenomena whose shape is considerably moulded by economics. The Loquentialist need not, for example, take up arms against the affectionately titled 'Yo-Ho-Heave-Ho' theory of the origin of language—according to which language developed out of the grunts and groans of cavemen as they toiled and strained. By insisting that production is the human essence, the Marxist is, to be sure, locating what is distinctive about human beings in a different place from the Loquentialist. But, as I argued earlier, such a difference in perspective, in stress, should not be taken as showing two accounts to be incompatible—in the sense that at least one must be false.

But there is another way the Marxist view of language, and its relation to production, might be read. One might take, very literally, the metaphor of language as a tool. It would be a tool, first of all, through having a particular function—that of oiling the wheels of co-operative, productive enterprise. And it would be a tool, secondly, through acting as the external conveyor or vehicle of the inner thoughts, beliefs and intentions that creative producers must be indulging in. With this picture of language as the external expression of an independently intelligible 'inner world', the Loquentialist must, of course, take issue. To claim that language is *simply* a tool—in principle, as expendable as the wheel or ratchet—is incompatible with the Loquentialist's insistence that the inner world of reflective, rational, mental activity is intelligible only as the inner world of *speakers*.

However, it is unclear that this objectionable view can be attributed to Marx himself, whose own position is at once more subtle and obscure. 'Language', he says, 'is as old as consciousness.' For him, it would seem, language does not become a necessary tool for expressing thought; rather, language and thought *together* are necessary responses to the need for social intercourse imposed by growingly

---

[8]  *Ibid*, p. 15.

complex methods of production. 'Consciousness is . . . from the very beginning a social product.'[9] This important adjustment will do something to appease the Loquentialist—but not everything. For we seem left with the picture of human beings *first* being engaged in complex social life and *then*, in response, developing reflective thought and language in harness. But this picture, if my earlier remarks were right, is not an intelligible one. Where it is proper to describe life in terms of the distinctive concepts of sociology (property, family, etc.), we are *already* describing the life of distant goal-seeking, hence rational, hence reflective, hence linguistic creatures. Again, it may well be that Marx himself would not disagree. There is the suggestion that, for him, one may only 'truly' speak of production and its social relations—expecially the division of labour—once consciousness has ceased to be 'purely animal'. On the assumption that the consciousness in question is the reflective language-involving kind, Marx's point seems a generalization of the one I made about property: that certain concepts employed in social description are properly applicable only given certain presuppositions about the rationality of the agents involved.

Loquentialism faces attack from several directions. We have already encountered at several places the most obvious kind of attack—that of the 'Mentalist' who sees language as at most a dispensable tool for outward expression of thought. As one Mentalist recently put it, angels, with their mutual empathy and infinite memories, would have no need to learn Latin.[10] I have nothing more to say about Mentalism; partly because my derivation of the role of language in human life, if well-taken, is a sufficient answer; partly because so many writers have already said so much on the debate; and partly because one would soon encounter arguments of such technicality as to render them inappropriate in an essay not primarily written for specialists.[11]

The attack on which I shall focus in these last pages is mounted by an opponent whom, at a superficial glance, the Loquentialist might be expected to embrace as an ally rather than do battle with as an enemy. I shall call the opponent the 'Symbolist'. It is important to discredit Symbolism, not only because it might be confused with

[9]   *Ibid*, p. 19.
[10]  J.A. Fodor, *The Language of Thought*, Harvester Press, 1975, p. 86.
[11]  Two good articles which argue at this fairly technical level, and in favour of the Loquentialist cause, are those by D. Davidson and W.V. Quine in *Mind and Language*, edited by S. Guttenplan, Oxford University, 1975.

Loquentialism; not only because it is thoroughly wrong; but because it is an approach that is threatening to dominate social science for the foreseeable future.

The Symbolist, like the Loquentialist, sees the human being above all as the possessor of a public, communicative, semantic system. But for the Symbolist, *language* is but one, not especially privileged, system among many. Or, better, language is just one possible articulation of an underlying semantic system which is realized in many dimensions —in ritual, music, mythology, eating and architecture, for example. Social anthropology has been the breeding-ground for Symbolists, and here is what one of its doyens, Edmund Leach, has to tell us:

> . . . *all* the various non-verbal dimensions of culture such as styles in clothing, village lay-out, architecture, furniture, food, cooking, music, physical gestures, postural attitudes and so on are organized in patterned sets so as to incorporate coded information in a manner analogous to the sounds and words and sentences of a natural language. I assume therefore it is just as meaningful to talk about the grammatical rules which govern the wearing of clothes as it is to talk about the grammatical rules which govern speech utterances.[12]

The expression 'analogous to . . . natural language' might lead one to suppose it is only a metaphor being offered. But not at all. The sole difference between a natural language and the various 'languages' of food, architecture, etc., that Leach notes is that the former is much more complex. Far from being offered a metaphor, we are asked to see each of the 'various modes of communication . . . (as) a "transformation" of every other [including natural language] in much the same sense as a written text is a transformation of speech.'[13] Everything that is communicated linguistically can, in principle, be communicated in these other dimensions because 'all our different senses are coded in the same way.'[14] If language enjoys any special status, it does so for purely utilitarian reasons. Words are easy to produce; they can be stored in the form of writing— and so on. A ritual is cumbersome relative, to a sentence, because its elements are more separated in time than the noises made in uttering a sentence. Still, the elements in a ritual are strictly analogous to those in a sentence—as is the nature of its 'grammatical' structure.

[12] *Culture and Communication*, Cambridge University, 1976, p. 10. Leach is clearly taking his cue from another Arch-Symbolist, Lévi-Strauss, for whom social anthropology is that area of 'semiology which linguistics has not already claimed for its own'.

[13] *Ibid*, p. 16.

[14] *Ibid*, p. 11.

For the Loquentialist, the above attitude intolerably lowers the status of language. It is no longer language, but that of which language is but one appearance, that identifies man. For the Loquentialist, language is the bride. If, for the Mentalist, it was merely the bridesmaid, for the Symbolist it is at best one inmate in an overcrowded harem.

So far I have studiously avoided saying what a language is. But this task must be faced if the claim is to be assessed that rituals, styles of architecture, etc., are languages. Certainly, I do not want to equate language with spoken language, nor with verbal language, if by a 'word' one means an element belonging to a natural language such as English. In fact, I do not want to equate language with any particular physical means for its realization. Clearly morse-code should count as a language; as should deaf-and-dumb systems. So the objection to Symbolism is certainly *not* that the materials mentioned —food dishes, clothes, rituals movements—are of an inappropriate kind to belong to a language. It is indeed for practical, not principled, reasons that we generally communicate by making sounds and not by manipulating potatoes, bowler hats or elephant tusks.

It is what is *achieved* by the structuring of elements, not their physical nature, which is crucial for language; and there is no clear limit on the variety of physical means whereby the achievement can be made. A language is, at heart, a system for generating propositions —true or false messages to the effect that *this is how things are*. For at least two reasons this is not an arbitrary focus on what is admittedly just one kind of message that languages typically generate. First, it would seem our understanding of other kinds of message is, standardly, derivative from our understanding of propositions. One understands a question, for instance, through understanding the propositions that would constitute answers to it. Secondly, our best theory of the meanings of individual elements—words, say—is in terms of the conditions under which propositions containing them are true or false. To understand 'red', for example, has surely to do with understanding the conditions under which sentences in which it occurs are true and false.

That language is primarily a proposition-generating system imposes definite requirements on the roles that elements and structures must play if they are to belong to a language, a semantic system. It is reasonable to require, *inter alia*, that some elements have the role of referring to things (as do names in English); that others serve to stand for properties; and that there be a structural device for generating messages in which properties are predicted of things referred to, telling us that so-and-so is of such-and-such a type.

A natural language like English—with its names, adjectives, copulas and so on—is paradigmatically a language, a semantic system. And we do not go far wrong by insisting that any other system is only a language to the extent that it can—perhaps only roughly and in part—be mapped on to English. We must be able to identify in these systems devices analogous to the ones, already mentioned, that we find in English. By this test, morse-code counts as a language, whereas the sounds of the sea, a horse's movements and the patterns on my tie do not.

It is important—lest the Symbolist scents an easy victory—to stress what is *not* being denied. It is not denied that in *special* contexts elements of the type mentioned by Leach—dishes, clothes or whatever —can be employed in ways strictly analogous to words to produce propositional messages. Think of the retired General refighting the battle of Alamein while dining at his club. The potatoes are divisions; the salt cellar is G.H.Q., and so on. By arranging the objects appropriately, and with the right stage-setting, he can inform his listeners that G.H.Q. was being threatened by an enemy division, and the like. Nor is it denied that some objects, because of the frequency with which they have been used in connection with messages, come to have, in context, a fixed significance in the way words have. Think of the black cap the judge dons before sentencing the prisoner to death.

None of these admissions is grist for the Symbolist mill. For the Symbolist, it is not only the retired general's potatoes and salt-cellar which tell a story, but the most ordinary meal that you or I eat. It is not just the judge's black cap, but footwear as well, which are meaningful elements. More generally, Symbolists do not restrict themselves to the harmless claim that, in special context, objects of various sorts can be used to convey messages. Their charge is that such objects, or combinations of them, always or ordinarily convey messages because they are outputs of a semantic system, even in usual contexts. Clearly the strong claim does not follow from the harmless one. That a race of giants *might* tear out trees and use them to pass messages does not show that a forest *is* a semantic system.

My faintly sardonic tone which is creeping in is perfectly intentional. There is, in fact, so much wrong with Symbolism that I can only pick up but a few of its defects—after which I shall suggest, briefly, some factors which may be responsible for the confusion.

Natural languages and their relatives are, I have stressed, systems for generating true-or-false assertions. From this, it follows that there are various questions about a language, its structure and its devices that it must be significant to raise. None of these questions I suggest, can be raised in connection with the 'semantic systems' promoted by the Symbolist.

A central linguistic device, we saw, was the *referential* device (for example, names in English or French). It must surely make sense to ask of any two referential elements whether they have the *same* reference or not. (Does 'Churchill' have the same reference as 'Britain's leader in World War II', for example?) For unless we understand what it is for two elements to have the same reference, we do not understand what it is for an element to have a reference at all. But when we try to raise a similar question about the elements in the 'languages' of food or architecture, nonsense soon sets in. Do my potatoes have the same reference as your beans? Is their reference wider or narrower than the African's couscous? It is no use, of course, pointing out very *special* cases where such questions may be in order, for if the Symbolist's claim about the 'language of food' is right, they should *always* be in order.[15] Nor, of course, is the point that we are simply *ignorant* of when gastronomic elements have the same or different reference. It is rather that the question is typically absurd, because there is nothing corresponding to the test for sameness of reference that we have in the genuine linguistic case. (The test, very roughly, is this: if you substitute one referential element for another in sentences (or messages), does the truth-value of the sentences (messages) remain the same?) Lacking such a test in the gastronomic or architectural case means we do not even understand the notion of sameness of reference in such areas. Hence we do not understand reference itself; hence the trumpeted analogy between these areas and natural languages is undermined.

Another consequence of the essential features of language is the significance of asking, of any two sentences or messages, whether they are paraphrases of one another or not. We tackle such questions by attending, first, to whether the two messages must have the same truth-value and, secondly, to certain structural correspondences. Once more it is difficult to see how nonsense can be avoided when we ask the same question of, say, two rituals or parts of rituals. What would it mean to substitute one ritual for another to see if the message is thereby changed? At the root of this and the previous difficulty is

---

[15] Here is an example, possibly, of a 'special case': the wafer has a different reference from the wine in Communion.

the problem of finding an analogue in the symbolist's 'semantic systems' to the true-or-false assertions generated by language. No doubt one may talk of a ritual being a 'true reflection' of a tribe's attitude towards its forefathers; or of a style of architecture 'truly expressing' the mood of the decade. But the connections between such talk, and saying of a sentence that it truly asserts how things are, are surely tenuous. The analogue to saying of a ritual or architectural style that it is a true reflection or expression is saying of a man's utterance that it truly reflects his attitude or mood—not that it expresses a true assertion, that it states something which actually corresponds to the fact it posits.

It should be no surprise that, special cases aside, we find no gastronomic or architectural analogue to the true-or-false assertion. Assertion, after all, is an intentional act. I assert when I intend my message to be taken as stating what is the case. It is difficult to see how agents can be described as making assertions unless they have and are aware of having such intentions. Yet the 'messages' of which the Symbolist is enamoured are, typically, ones whose transmission and alleged content the agents are unaware of. It is only the anthropologist, it would seem, who recognizes and understands these 'messages'. To accept the Symbolist thesis is, as Dan Sperber stresses, to swallow 'that the mass of humanity obsessively manipulates tools whose usage it does not know and reiterates messages whose sense it is ignorant of.'[16] The point is not that there is *no sense* of 'message' in which people or animals (or even mere objects) may convey messages they are ignorant of.[17] It is rather that this must be a sense totally different from the one in question when we speak of the messages generated by language—for these messages are understood precisely in terms of the conscious, assertive intentions of agents. The massive distinction between language and the Symbolist's 'semantic systems' is being masked by a shoddy play on the vagueness or ambiguities of words like 'message'.

How should we explain the appeal of Symbolism when, if my arguments are cogent, it is such a mess? I shall briefly mention a couple of considerations which might help. The first is simply a generalization of the point made about the word 'message' in the last paragraph. It is an unfortunate fact that many of the crucial terms that occur in the semantical study of language—in which area they

---

[16]    *Rethinking Symbolism*, Cambridge University, 1975. p. 22.
[17]    One hears, *inter alia*, of neurones sending messages to cells, receiving messages from pulsars, and of chest pains being a message to take things easy.

have relatively narrow meanings—also occur outside but with much wider or quite different meanings. I have in mind such terms as 'message', 'communication', 'reference' and 'meaning' itself. It is only too easy to suppose that because these terms can be employed in the description of both linguistic behaviour and other activities, such activities must all be essentially analogous to using a language. One might as well suppose that the behaviour of nations must be essentially analogous to that of the particles studied by physicists, on the ground that expressions like 'force', 'power', 'affinity' and 'atrophy' can be used in the descriptions of both.

The second consideration concerns the notion of a *symbol* in particular. Taken the right way, and for certain purposes, there should be no objection to describing many of our activities—including our eating, our building, our dressing, etc.—as symbolic. Indeed, such a label can be valuable. For one thing, it serves to stress that many features of such activities are to be explained in terms of social conventions rather than natural necessity. (One could not get a full explanation of why we eat as we do in terms of natural resources, palates and gastric juices.) It stresses, too, that there are no doubt many loose but interesting connections between the ways these activities are conducted in a society and the various attitudes, beliefs and emotions found in that society—ones of a religious sort, for example. But it is both easy and fatal to slide from harmlessly labelling an activity 'symbolic' to claiming that such an activity must largely consist in using *symbols*—about which we can ask the questions asked about linguistic elements: 'What do they refer to?', 'What is their meaning?'—and so on. Despite the air of paradox, it is an important truth that 'there is no need for an analysis of the symbolic phenomenon into symbols.'[18] To take an analogy: someone engaged in the activity of dancing need not, during that time, be executing *dances* (for example, a samba or a tarantella). Isadora Duncan, I imagine, could happily dance all afternoon without our being able to identify *a dance* in any of her movements. Similarly, the fact that we may, perhaps usefully though vaguely, describe an activity as symbolic does not entitle us to suppose that it is so structured as to contain discrete elements deserving the title of *symbols*.

Symbolism, as I depicted it, cannot replace Loquentialism as an account of the human essence. Semantic man is linguistic man—not gastronomic, ritualistic or architectural man as well. As the preceding

---

[18]  D. Sperber, *op. cit.* p. 50.

remarks suggest, however, there is a much weaker thesis that might be labelled 'Symbolism'—the thesis that we should see the human essence as consisting in the conventional nature of human life. It is the fact that human activities are not, like those of animals perhaps are, explicable in terms of natural necessity. But if earlier remarks of mine are correct, this view—like that of the Marxist who stresses the productive side of human life—cannot go deep enough. To see and describe human life as conventional, rule-governed and the like is already to see it and describe it as the life of creatures with a distinctive rationality. And to see it that way is to perceive it as the life of creatures who, necessarily, command a language.

# Essay 6

## Hiram Caton

*Two friends met on a city street.*

Ian: It's been ages since I last saw you, Myles. How are you keeping?

Myles: Well, thanks. I've been working in the garden this spring. It is flattering to have plants responding to one's care. And the wife and children are well. Of course, the household is a perpetual tumult with two energetic teenagers on the loose. How about you and your family?

Ian: Linda's been down lately with a nasty bug that's been about, but looks like she's on the mend. I've been too busy to be sick.

Myles: I suppose you've heard the news about Frank Roberts?

Ian: I did, and I was shocked. In the prime of life, enviably successful, and then suddenly, dead. I suppose Kathy is passing through a difficult time now. I mean to write her a note in a week or two, when things have settled down. I gather from the news reports that the crash is something of a mystery.

Myles: Yes, still unsolved. You probably read that a farmer heard the plane overhead and noticed the engine cut out; he looked up to see it plunging silently to earth. The autopsy showed that Frank hadn't suffered a heart attack or anything like that. And no mechanical faults were found in the wreckage of the plane. So it's a puzzle, considering Frank was a good pilot.

102

When I went down to Melbourne for the funeral, I found Kathy was putting a brave face on things but was deeply disturbed. She suspects Frank committed suicide, and has taken it into her head that she bears some responsibility.

Ian: Ah, how distressing; and yet so common with those who lose a loved one through suicide. I must write to Kathy immediately. But you knew him well, Myles. What do you think? Could Frank have committed suicide? What could his motive have been?

Myles: It's difficult to imagine, though believe me I have tried. Ian, are you free for lunch?

Ian: As it happens, yes. Would The Cellar suit you? It's my regular place.

Myles: I'm at your disposal.

*The two men, one a judge, the other a publisher, found a quiet corner in The Cellar.*

Myles: To tell the truth, Ian, I'm shaken by Frank's death. I lost my best friend. And then, like Kathy, I've become obsessed with this suicide possibility. It made me wonder. He had everything. An international reputation as an architect, many friends, worthy enemies, a happy marriage and lovely children, good health, wealth—what more could anyone want? It occurred to me that if he could commit suicide, maybe I'm not immune to whatever malignant spirit got at him. For several days I've been diligently searching the past . . . our school days together, our many late-night conversations . . . looking for clues.

Ian: Yes, I understand. If Frank did commit suicide, he'd make it look like an accident. He was too proud to admit he was beaten by anything, don't you think? He might not even admit it to himself. Some say that a good many traffic fatalities are disguised suicides. But tell me, did your ruminations bring you to any conclusions?

Myles: I have some ideas, but no conclusions. I'd never really thought about the subject before this. Only once have I contemplated suicide. I was eleven, and the family visited relatives in Sydney. It rained the whole time, so I was left to play with my cousin in whatever ways we could devise to amuse ourselves. He showed me the family heirlooms in Grandma's jewelry case. I took a great fancy to a gold pocket watch, and reckoned that it wouldn't be missed from all that loot. So when the opportunity arose, I stashed it in my dirty linen.

Well, the theft was soon discovered and the culprit identified not long after. I was mortified beyond telling. Not only had I disgraced myself, but also my parents. There was no solution, it seemed to me, but to throw myself from a third floor window of that old Victorian house. I settled instead for tearfully imploring God to obliterate the memory of my vileness from the minds of all who knew it. But God had other ideas. No one forgot the incident, and my iniquity was visited upon me from time to time when the story would be dragged out and rehearsed for the amusement of others at my expense.

Ian:    Well, it's an amusing story, Myles. Instructive too. Your childhood experience is not so different from the experience of those convicted of criminal charges. Sitting there on the bench, pronouncing sentence, I often feel I know what must be going through the man's mind. His life is shattered. He's been disgraced before the world, and he is about to be deprived of his freedom. He is in debt and has no idea how he will provide for his family. The agony must be terrible. It is striking, when you think of this drama, that judges enjoy such respectability and that convicted felons so rarely suicide. I've sometimes wondered whether I could endure the disgrace of conviction for a criminal offence. I certainly cannot imagine how I could adjust to prison life.

Myles:    And yet, you know people like yourself have done it. I think time is the main factor. When the market crashed in '29, thousands committed suicide. And there was a rash of suicides when Orson Welles did his radio dramatization of *The War of the Worlds*. Many people believed it was an actual newscast of the invasion of the earth by horrid Martians. Yet declarations of war don't produce waves of suicides, nor did the explosion of the first atomic bomb.

Ian:    How does time get into that picture?

Myles:    This way. When the market crashed, many people suddenly went from riches to rags. Among them were some whose sense of self and their place in the world was so bound up with high status that the loss of wealth was a world-shattering experience, a kind of life-trauma. Because the crash came without warning, they had no time to become accustomed to their changed status. They had no time to adapt their self-image to a new way of life before they were thrown into it. The same is true of Welles' broadcast, except that the entire thing was imaginary, and the people who suicided did so from fear of imagined evils.

Ian: You seem to be saying something like this: people have their own particular sense of self, related in various ways to people and circumstances around them. The total ambience of self and world is like an ecological niche individuals have worked out for themselves. Therefore, a change in the environment forces individuals to change their self-image and find a new niche, including an adapted sense of self. But adaptation takes time; it's a gradual process of getting used to a new idea. Sudden environmental changes are apt to produce great stress, and in some instances, suicide. Is that the idea?

Myles: I think you've said it better than I could.

Ian: And your notion is that in 1929 everyone who lost all and whose sense of self was tied up with wealth was under stress, but of those only some couldn't make the adjustment?

Myles: That's it. All of those who were under stress had to adjust after the event, and some couldn't do it, or perhaps didn't care to.

Ian: Well, on that theory, shouldn't the sudden out-break of war and invasion produce the same effect?

Myles: Yes, unexpected wars probably do. But what government would publicize a rash of suicides at the outbreak of a war? And I imagine that some people suicide in those circumstances simply by not bothering to take cover. It would be like the suicides enumerated as traffic fatalities.

Ian: How does this relate to Frank's case?

Myles: My guess is that Frank's case is rather the opposite. The decision to suicide—if that's what it was—came after years of secret frustration and disspiriting experience; and the decision would have been as cool and collected as a court order. I'm sure Frank didn't see himself as a failure. But

I am beginning to suspect he thought the world had failed him. He never quite put it that way, but I recall a metaphor he once used to describe his frustration. He said that urban planning in Australia was a brittle medium that resisted all the artist's attempts to impose a form— like a grainy block of marble that splits with the first touch of the chisel. Frank was the artist who came to believe he would be denied the marble needed for the perfect work of art conceived over the years. Then life lost its allure and savour. So he decided to get out altogether rather than accept second-best. I imagine the mood of the decision would have been toned more by resentment than by regret. Anyway, all that is my speculation.

Ian:     What you say is elusive. Do you mean he regarded all his work as second-best?

Myles:   Not quite. He regarded some of his buildings as studies for the perfect work of art. But here is the catch. Frank did not conceive the perfect work as just one building. For him individual buildings were not artistic units. The architectural artistic unit, he believed, was the functioning whole that a collection of buildings, such as a city, compose. For him, that's what the perfect work of art was —a city or town.

Ian:     What amazing ambition!

Myles:   Not a large city, mind you. Frank thought modern cities are horrors and he was belligerent on the subject of skyscrapers. But he did dream of building a city—an Australian Alexandria, he used to call it.

Ian:     For that he would need an Alexander.

Myles:   I said that to him once, and he had a come-back. All he needed, he claimed, was a genuinely reform-minded social-ist government. After a pause he added: 'And they are rarer than Alexanders'.

Ian:     A disarming admission. But then he was a charming man. I didn't know him well enough to fathom his politics. My impression is that he was rather more superficial than naive, for he was certainly realistic about trade-union leaders. It seemed to me his socialism amounted to little more than loose identification with the people who decry necessary evils. But what you've been saying suggests that perhaps he was a socialist from artistic self-interest.

Myles:    My goodness, there's a large subject. Frank and I were scarcely able to talk politics without ending up in a brawl, with him accusing me of cold opportunism, and me accusing him of hypocritical righteousness. There was a time when we didn't speak for six months. Then one day he rang to ask whether I'd care to fly up to Cairns for some capitalist fishing; that ended the severed relations.

    Yes, there was a connection between his socialism and architecture—it was town planning. Left to his own devices, Frank would have planned everything, right down to the shoe leather of the least street cleaner. Seriously. He wasted God knows how much time designing clothing for the populace of his dream city. He showed me some of the designs. Often the ideas were good, and sometimes brilliant, but the setting was a nightmare. I would say to him: 'Frank, that's all very well. But who is going to live in this town? Robots? You've over-prescribed. You can't clap human beings into fixed moulds. If you manage to keep them there, they will die like pot-bound plants. But the chances are you won't keep them there. Life is growth and change, Frank—individual growth and change. Just think of yourself.'

Ian:    What did he say to that?

Myles:    Different things on different occasions. There was a time when he was enthusiastic for regimentation, claiming it was just what human beings need most. Of course, he called it 'community', not 'regimentation'. He said Mao's communes and the Prussian officer corps in the old days were fine communities. When I countered that he ought to include British Military Intelligence and the KGB, he said that was all right with him. In arguments like this his obstinacy was exasperating. He had no knowledge of China, and the Prussian officer corps was probably picked from the air just to underscore the point that he meant *any* disciplined community. But he disclaimed interest in 'pedantic facts'. All he needed, he claimed, was the idea; the details he would imagine for himself.

Ian:    Sounds like some lawyers I know.

Myles:    And like some reporters I know. Anyway, his enthusiasm for regimented communities didn't last more than a year. Not that anything I said changed his mind. He was

|        |                                                                                             |
|--------|---------------------------------------------------------------------------------------------|
|        | unmoved when I pointed out that people as jealously independent as himself would be miserable in a commune. He dismissed it by saying that his hankering for independence was a product of his upbringing; that he'd be much happier had he been born in a well-ordered community, and so on to that effect. What changed his mind was a book by a French crackpot by the name of Fourier. Have you heard of this chap, Ian? |
| Ian:   | Do you mean Charles Fourier, a contemporary of Napoleon?                                     |
| Myles: | That's him. I'd never heard the man's name until Frank delivered a long encomium on him one night in a Perisher Valley ski lodge. He made me promise to read him. Well, I did, and never in my life have I come across such amusing nonsense uttered in so solemn a manner. You know about the phalansteries, Harmony and all that, I suppose? |
| Ian:   | Yes, I must confess a liking for utopian books.                                              |
| Myles: | I wouldn't have guessed that of you, Ian.                                                    |
| Ian:   | You say that as if I'd confessed a wicked habit. I suppose I can't avoid admitting to at least depraved taste, since I balance utopian books with science fiction; and, as you know, science fiction stoutly defends the old Adam against ingenious utopian contrivances. |
| Myles: | That's certainly true. As they say in the publishing trade, 'Scratch a science fiction writer and you'll find an individualist'. But you were about to say . . . |
| Ian:   | Utopian books are political science fiction. The aim of the genre guarantees in advance that the population of Harmony, or whatever, won't be recognizably human. It's a pastime of mine to figure out in each case just why the population isn't human. Still more interesting is the next step of figuring out why the author believed that this or that imagined ideal situation is more desirable than the actual human situation. |
| Myles: | Sounds as if you have your pastime worked out to an art.                                     |
| Ian:   | Well, I do make notes. But Linda, who is something of a utopian herself, dismisses the preoccupation as the defence mechanism of a judge.                                   |
| Myles: | Your friends can afford to be more generous than your wife. We will say you are only finding good reasons for doing your duty. But tell me what you think of Fourier. |

Ian:     An interesting case, actually. Before automation, most utopians felt they had to make up their minds about the significance of work and abundance. If they believed most work could not be made pleasant, they had to persuade themselves that human beings could be happy with relatively modest means. But if they thought significantly greater wealth was required to support happiness and develop human faculties to the full, they had to persuade themselves that work could be pleasant. Fourier unflinchingly admitted that work for the most part is inherently drab and that considerable wealth was needed to support happiness. He rescued the situation by arguing that the drabness of work was mainly because of its repetitiveness, which could be reduced by letting the Harmonions shift to a new job every hour or so; but more important than that, he thought, was the organization of labour into voluntarily associated teams based on mutual attraction amongst its membership. The teamwork principle turned work into harmless games of rivalry, with greater rewards going to the most talented and productive.

Myles:   Yes. Fourier strained his ingenuity to make matches between necessary work and fugitive human desires. One would suppose that tending refuse and sewerage is the sort of job none would choose. But he believed that boys, at a certain age, delight in filth and that they would happily volunteer to clean the sewers.

Ian:     Fourier was probably as attentive to the variety of human types and desires as any utopian. He had calculated there are exactly 820 possible personalities, although most of these don't occur often. At first glance that seems a considerable variety. But if you think about it, you see it falls short by an infinite number. You recall how he arrived at his calculation. First he enumerated the basic passions—there are twelve—and then computed the number of possible combinations of their occurrence when one or more passion is dominant. That calculation is an instance of how the comedy of unreality creeps into his theory. He thought such a deduction was legitimate because he had decided that Newtonian mechanics must be applicable to the animal kingdom. But the part of the animal kingdom I deal with is very different. Supposing there were exactly twelve basic passions; the number of personality types would still be infinite because small variations in degree and tonality of passions can produce great differences. Two solicitors who in other things are equal—and of course they never are—will differ markedly in their handling of a case, according to their characteristic mix of confidence and caution. But all that is secondary to his general theory of the passions.

Myles:    The general theory was what excited Frank's interest and what seemed maddening to me. The idea that the passions are inherently benign and pleasant, and that they become cruel and aggressive only when they are frustrated seems to me so contrary to experience that I had to wonder whether Fourier and I were experiencing the same species of being.

Ian:    You can spare yourself the effort. The notion of the benignity of the passions was another deduction from his model of a Newtonian social science. He argued that in the animal kingdom there must be a harmony of attraction analogous to the harmony produced in the heavens by gravitation. Never in human history, he admitted, has the supposed harmony occurred—otherwise, a utopian scheme would be unnecessary. But Fourier believed that he had discovered the principles of the scheme, and that they could be implemented.

Myles:    I used to become furious with Frank about that analogy to celestial mechanics. I said to him: 'Frank, even with my layman's knowledge I can see the harmony of attraction business is pure rhetoric. Gravitational "attraction" was a metaphor Newton used to designate what he could not understand—the inscrutable "action at a distance". If "attraction" was to mean anything in physics, it had to be explicable as force. Substitute "force" for harmony, and the allure of the analogy vanishes. It is sheer self-deceit for you, who know much more about physics than I, to be taken in by mere words.'

I remember the occasion vividly. Our political arguments had been slowly mutating from stimulating differences of opinion and attitude to incompatibilities of character. As boys and youths, each had been the confidant of the other. We shared the excitement of discovering ourselves and the world, we advised and consoled one another in defeat, we took risks for one another. We were an intimate, exclusive club of two. But now we seemed to value incompatible things and it strained our relationship.

That was the background of my strong words about self-deceit. I realize now it was a plea for him to give back the old Frank I admired. His response, which I expected to be hostile, took me by surprise. He said that the inconsistency hadn't occurred to him and that he would need to think about it. I was astonished a man of his intelligence could have made such an oversight. It set me thinking.

Ian: Were you really astonished? What have you learned from experience if not that intelligent human beings are the sources of the greatest errors as well as truths?

Myles: I admit the naivety of it, Ian. You are more studious than I, and you probably comprehend your experience better. In any case, this realization assumed great significance for me. Previously I had believed, probably because everyone said so, that differences of value judgements are not arguable; they just are. Now it seemed to me that truth and falsity must play a great role in determining what one values. I remembered a book we'd published on the concept of nature in French literature, and picked it up from the shelf. I found what I was looking for. Fourier was neither the first nor the last to preach some doctrine of the harmony of the passions based on the assumption that the passions are part of a deterministic world mechanism. But there is a greater paradox still. These philosophers believed that human thoughts and actions are as rigidly determined as the impacts of billiard balls. Yet they generally championed freedom against despotism and advocated forms of government that reduced the use of coercion to a minimum. It's the same in Fourier, except he goes to extremes. There is no coercion whatever in his phalansteries, everyone does everything voluntarily—not even self-control is demanded—and the whole of Harmony is elaborately contrived by the wise social scientist. And yet every action is mechanistically determined. Tell me, Ian, who can't see straight here, me or them?

Ian:          I have no head for these abstract questions, Myles. I can't
              pronounce upon them with any assurance.

Myles:        Are you being coy?

Ian:          Not in the least. Lawyers make poor philosophers. Their
              training saturates them in particulars of human conduct
              and trains them to think always in terms of relevance to
              particular cases. The legal mind can cope with the notion
              that individuals might be *non compos mentis* and therefore
              not answerable for their actions. But it cannot cope with
              the idea that no individual is responsible for any action.
              I express the bias of my profession when I say I cannot
              assign any concrete idea at all to the notion that all action
              is completely determined. To me those are mere words at
              cross-purposes with experience. I do not deny that people
              of outstanding ability have advanced such views. They say
              the intimate and direct experience of freedom is an illusion.
              But to me the experience is real and the explanation
              illusory. Do you see what I am driving at? The
              philosophers have heads for abstractions. To them, the
              concept of a mechanistic universe is very real—maybe the
              most real thing of all. And you must admit they can't be
              completely mistaken because, after all, there is physics with
              its demonstrated laws. Then the logic goes to work. The
              human being is a part of nature—undeniable. Therefore,
              human conduct is completely determined, like nature. The
              conclusion is compelling, even irresistible, once you grant
              the initial premise. But the lawyer in me says these
              cosmological speculations cannot be made relevant to law
              through the slender thread of deductive argument. There
              must be experiential evidence enabling me to see directly
              that freedom is an illusion.

Myles:        For a man with no head for philosophy you seem to get
              on well enough.

Ian:          I don't deceive myself on that point, Myles. For many
              decades various philosophies have invaded law, partly via
              psychiatric testimony, partly through jurisprudence, partly
              through ethics. Taken all together, they seem to me to be
              the thin edge of the wedge that will destroy law. Conse-
              quently, I look upon philosophy with great mistrust.

                  From time to time I become angry about it and fall into
              my punitive mood. Take this matter of the harmony of

the passions. As you suggested, there are many versions of the theory, the best-known being the idea of the invisible hand which produces from the self-interested conduct of each the harmonious well-being of all. But, as you also suggested, this is a providential supplement to the mechanistic theory, not a part of the theory itself. From the same theory, one could read out an opposite theology—that nature is violent, not benign; that it is mindless, not providential; that it favours chance, not design; that the most depraved criminality is as natural and justified as high-minded dignity.

Some writers actually said such things. I recall an extraordinary dialogue that grinds all dignity and feeling to bits in the mill of Newtonian cosmology. It was by a Frenchman named Diderot; anyway, its excess is very un-British.

If such theories were spun out for the private amusement of their authors, no one could object. But they are published, and invisibly eat away like some disease at the vulnerable body politic. The dissemination of this sort of writing is irresponsible and produces no end of confusion and chaos. Especially today. In the 18th century the temerity of the intellectuals was at least moderated by censorship. But meanwhile they have taken over educational institutions, converted them to fortresses invulnerable to criticism, not to mention prosecution, and have created an atmosphere in which the most outrageous opinions are applauded loudest. There is a great and portentous significance in this development.

Myles:    You put the case rather strongly—perhaps too strongly. Mind you, I hold no brief for the radicals. But they are a small minority. Most academics are honest people, even dull.

Ian:    It's not the radicals that I mean. No one takes them seriously. I do mean your rank-and-file academics. Of course they are dull, but perhaps you underestimate the power of persistent mediocrity, especially when it is tenured.

Myles:    What do you mean by that?

Ian:    It's difficult to explain, for it has as much to do with attitude, mood and expectation as with opinions. Maybe

Fourier will serve as an analogy, although at first sight the example seems inapt. You know, don't you, that he was self-taught and that his theory was spurned by the leading lights of his day. But not completely. Perhaps just because of his novelty, some writers began to air his views with a bemused innocence. But that is not especially relevant.

The relevant matter is the significance Fourier attached to his work. He boasted he was a second Newton, but otherwise he acknowledged no teachers or precursors. His utopia became so real to him that he used it to judge the past, present and future. All the experience and wisdom of time he called 'civilization', and he execrated it as utmost ignorance and viciousness. He and his utopia alone were rational, humane, beneficent.

Myles:     Yes, these claims make one blush. I suspect his isolation pushed him to the point of madness.

Ian:       Madness? But what manner of madness? Fourier was a man of modest endowment, yet he flattered himself he was a great genius. His grasp of human things was imperfect, yet he dared to repudiate civilization as of no account. Yes, it is madness to reject civilization for your own uncertain cogitations. But the conviction that one knows more and better than the sum of human experience and of a long tradition of highly refined minds—here vanity metamorphoses into something new. I don't know what to call it except the barbarism of the half-educated, who enter the temple of wisdom and trample underfoot in a destructive rage everything that offends their vanity or resists their understanding. Unable to discern the variegated eternal logic of human affairs, he saw nothing but a mass of malevolent inconsistencies. And he said to himself: 'What is this? Fie! Away with the infamy!'

But how, Myles, did this pretentious wart find the hide to oppose himself to civilization? What fortified his vainglorious temerity? Fourier believed in Scientific Reason, which pays no homage to belief, however venerable, nor to received practice, no matter how ancient. What is more, he believed that by a special providence—such as Newton had received—Scientific Reason had chosen Charles Fourier to declare the truth about human affairs.

All this would be mere curiosity, a pathetic case of delusions of grandeur, were he unique. Alas, he is not. He is part of a barbarian horde, all calling upon the name of that new Moloch, Scientific Reason, to declare that law, civil institutions, class, the state, morality and religion are one and all a tissue of lies and prejudice. And they espouse a new order of things, totally at variance with all practice hitherto, in which human beings will at last attain their 'true humanity'.

It's virtually a truism to say that any civilized person rejects this sort of thing as impertinent rubbish, and dangerous rubbish. For in practical terms it means that if a people can be lured towards the empty objectives of the scientific reasoners, the repudiation of civilization demanded by the doctrine guarantees the most brutish and bestial politics imaginable—just because it has thrown off all the 'repressive fetters' of civilization which restrain, among others, despots and potential despots.

For some time this nonsense was spurned by cultivated people, and circulated only as political oratory. It was even a useful check upon the complacency and arrogance of those who governed at the time. But when radicals were assimilated politically into the parliamentary system and achieved respectability, they naturally brought their gospel with them. Then by slow degrees it became fused with the established learning until at last hardly anyone in tertiary institutions, least of all teachers of law, remembered the reasons why the institutions of civilization are civilizing, or how they exercise their civilizing influence.

Myles:   I'm not sure I follow what you are saying. Is it that Fourier illustrates a mentality that has attached itself to the established learning?

Ian:   Yes.

Myles:   And because this mentality is barbaric, the established learning is like a disease eating away at the vitals of our social order.

Ian:   Yes, our social order; but it is also incompatible with any social order.

Myles:   Well, there are two things I don't understand. What is the connection between scientism, utopianism and conceit in Fourier? And secondly, how has this connection mutated into the non-utopian attitude of the established learning —for you would agree, wouldn't you, that it is non-utopian?

Ian:     You pointed out yourself that there is no logical or substantive connection that links scientism with utopianism. As far as I can make out, the connection runs through back doors. One of the doors is a sort of torpor artificially induced by the attempt to understand the human being scientifically. Because it can't be done, the scientific and philosophic thinkers invent a new being which they call man, such as the 'man-machine hypothesis'—'hypothesis' sounds very clinical and innocent, doesn't it? Because the scientifically invented human being is incompatible with real human beings, scientific reasoners are free to impose whatever characteristics on their model their fancy, anxiety, vanity, ignorance or envy may suggest. This is where utopianism gains its entrance. There is a touching and, in its own limited way, noble wish which seems to arise spontaneously in the hearts of people that all their desires should be fulfilled, that they should live together in peace and be exempt from the onerous hardships and vicissitudes of life. It's the idea of the Garden of Eden, interpreted now one way, now the next.

In the Bible, utopia didn't last long; Adam acquired the forbidden knowledge of good and evil and had to be expelled from the earthly paradise. The enlightenment philosophers used to reproach the cruel inhumanity of the old God of the Hebrews who cast his most perfect creation into misery. But similar stories were told by Indian sages and Greek poets, and they believed that, contrary to our naive feelings, Yahweh or Zeus did the right thing. What they meant, I imagine, is that to be human *is* to possess knowledge of good and evil, and that such knowledge is contrary to the spontaneous utopian wish everyone sometimes feels. To know good and evil is to know ourselves, and those who have that knowledge would decline to enter utopia unless they were weary of their humanity and sought to cast it off.

Myles:   In other words, Adam gained his humanity when he lost paradise?

Ian:      Exactly. All the old stories are clear about that, I think. By reversing the process and restoring human beings to paradise, the utopians confirm these stories when they people their gardens with beings who are not recognizably human.

Take the utopian belief that all desires should be gratified, and the related view that restraint, whether imposed by oneself or in some other way, is repressive and therefore ought to be done away with. This belief passes for evident truth in much public discourse and in the established learning. And yet, it is difficult to imagine a belief more at odds with our humanity, with the good and evil in our nature. What manner of monsters would we be if we did not restrain pride, envy, revenge, cupidity, the will to dominate and the like? You can read about such beings in history books.

Myles:    The utopians maintain that these passions are awakened only by frustrations and hardships imposed by corrupt or exploitative socieites, and therefore will not exist in the harmonious utopia where everyone is satisfied.

Ian:      Have you ever met a human being who was satisfied from the cradle to the grave?

Myles:    Scarcely.

Ian:      Can you imagine such a human being?

Myles:    Frankly, no. A completely satisfied person would have no desires; would lack all motive and ambition; would be inert —dead in effect.

Ian:      So when you look the matter straight in the eye for a moment, you see that satisfaction makes no sense without its contrary. For the sake of utopia, then, utopians admit just a little bit of non-utopia into the Garden. There needs to be just enough hunger to create robust appetites, just enough sexual denial to redeem the act of love from boredom, just enough toil to sharpen the pleasures of leisure, and so on. Well then, there must be a regime and a routine in utopia with imposes temporary denials, because if all individuals were allowed to choose for themselves between instant gratification and postponement, experience teaches that significant numbers would choose instant gratification, until they learn—if they learn—from the destructive consequences that their choice was unwise.

Some measure of communal discipline and sense of self-restraint must then re-enter the picture. And if they are consistent in the use of the utopian terminology, they shall need to admit that at least a dose of 'repression' or what we would call 'good manners' is required in order to live recognizably human lives. Since utopians aim at the maximization of pleasure, and do so because they believe pleasures and pains can be neatly classified and distinguished from one another, they do not look gladly, if at all, on the necessity of admitting some pain into the Garden. In real life, however, pleasure and pain cannot be disentangled. There are many pains that can be experienced as pleasant, and conversely; similarly, few are the pleasures that do not have an antecedent pain, and conversely. Youths and athletes, for example, actually take pleasure in the rigours of physical training, even as they suffer from it, not only because pleasant physical feelings mingle with painful ones during the exercises, but also because of the delight they take in strengthening and gaining control of their bodies. And I imagine that the case is the same for all those who achieve anything in art or science or statesmanship or learning.

The utopians believe that, like pleasures and pains, motives and passions can be neatly divided into good and bad, and that in the Garden it will be possible to have the one without the other. They imagine there will be a spirit of equality, but also rich variety of persons and certainly not boring identity; all will have a sense of their own worth and dignity, but none will be proud or overbearing; there will be love, but no jealousy or broken hearts; there will be joy, but no sadness to speak of; victory, but no defeat; there will be desire, but no envy, revenge or frustration; there will be perfect order and justice, but for that reason no magistrates or rulers and no punishments; there will be intellectual inquiry and science, but there will be no discoveries that threaten the beliefs upon which utopia is based; all will be free to develop their natural powers, but a whole range of possibilities—from the sombre creative melancholy of so many painters, to the fiery righteousness of the prophets, to the stern glory of the warrior—will be excluded; utopia will exist within the flux of changing nature, but no new ice age, no pestilence or disease, nor any other natural calamity will endanger the soft peace of utopia.

If you point out to the utopians that their vision supposes a saltus in nature and human nature such as had never been seen, they reply blandly: 'As for nature, science will take care of that.' They don't seem to realize that the powers that science lays in the hands of human beings, while sufficiently great to surpass our wisdom to use them well, are nevertheless as nothing compared with the powers of nature. Nor do they realize that science, which in the utopian wish fantasy is supposed to give human beings control over nature, is now itself quite out of control, like a genie from a magic lamp. But more fateful still is their conviction that by magic—whether called 'progress' or 'revolution' or 'behavioural engineering' is no matter—a saltus can be achieved in the contrariety of the passions as we have hitherto known them. The magic will separate the good passions from the bad, and the latter will be eliminated, despite the fact that all sustained approximations to utopian desiderata confirm that good and evil can no more be separated from one another than life can be separated from death.

Myles:  Can you think of examples?

Ian:    Well, consider various religious orders that have for centuries and still do live the life of communal solidarity, preserving the right proportions of work and prayer. Not to mention the 'repression' of such regimens, which we cannot imagine is always accepted gladly, these orders exclude from their midst certain carnal things without which the orders themselves cannot exist—such as sexual reproduction and laws and arms to defend the monasteries.

Or consider the kibbutz, which is inspired by secular utopian notions. The fraternal solidarity of the kibbutz is not the community of human beings as human beings, but of a special category of people created by a unique history of persecution that burned the distinction between 'them and us' on the Jewish soul. That distinction, and the enormous solidarity it created, has been kept alive by repeated wars and the constant threat of war. Yet despite

Fortress Israel, the kibbutzim have had to struggle to preserve their spirit against the allure of prosperity and individualism; and I would wager that dedication to the asceticism of kibbutz life will disappear when the challenge to which it was a response disappears.

All these communal experiments prove that community is purchased at the price of a degree of conformism incompatible with even 'innocent' variety. As a wise student of law discerned long ago, at bottom they all depend upon an enemy against which they are in arms. Mind you, I am not decrying conformism nor its martial spirit. Frank appreciated its allure for a while, and it has been the condition of many worthy societies. I'm only pointing out that you can't actualize all *worthy* human possibilities in any conceivable community. There are always some who are left out, or what is more likely, some aspect of the humanity of all will be banned. And some one or few will discover this fact, and they will begin to murmur; and ambition, which will have been repressed, will raise its head to champion justice, and the conflict will begin.

Myles:     Now I think I understand better what you mean. First comes the blindness to knowledge of good and evil induced by scientism, and then the substitution of spontaneous, naive wishful thinking for knowledge. And in intellectuals this takes on the quality of the drive to create the world anew. We seem on the verge of characterizing knowledge of good and evil, but as yet it eludes me.

Ian:       You mean a general characterization?

Myles:     I think that if I had that, all you have been saying would become clear.

Ian:       I'm afraid I can't help you. I'm no good at abstractions. Besides, they readily reduce to catch-phrases which become impediments rather than aids to understanding. I prefer to keep my eye on particular cases. Restraint is harsh; therefore banish it. But then you banish power of soul and achievement. Love is good; therefore base utopia upon it. But love is exclusive and jealous; therefore invent a new kind of non-possessive love and call it 'truly human'. Self-esteem is a good thing, but it involves invidious comparisons and inequality. But inequality is a bad thing, for it offends the envious. Therefore invent a new kind of self-esteem based on nothing more than respect for the humanity in oneself and others, and do not pause to consider wherein precisely this humanity consists. Democracy is a good thing because everyone has a say, but actual democracies presuppose hierarchies of merit, of decision, of status and a host of other inequalities; therefore inveigh against actual democracy as oppressive elitism and invent a new democracy in which human beings miraculously determine themselves individually through some collectivity. Science is a good thing, for it enables us to control nature to our advantage. But science concocts modern weaponry; therefore decry the misuse of science and invent human beings who would neither wittingly nor unwittingly abuse its enormous powers. Industrial production is a good thing, because it abates the rigours of natural scarcity. But the more we acquire, the more we want. Therefore reprobate this tendency as a transitional historical phase of greed and invent a future in which greed will vanish. In doing so, however, be careful not to examine the motives of the heart, for that would give the game away. Instead use unintelligible abstractions such as 'capitalism' and 'socialism' to obfuscate the real questions. Reason is a good thing, for it enables us to defeat ignorance and prejudice and to control our lives. But in its actual existence in people, it is not exempt from error, vanity or avenging dogmatism, and it has been known to oppose itself to all the world. Therefore conceal the character of actual reason by protesting that it can be fettered to 'social responsibility'.

The utopian's misapprehension of good and evil is like the mistake of someone who wanted dawn with darkness of night; who loved children, but not their demanding dependence; who relished adventure, but would have it without risks. They do not know that to be human means to plant our abode in the golden circle of the divine laws of contrariety.

*Myles listened to this diatribe with fascination moderated by a muffled sense of alarm. After a long pause he said, almost in a whisper:*

What you say, Ian, is . . . incredible. Do you really believe it? But that is a silly question. I've been turned into myself . . . the implications are so vast.

Ian: Believe it? No, I do not *believe* it.

Myles: *Don't* believe it? But the conviction, the fervour . . . why?

Ian: Beg pardon, Myles, I don't mean to play at paradox. Yet if I agreed that I *believe*, I would have misstated my thoughts. How can I say it? To my mind, belief, like reason, is for philosophers and others of that sort. Reason, belief, opinion—these are more abstractions; fickle, arbitrary, anaemic, remote from life. Comprehending life rationally—that sounds to my ears like a proposal to capture butterflies with a fish net. What blunt instruments these rationalists use to dissect their specimens! First they locate what they call a 'problem'. A problem is a state of affairs someone wants to change, or a question that can be answered with the support of objective data. The only sort of enquiry the rationalists know is 'problem-solving'. But what if there are insoluble problems and unanswerable questions? What if the 'insoluble problem' of contrariety lies at the centre of existence? Well, there go the butterflies through the net. Then there are those objective data marshalled by logical arguments. Much of the data are of dubious relevance at best. Myles, I wonder whether you know that tens of thousands of scientists have spent hundreds of millions of dollars researching the behaviour of rats?

Myles: You mean the white-frocked psychologists who believe that mice are men, only smaller?

Ian: The same. Their idea is that in order to have objective knowledge of human beings, why, you must study non-human subjects. If that seems paradoxical, it is only because it takes practice to appreciate the splendid logic of objective reason. For the point of studying non-human 'subjects' is to eliminate from research any contamination by subjective human psychology; in other words, the psychologists concoct a science of the human being that leaves the human being out, because the specifically human cannot be treated objectively; although 'objective science' is, as far as anyone knows, purely human and therefore contaminated by anthropomorphic biases. But I believe that these psychologists are correct that objective reason cannot deal with the specifically human. Rather than pretending that the human being is reducible to the rat, I believe that their conclusion simply exposes the scientific prejudice of objective reason.

Myles: I'm not very well informed on these matters, but I have the impression the school of thought to which you refer is only one among a number. Certainly most academic books we publish say nothing about rats.

Ian: True enough, but that's not my point. Regardless of how many academics are active behaviourists—and I have the impression that many are—the fact is that behaviourism has been more than tolerated; it has commanded great prestige and large research budgets. The study of literature or religion, by comparison, have not. Why? Because behavioural science is thought to meet the formal criteria of objective knowledge, whereas the latter two subjects do not. And what is true of psychology is true of other disciplines as well. They may not study rats, but by going about their business objectively, they obfuscate the subject matter they are supposed to be studying. I see this clearly in my own field. First, law was invaded by sociology or, I should say, academic lawyers were seduced by sociology. This was the phase in which law was interpreted to be an instrument of 'social control'. No one seemed embarrassed by this new conception; on the contrary, it was greeted as a great enlightenment: the nature of law had at last been understood. In reality, I at least cannot imagine a greater perversion of legal understanding.

Myles: Those are strong words, Ian. What is so insidious about such a definition?

Ian: Yes, I do seem to be in my sentencing mood today. I take it that law is rooted in the ethos of a people, its experience, its painfully acquired consensus about right and wrong. To construe law as social control, however, detaches it from these roots and interprets it in a purely technical sense as one means among many of getting your way. Other means are kangaroo courts, secret police terror and genocide. But law is what it is because it authoritatively affirms ethical distinctions between legality and arbitrary measures. The classification of law as a means of social control is like classifying atomic particles as imaginary beings. The generality of the abstraction lends it a certain appeal.

But that was only the first phase of reform. Next it was decided to increase objectivity by introducing behavioural concepts that can be measured. The result is the science of jurimetrics, which a colleague of mine calls 'the academic numbers racket'.

Myles:     A psychology that knows nothing of the soul . . . A legal science that abstracts from ethics . . . I think I see what you mean about the barbarism of objective reason.

Ian:       Often objective reason is little more than a high-sounding honorific for the mechanistic prejudice. For years now the social scientists have been advertising themselves to the highest bidder, saying 'Here are we, your friendly social engineers. Problems solved.' And then in fine print: 'Permanent solutions not guaranteed.' You see the utopianism of it. The human world is a machine whose worn gears can be replaced by the latest automatic equipment, known in the trade as 'mass man'.

The paradox of it all is that because the soul is inscrutable to objective reasoners, they cannot learn anything substantial about the human being from their studies. This they admit when they declare there can be no 'objective knowledge' of good and evil. Nevertheless, objective reasoners are also human, so they must take their orientation from somewhere. In lieu of knowledge, they appropriate utopian aspirations and orient research around that.

Myles:     I see. There's a double-bind syndrome here. One knot in the bind is the element of hard-nosed realism. This is the juncture where the objective reasoners say 'All right, enough of this pre-scientific lore and value-laden judgement. Let's get serious about the science of human beings and consider them coldly in the light of the appropriate mechanistic assumptions and models.' There is much self-congratulation and seemingly malicious glee at how 'cold-blooded' they are about the whole business. It's as if they entertained a vast contempt for the human being.

Then there is another knot. In addition to the cold-blooded contempt of the human being, these objective reasoners also entertain deep sympathies for human suffering and are sometimes maudlin and sentimental to the point of absurdity. They also want to improve people and their estate, to turn them into the green pastures of paradise. That's one bind. The other bind is that because the objective approach to the human being is barren, sentimentality is covertly injected into objective science to give it some concrete content and reference.

Ian:  The double-bind syndrome—I like that. You see it also in the two faces academics present to the public. On the one hand, they are politically committed and like to think of themselves as the vanguard of progress. On the other hand, they claim to be impartial investigators carefully sifting facts and drawing conclusions irrespective of whatever party, interests or sentiments their research may flatter or offend. As political partisans, they exist in the political milieu of conflicting claims about the good and the just, and conflicting views about what human beings are. But as experts who advise governments and teach the youth, they say to the public: 'We have no political interests of our own and do not take sides. Our sole aim and duty is to discover truth by methods as impartial as possible. Let the community make such use of our knowledge as it sees fit.' This attitude they call their 'value-neutrality'.

Any lawyers with their wits about them would recognize the special pleading here. The so-called value-neutrality is actually a statement of commitment to truth as the highest value—truth, no matter what the costs and consequences. It is a plea that the public should tolerate enquiry, even though the advance of knowledge is bound to hurt when it collides with some cherished opinions; there is no guarantee it will not demolish all cherished opinions and stumble into a desperate night of total nihilism. Why then should the public expose itself to such hazards, putting itself, as it were, in hostage to what academics and their muse Scientific Reason declare the truth to be? 'Because', they say to parliamentary committees, 'knowledge is socially useful; it enables the polity to eliminate social evils and advance towards a better society.' Well, you see that all the important questions are begged here, and value commitments of the value-neutral reasoners multiply like rabbits. So assiduously do they scour all points of view that it doesn't enter their heads to consider some truth might be injurious in the highest degree; or attempts to eliminate certain evils may be worse than the disease.

To support their point of view, academics conjure up a vast mysterious planetary mechanism called 'social progress' and many other names. The mechanism, we are assured, grinds out change after change, to which individuals and societies must 'adjust'. Academics are needed to predict the behaviour of this implacable mechanism, and advise us how to adjust, lest we be damned to obsolescence by the unyielding decrees of the *Zeitgeist*. The absurdity of it all is writ so large that by itself it is a singular proof that if mankind is to be saved from itself, it won't be thanks to the cogent intellect of the objective reasoners. They say values cannot be validly deduced from facts, and yet the practical usefulness of their research—and they do keenly desire to be useful—depends upon governments and institutions deducing policy objectives from research. Indeed, the research report more often than not concludes by pointing out practical implications. Needless to say, the implications are invariably progressive. For example, economics invariably supports continued growth, because growth is required by the regnant notion of social progress. I am told this assumption is so deep in economics that it cannot even deal with a steady-state economy. Similarly, the study of class and status is ostensibly neutral to the question whether inequality is good or bad; nevertheless, it is rare for research not to assert the existence of inequalities, as if no-one had noticed them, and to argue that they ought to be eliminated as being incompatible with our democratic ideas. Or take criminology and study of the causes of crime. The causes are invariably said to lie outside the criminal, who is considered to be an unfortunate victim of the law, who happens to have become the unfortunate locus of contrary social forces.

*Myles relaxed in the abundant space of his padded leather chair, and looked pensively across the room at nothing in particular. After a time, he spoke:*

Suppose you believed you were only the chance effect of the accidents of birth, socialization, industrialization, the world market and so on. How would that affect you? You would think of yourself as a helpless pawn in a meaningless game of chance, as stripped of any responsibility for your actions—provided you were consistent. Wouldn't you then be contemptuous of yourself to the point of self-hatred? Or perhaps you would turn the hatred outward upon others, and upon 'society'. And suppose chance had dealt you a weak hand, while others held aces. Wouldn't envy of them turn into a poisonous hatred? Could it be that objective reasoners are perpetually in an adversary relation to the real world out of sheer resentment?

And what about Frank? Was this the malignant spirit that beset him? He was too proud to turn the destructiveness outward upon a scapegoat. His suicide would have been an act of pride, an act of self-assertion, a redemption of his humanity . . .

Ian:    For his sake and for ours, let the silence we cannot penetrate guard his tomb.

## Essay 7

## Christian Bay

Minimally, what it means to be human is to be capable of asking this question. I understand, from people who claim to know, that for all its massive brains a whale isn't capable of asking what it means to be a whale. *Homo sapiens* presumably differ from all other species in our ability to develop a consciousness of our own being. Many kinds of animals can exercise 'judgment' as they relate to, attack or avoid other animals; the human being alone is capable of judging himself, or herself. Moreover, the human being alone is capable of developing cumulative systems of judgment, on levels of abstraction that permit deductive as well as inductive reasoning. Minimally, the human animal is capable of social and political consciousness: capable of judging relations between self and others, and of judging the realities of social existence in terms of conceptions of how human and social life ought to be lived.

In this essay my concern will be, however, with what it can mean *maximally* to be human. Man's vocation, writes Paulo Freire, is humanization.[1] That is, our joint endeavour ought to be to struggle to become more fully human. But what does this *mean*?

There is no way to get around the question of human nature, if we want to understand the meaning of this endeavour. But the question must not be put so as to invite ontological answers or theological answers—about the essence of the human being, or about the assigned

[1] Paulo Freire, *Pedagogy of the Oppressed*, Seabury Press, New York, 1974 (1970), p. 28 and *passim*.

mission of mankind. Answers of these categories are like intellectual short-circuits: they do not require sustained reflection, let alone empirical inquiry, even if they may be elegantly phrased and embellished with articulate justifications; they encourage premature closure of inquiry.

What we can attempt to formulate in positive terms about the nature of human nature must be very open-ended. First, we must assume that there *is* a basic human nature, in the sense that there is likely to be at least a rudimentary instinctual equipment common to all mankind, along with some basic reasoning capabilities. Obvious examples of human instincts are sexual attraction, joy of parenthood and solidarity when threatened by other species or the harshness of natural elements.

Secondly, if we can draw inferences from observations of how most people act and behave, there appears to be a social tendency in most human beings: individuals tend to be members of families and/or clans or communities, and to collaborate on joint tasks, voluntarily or involuntarily. Thirdly, at least in the modern world, there is also an individualistic tendency to be observed. Each person likes to have a name of one's own, a sense of freedom to choose between options, in work and in leisure, and a sense of development or growth.

But it must be conceded right away, and indeed given much emphasis, that the inferences we can make from observations of acts and behaviour may be quite misleading as a source of knowledge of human nature. They might alternatively, or in part, be attributed to the human condition, to the socio-economic system or to any number of combinations among all kinds of cultural and historical circumstances, or to factors of individual psychology and experience. Even that great work of Thomas Hobbes, the *Leviathan*[2], so often referred to for its pessimistic account of human nature, may alternatively be construed as revealing more about the human condition or about life in 17th century England.

In short, the 'power of positive thinking' about human nature is extremely limited. Human nature can never be observed; inferences drawn from motivations that the observer attributes to given acts and behaviours are always to a considerable extent speculative, and influenced by the observer's or interpreter's own kinds of motivations. There are always many alternative kinds of determinants and

---

[2]  Penguin, Harmondsworth, 1968.

combinations of determinants that could have been taken to account for one's available data.

In addition, there is the consideration that human nature, whatever it 'is', is in the process of development, towards destinations largely unknown. As human nature presumably has evolved from ape-like and then humanoid nature, so we may hope it is on its way towards a 'more fully human' nature. While the transition from ape-like to humanoid nature presumably served the cause of survival under the 'law of the jungle', it is much harder to extrapolate future directions of development, now that much of mankind has escaped jungle-like conditions of life, at least in the ancient sense of that phrase. Moreover, man is, in Marx's phrase, an '*active* natural being'[3]: a species in the process, not only of adapting to changing environments—as other animal species, and plants as well, must do—but in the process of changing the environment too. To the extent that these changes are for the better, they may increase the range of options for the continuing development of our human nature and needs. Marx was an optimist on this score, untouched by a later age's ecological pessimism; but he thought it would be foolhardy to forecast, even for the next century, what human beings could become after the end of capitalism's alienating conditions of life.

Clearly, positive thinking about what it will come to mean, maximally, to be more fully human cannot take us very far. Let us now attempt instead some 'negative thinking'.

What is empirically given, I think, is not what it can come to mean to be human; that is still a figment of the political imagination of philosophers and other reflective men and women, relatively few in number. What it means to be *in*human, on the other hand, is widely perceived and understood. We can make well-supported statements (that is, backed by much evidence) about inhuman acts and behaviour; and we can go about studying their incidence under varying circumstances, with hypotheses in mind about what induces such kinds of activities. About optimally human behaviour there is not only the difficulty that its incidence, even in approximation, is relatively infrequent. That is a surmountable problem. It is a much greater difficulty that the *concept* of 'more fully human' is hard to make precise enough for research purposes.

Let us start at the negative end, therefore, and observe first of all that in the Beginning was the Jungle. Our ancestors were non-human,

³ Karl Marx, 'Economic and Philosophic Manuscripts of 1844' in *The Marx-Engels Reader*, Robert C. Tucker, ed., Norton, New York, 1972, p. 93.

and subsequently, for many thousands of years, humanoids. They were all 'inhuman' in the sense that they would perpetrate what we today would call pillage and rape and murder on one another without any inhibitions other than considerations of prudence. They were engaged, as every other kind of animal, in the struggle for survival. Their basic needs were for sustenance, shelter and safety.

The first prerequisite towards becoming human, or more human (whatever that *means*) surely is to leave the conditions and mentality of the jungle behind, or more completely behind. In Maslow's terminology, sustenance and safety needs must be met first of all. They are deficiency needs. 'Higher' needs cannot become activated before the constant preoccupation with basic physical needs ceases.[4]

It is worth noting in passing that this appears to be true for many other species of animals as well. Most of their species–members still live in the jungle, literally, except for the millions of pets and other domesticated animals which relate most of the time to at least a few human beings without fear or aggression. Even lions, tigers and other 'fierce' animals can become socialized to develop trusting relationships with human beings, if they grow up in a well-kept zoo or in some other sheltered setting removed from the terms of life of the jungle.

There are few well-kept zoos for human beings, even for elderly persons. But most of us are familiar with schools, and it may be worth taking a moment to state how most schools are like zoos, and how they differ from zoos. They are similar to zoos in that they shelter our human children from violence and threats to their lives and health; also in that another 'species'—the teachers/custodians—make all-important decisions affecting day-to-day activities. But schools are unlike zoos in that they prepare their charges for life 'on the outside' for the years to follow after their years in school. School children,

---

[4] A.H. Maslow, *Motivation and Personality*, Harper & Brothers, New York, 1954, Chapter 5. In this early paper, first published in 1943, Maslow lists five categories of the most basic needs, in this order: (1) physiological; (2) safety; (3) belongingness and love; (4) esteem; and (5) self-actualization. I am indebted to my friend David J. Baugh for the idea of collapsing, for present purposes, the first two and the next two categories, thus coming up with three tiers of basic needs instead of five: (1) basic physical needs; (2) belongingness or solidarity needs; and (3) subjectivity needs. This choice of terminology, too, is influenced by Baugh. In a later book Maslow developed his distinction between 'deficiency motivation' and 'growth motivation', the former encompassing the first four of his basic need-categories and the latter the fifth one. See his *Toward a Psychology of Being*, Van Nostrand, Princeton, 1962.

unlike zoo animals, are expected to graduate, unless they are severely retarded or otherwise mentally handicapped.

What kinds of life are children educated *for*? Their destination is to become 'useful citizens', as the phrase used to be in Norway's legislation governing the public school system. Less revealing phrasing is used in current legislation, there and elsewhere, but I am sure the basic purpose remains the same, in all countries: schools are *socializing* agencies, helping 'society' (that is, the state and its principal sponsors and beneficiaries) to remain as stable and unchanged as possible by programming lively youngsters into stable and useful adults—adults with useful skills and attitudes, people who will perform well in the tasks assigned to them or, more strictly speaking, in the occupations and careers in which they will compete for jobs and advancement. Could it be that in important respects most schools make children *less* human?[5]

Zoos make lions less lion-like and tigers less tiger-like, or so it appears. Or could one speculate that, on the contrary, life in a good zoo can bring out a 'higher' nature, even in animals of species whose living members for the most part are doomed to remain 'under-developed' in the jungle? Does the famous Elsa demonstrate that one lucky lioness could develop a higher 'lion-nature' compared to her wild cousins?[6]

Fortunately, I am not expected to write a paper on what it could mean, maximally, to be a lion. It is a less forbidding task to write about possibilities for our own species—not only on account of being a member, or an insider so to speak, but because much information has accumulated on how human beings live and behave under many kinds of conditions: from the most violent ways of life in the jungle to the largely nonviolent ways of life we find, for example, in most monasteries, some universities and quite a few schools.

'Violence' is a term that calls for some discussion, for it is a crucial one in any substantial effort to reason our way up from the negation of 'what it means to be human'. That negation is found most clearly in the jungle. What is bad about life in the jungle is its violence. 'Violence' means, as I understand and shall use the term here, the

---

[5] For an eloquent description of how schools can make children less human, see John R. Seeley, *The Americanization of the Unconscious*, Lippincott, Philadelphia, 1967, pp. 292–295.

[6] See Joy Adamson, *Born Free: A Lioness of Two Worlds*, Pantheon, New York, 1960; *Living Free*, Harcourt Brace, New York, 1961; and *Forever Free: Elsa's Pride*, Harcourt Brace, New York, 1963.

deliberate or negligent harming or destruction of human life, health or freedom.[7] I shall also speak of violence against animals, mainly sentient animals: by 'violence (animals)' I shall mean the taking of lives or the damaging of the health of animals. Violence (humans) or the threat of violence clearly blocks the possibility of achieving freedom to develop whatever it may take (or mean) to become fully human. To overcome violence may not be a sufficient requirement for achieving one's full humanity, but it is surely a necessary requirement.

Now there are many kinds of violence. There is the predatory violence (humans and animals) of the animal kingdom, where one animal kills another to obtain food or safety. And there is the much larger-scale violence of wars between human beings, or the killing of immense numbers of animals by human beings for trade, manufacturing and profit. Then there is also the *structural* violence in most human—as distinct from humane or humanistic—social orders, not unlike a macro-counterpart to the violence against runts in litters of piglets: some classes are doomed to live 'nasty, brutish and short' lives because they are without political or economic power. Much of the Third World today is ruled by small coalitions of aggressive entrepreneurs, who make deals with foreign superpowers and large multinational corporations. In effect these deals doom once-independent peasantries to lives oppressed by poverty in urban shantytowns, with their youngsters often subsisting on diets insufficient for full mental development.[8]

What happens meanwhile to the people of the corporate elites, the so-called upper-middle classes in the First World, with material living standards beyond the hopes of kings in centuries past? Are *their* lives as 'fully human' as possible, in being removed this far from the human jungles of the Third World? I should think not, for two main reasons: first, they are trained to do violence to one another whenever the

---

[7]   In an earlier paper I have defined violence as 'any cause of any needless reduction in basic freedoms for any human being'. 'Violence as a Negation of Freedom', *The American Scholar*, 40 (1971), pp. 634–641 at 638. Italics omitted here.

[8]   Michael Harrington estimates that as of last year there were some 70 million people in the Third World in immediate danger of starving to death, another 400–600 million with stunted brains on account of caloric and protein deficiencies, and two billion living in want. See his *The Vast Majority: A Journey to the World's Poor*, Simon & Schuster, New York, 1977. On the activities of multinational corporations, especially on their part in causing Third World hunger, see especially Frances Moore Lappé and John Collins, *Food First: Beyond the Myth of Scarcity*, Houghton Mifflin, Boston, 1977; and Susan George, *How the Other Half Dies*, Penguin, Harmondsworth, 1976.

'necessities of the market' seem to dictate; they must strive constantly to please customers and the higher-ups in their corporations, and still risk losing out or being fired or demoted; and, secondly, they are trained to do violence by exploiting their own employees, or the general public, or the Third World poor (whichever is applicable), for they are all parties to a system of business that serves to maximize corporate profits at the expense of the dire needs of those who can least afford to pay or who need work most badly.

The Socratic argument that it is worse to inflict evil than to suffer evil is, to be sure, not a part of the liberal creed—even if most professing Christians claim to agree with Socrates, and a few actually do. It is not necessary for my argument to claim that inflicting violence is always worse than being at the receiving end; all I need to argue, and I shall, is that violence in itself sets back the process of becoming more fully human, both for the perpetrators, with their accomplices and willing beneficiaries, *and* for the victims, whether they are targets of deliberate acts of violence or victims of structural circumstances.

Why is that? Because there are at least two main obstacles to our freedom to become more fully human: first, violence; and secondly, alienation from trust in ourselves and in one another as human beings. So-called primitive and backward peoples may develop only rudimentary social institutions, when severe deprivation has made it impossible to develop a sense of solidarity with people outside the immediate family.[9] And so-called modern corporate liberalism has promoted the orientation of possessive individualism: to consume and to own things are said to be what the good life is about, more so than achieving friendships and communities based on giving love and trust. The road to affluence in our system is paved with prudential but 'inhuman' decisions: to the extent that the laws permit, one exploits as far as practicably one's employees and outsmarts one's competitors; business decisions are supposed to be in quest of profits, divorced from issues of morality or justice, guided by prudence only. It is a new kind of jungle, bestowed on us by liberal/corporate capitalism.

While capitalism has wrought many wonders, it has wrought havoc as well: blood, sweat and tears and the actual destruction of countless human lives, so that business firms and ruling classes might prosper. Today large sections of the working class in First World countries

---

[9]    For examples, see Allan R. Holmberg, *Nomads of the Long Bow: The Siriono of Eastern Bolivia*, Smithsonian Institution, Washington, DC, 1950; and Edward C. Banfield, *The Moral Basis of a Backward Society*, Free Press, Glencoe, Ill., 1958.

also prosper, relatively speaking; but majorities in many Third World countries suffer deprivations so extreme that most liberals and conservatives in our part of the world seem incapable of registering in their minds what is going on. They cannot plead ignorance, as many Germans claimed regarding the Nazi extermination programmes. I think the kindest interpretation of their liberal acceptance of Western-powers-dominated world trade patterns is that a fundamental decency blocks their vision of the many well-reported and well-documented recurrent Third World famines—even in the same countries from which our multinational corporations continue to extract food exports and large profits.[10]

By 'alienation' I shall here understand the suppression of human solidarity needs and feelings. The *problem* of alienation is structural and therefore large-scale. It does not exist in the primeval jungle, for the dictates of the primitive struggle for survival make competition for scarce food resources appear obviously necessary. For many kinds of animals, solidarity with the species, beyond caring for the young, is not compatible with survival. While violence was always there for humanoids and early human beings, it is 'civilization's' accumulation of wealth, with the power to exploit the property-less, that has brought us alienation.

Under the feudal system the lords of the manor sometimes—as in Leo Tolstoi's case—became dedicated to the welfare of 'their' peasants; but more frequently there was alienation, with callousness from above and either hatred or resignation from below. So it was in the antebellum United States' South too, and so it remains on countless haciendas and similar estates in many countries today.

With the capitalist system, alienation became as ever-present as violence was in the primeval kinds of jungle. As Marx observed with such insight, the working class under capitalism was reduced to a category of commodities: for practical purposes a worker's life was no longer an end in itself but a means in the production of surplus-value; the measly value of the worker's life under capitalism was determined by the fluctuating worth of his or her labour–power in the capitalist marketplace.[11]

The capitalists, too, are alienated, more so than the feudal lords who had preceded them as the ruling class. For feudal families could relate to one another with solidarity and friendship, without

[10] For well-documented examples, see Lappé and Collins, *ibid.*, and George, *ibid.*
[11] Marx's influential essay on 'Estranged Labour' is reprinted with other selections from his 1844 Manuscripts in Tucker, *ibid.*, pp. 52–103 at 56–67.

contradicting their own 'interests'. But under capitalism there can be no anticipation of human solidarity, even within the ruling class, except as some individuals transcend the norms of the competitive *system* and thus violate their own supposed interests. Trusting friendships do occur, as do less stable truces and coalitions, but the jungle-like dictates of short-term and private self-interest prevail, with continuing alienation. 'It's a dog's world' is a saying more appropriate to the feudal order, from the peasant's perspective. 'It's a shark's world' is an appropriate paradigm for our kind of social order; whales and the biggest fishes are reasonably safe from the sharks, but not the smaller ones. The capitalist's potential as a human being is blocked, even when he is one of the biggest fishes; 'greed, cruelty and hypocrisy emerge from his dealing with competitors and customers as well as with workers.'[12]

In times of expanding economies there could, to be sure, still be a livable (if alienated) life for the industrial working class. But in our own time, when it is becoming clear to more and more influential people that ecological limitations require an early end to population growth, industrial expansion and waste of energy and raw materials, the commodity of labour power has become very cheap—especially in Third World countries, where there is no end in sight to massive structural unemployment. Does it matter to influential people in the First World whether Third World peasants and workers live or die? The alienation of some First World liberals has reached the point where several prominent academics now advocate 'lifeboat ethics', sanctioning the likely death by political negligence of millions of human beings in disadvantaged countries.[13] Others argue, just as complacently, that we should take it in our stride if the consequences of our wasteful economic system should be that human life must come to an end at some point.[14]

What does it mean to be human, maximally? The first part of my concluding reply must be simple: it means to be responsibly, universalistically humane—that is, impelled to care maximally for the

---

[12]  See Bertell Ollman, *Alienation: Marx's Conception of Man in Capitalist Society*, University Press, Cambridge, 1971, Chapter 23, at 157.

[13]  Garrett Hardin, 'Lifeboat Ethics: The Case Against Helping the Poor', *Psychology Today*, 8 (September 1974), pp. 38–43 and 123–126.

[14]  Wilfred Beckerman, 'The Myth of "Finite" Resources', *Business and Society Review*, 12 (1974–75), pp. 21–25 especially 22. For a scathing comment, see Robert L. Heilbroner, 'What Has the Future Ever Done for Me?' in his *An Inquiry Into The Human Prospect*, Norton, New York, 1975.

survival, health and basic freedoms of others, of all others. The least alienated are the most human: those who not only feel a distaste for violence against the weak or the nonviolent but who refuse to tolerate it because they experience a strong and activating revulsion. The most human persons must in Camus's sense be rebels, *hommes révoltés*.[15]

It is often said that it is 'only human' to care for our own family and friends more intensely than we care for strangers. Perhaps so. But I submit that it is possible to bridge and reduce this distance, in a non-alienating society in which we are secure and free enough to see the beauty of other people's children as well, and indeed come to appreciate the unique qualities of human beings everywhere.

In the Christian Scriptures we are admonished to love our neighbours as we love ourselves, and we are given to understand that all people everywhere are our neighbours. Some saintly persons are able to approximate this understanding and this way of life, even in our kind of society. A few even feel compassion and concern for all the children yet to be born, on a much worse-plundered planet than our generation inherited. But these are not the kinds of outlook encouraged, or even widely tolerated, in our alienating system of competition, exploitation and private-profit-orientation. More compatible with survival, and certainly with private safety and property accumulation, are maxims like 'Screw thy neighbour' or 'Do unto others before they do unto you'. And yet, capitalism's effective media of communication and information technology have created the objective possibilities for a revolution in every human being's comprehension of the evils perpetrated and tolerated, up to now: the evils of starvation and other extreme structural violence, of massive exploitation, and of a stupidly short-sighted waste of natural resources and needless destruction of air, water and soil.

To the naive among us—those of us who believe that even alienated persons can be revolted by a new awareness of monstrosities previously invisible to them or explained away—it would seem that improving standards of press and television reporting (and they *have* improved since the Vietnam war) could take us a long way towards building up a sufficiency of revulsion and revolt against our profit-serving system, simply because it serves human needs and human concerns

[15]    Albert Camus, *The Rebel: An essay on Man in Revolt*, Vintage, New York, 1958 (1956). The original French title was *L'Homme Révolté* (Gallimard, Paris, 1951); it could alternatively have been rendered 'man in revulsion' and this double meaning was without a doubt intended by the author.

so badly. Will the new official American concern with human rights in unfriendly countries eventually backfire, as more and more Americans begin to insist that the basic needs of human beings should take precedence over other public policy objectives—even over the interests and allegedly sacred property rights of the giant corporations?

In a political system directed to serving human needs according to rational priorities—that is, according to how essential each kind of need is to human health and well-being—how 'human' could human beings become? It is fun to speculate about this, if I am allowed to end this paper rather frivolously. I think frivolity is a human need, too, even if it must take its place in line well behind more basic needs. Physical survival needs must come first, I have been arguing, followed by social belongingness and solidarity needs; only in the third place come the subjectivity needs, the need to express individuality, both seriously and frivolously.[16]

One way to restate and elaborate on this orientation to human priorities is to draw on Hannah Arendt's distinction between labour, work and action[17], and place these kinds of activities as middle categories between the two extremes of warfare and play. Then we have a five-rung ladder that will take us all the way from the miseries of life in the Jungle to the bliss of a humane existence in Utopia.

Enough has been said about the Jungle. Even the most oppressive conditions of labour must be seen as an improvement over spending one's life killing or being killed. Yet our modern technology has made alienating heavy toil increasingly superfluous too, with modern machinery capable of substituting for wage slavery. Arendt distinguishes the 'work of our hands' from the 'labour of our bodies'[18]; I shall prefer to define 'work' as productive creative activity that results in bringing about some useful product or service. Unfortunately, modern technology in our social order produces optimally marketable commodities instead of optimally useful products and, instead of creative work, requires monotonous, inherently unrewarding labour, with workers and technicians becoming like automatons, extensions of the machines they serve. In our society only some of the surviving small farmers, crafts-people and co–operative communes can still

[16]   See note 4. See also various contributions to Ross Fitzgerald (ed.), *Human Needs and Politics*, Pergamon Press, Rushcutters Bay, Australia, 1977.
[17]   Hannah Arendt, *The Human Condition*, Doubleday Anchor, Garden City, N.Y., 1959 (1958).
[18]   *Ibid.*, p. 119.

engage in unalienating, creative work—apart from 'intellect-workers' whose 'products' may not always be easy to pin down.

Marx thought of work as a prime need in an unalienating social order. In my terms, work must be seen as one essential way of gratifying our basic solidarity needs. With freely given work we contribute creatively to our common good; this is gratifying to the worker/contributor, quite apart from the value of the product or service. For this reason, at least, we all need to work. It is the most basic reason why unemployment is a disaster in any kind of society, even in one with relatively adequate welfare services.

Action expresses individualities and meets subjectivity needs. The ideally democratic community makes political action possible for all; the so-called democratic state, by contrast, normally makes political action possible for only a few, except for the type of self-defeating tactics by which most citizens define 'lunatic' fringe groups. The 1960s in the United States was an exception of sorts, in that sizeable minorities of students engaged in political action; they could do this because the magnitude of perpetrated evils and the deepening embarrassment of the regime had become so starkly visible.

In Utopia most men and women will want to act, as well as work. Political action against anti-social behaviour will tend to be effective, for practices of open access to information will render evildoers readily accountable. There will also be experimental social and political action of many kinds, to test new ideas for improvement in patterns of work and interaction.

Also, people will play. In Utopia there will be a new and much deeper sensitivity to beauty, just as our ethical and compassionate perceptiveness will be more alert and lucid. With cruder forms of violence now a historical curiosity, there will be a stronger sense of revulsion against exploitation of many kinds, including what we now would term mildly alienating behaviours. As Camus saw, the need for revulsion and revolt will never end, for there will never be an age of permanent, monotonous perfection.

But as the incidence and grievousness of violence and alienation recede, the scope for play will become wider. *Art pour l'art* will cease to be an essentially elitist maxim, for the cultivation of aesthetic values independently of ethical concerns will now be compatible with responsible humanitarianism. And unheard-of possibilities for sensuality and frivolousness will add spark and colour to most people's lives.

In this context it is worth returning, as Gad Horowitz has done recently, to Herbert Marcuse's analysis of repression in his *Eros and*

*Civilization*.[19] Marcuse argues that Freud had mistakenly attributed man's internalized oppression to the weight of civilization itself on our libidinous instincts; and Marcuse proceeds, drawing implicitly on Marx, to distinguish capitalism's *surplus-repression* from the existential basic repression which, he concedes, had to remain in every kind of social order.

Marcuse believes that not only our minds but our bodies as well have become alienated from their social and subjectivity potentialities for creativity and gratification; our bodies have been harnessed by capitalism to retain their capacity for erotic pleasure only in the genital zones, where pleasure serves the aim of producing new human beings, or new labour-power commodities. Marcuse envisages the objective possibility, after capitalism, of the re-erotization of the whole body. (For the newborn infant, he argues, the whole body is still sensitive to erotic pleasure, in the broad sense of that term.) When we are enabled to become more fully human, in other words, we will want to play as never before; the joys of sensuality and frivolity will come to enrich most people's lives beyond our contemporary imagination, even after the so-called sexual revolution (about which Marcuse incidentally has expressed himself rather critically, objecting to the 'commodification' of sex).

Following a careful re-examination of Freud's argument as well as Marcuse's, Horowitz concludes that Marcuse's qualified optimism is well founded, not to be dismissed as an utopian frivolity[20]; indeed, that it is more solidly based than Marcuse's own critique of Freud allows. Like other non-Marxist thinkers, Freud accepted capitalist surplus-repression as 'fate' or as dictated by 'eternal Nature', writes Horowitz, and he continues: 'The necessity for alienated labour, toil, a historical necessity, is erroneously assigned the same "dignity" and eternal validity as the necessity for work, which arises from man's biological dependence on the material environment.'[21]

Beauty is in the eye of the beholder, as is vice. To become maximally human, I submit, is to become minimally vicious—not only in the sense of being revolted by violence and resistant to alienation, but also

---

[19]    See Herbert Marcuse, *Eros and Civilization: A Philosophical Inquiry Into Freud*, Vintage, New York, 1955; and Gad Horowitz, *Repression: Basic and Surplus Repression in Psychoanalytic Theory*, University of Toronto Press, Toronto, 1977.

[20]    See, for example, Philip Rieff, *Freud: The Mind of the Moralist*, Doubleday Anchor, Garden City, N.Y., 1961 (1959), p. 256; Alasdair MacIntyre, *Marcuse*, Fontana-Collins, London, 1970, Chapter 4; and Erich Fromm, *The Anatomy of Human Destructiveness*, Fawcett, Greenwich, Conn., 1973, p. 512.

[21]    Horowitz, *op.cit.*, p. 157.

in the sense of being revolted by violence and resistant to alienation, but also in the sense of being minimally troubled by those alleged vices that victimize nobody.

When there are no more victims, in a humane social order, our eyes and hearts will become attuned and attracted to the full range of beauty in all kinds of human beings, and in animal and plant life as well, throughout our richly endowed planet.

# Essay 8

## Richard Gelwick

There is a point where the essence of our humanity appears with dazzling light, but it is only in our century that we are beginning again to be able to look at it. After nearly three centuries of analytical dissecting of our human nature, we are turning to a more whole view of ourselves within the cosmos. Consider for a moment two examples of human creativity and their significance for us. First, take the vault of the Sistine Chapel painted by Michelangelo. It is one of the marvels of art in both imagination and execution. Accomplished within four years while Michelangelo painted alone, lying most of the time on his back, this gigantic work comprehended the Biblical drama with such beauty that believer and unbeliever alike can never see it enough. Besides the careful detail and unsurpassed elegance with which Michelangelo painted these figures, there is also the genius of his comprehension of the familiar subject matter of the Bible. His illustration of the theme of creation has fixed itself in the memories of its beholders like an archetype. Adam lying on the ground is posed with dignity and handsomeness, and his arm rests naturally on his knee as he extends his hand. The creator God approaches in a billowing mantle surrounded by his angels. As God stretches out his hand, we can almost see the birth of the human spirit as the divine hand nearly touches that of Adam. But in God's hand, the extended forefinger just nearly, not completely, contacts that of Adam. In this remarkable way, Michelangelo suggests both the power and the mystery of creation.

For a second example of human creativity, take the discovery of the structure of DNA or 'the genetic code'. This revolutionary breakthrough was the culmination of a number of brilliant scientific achievements. A key turning point came in 1944 with Avery's showing that nucleic acid was a genetic substance, not protein as many had supposed. Still, the way genetic information could be contained and passed on was not understood. Chargaff helped towards the solution in the late 1940s with his breaking down the chemistry of the nucleic acid molecules, finding a symmetry among the component chemical groups. Maurice Wilkins and Rosalind Franklin applied the technique of X-ray diffraction to the crystalline aggregates of the DNA molecule in the early 1950s, and Pauling about the same time developed his theory of the helical structure of proteins. The situation was now ripe for the act of intelligent and creative imagination that would produce the major breakthrough. Francis Crick and James Watson undertook the problem using the insights of their colleagues and predecessors, and they were guided by 'the belief that the truth, once found, would be simple as well as pretty'.[1] They avoided the complicated approach and surmised that the DNA molecule might be helical, like the protein model of Pauling. They played with 'a set of molecular models superficially resembling the toys of pre-school children'.[2] Eventually, they arrived at the model of a double helix, partly to account for the findings of Chargaff earlier. From this double structure came the solution as to how replication is possible and how genetic heritage is transmitted. This discovery has opened many new avenues of understanding the development of life and has startled us with its beauty and profundity. It now appears that all forms of life are built upon this structure and that the code is universal, so that the variation in basic chemical components among animals is slight.

These two feats take us in different directions, one to art and the other to science, but they are joined by a common phenomenon, the creative achievement of the human person. In each case, we enjoy and participate in the recital of these accomplishments because they inherently touch upon our own being as persons who can explore and break out into new levels of understanding and living. We may not understand the technical elements involved, but the story of human development and greatness in new horizons of the truth is compelling and involving; it holds our attention because it represents our

[1] James D. Watson, *The Double Helix*, The New American Library, New York, 1968, p. IX.
[2] *Ibid*, p. 38.

humanity. People have observed that when the birth of a baby is announced there is unanimous response of pleasure and affirmation. The sharing of a discovery, or even the recounting of its attainment, evokes a response similar to that towards the birth of a new human life. We are assured and reminded of our distinctive human quality: to know and to pursue truth.

What we have, then, in the act of human creativity is of ontological, epistemological and ethical significance. Creativity touches us at the heart of our being and directs us afresh to our human vocation, to seek the truth and state our findings. In order to comprehend this thesis, we have to do much more than assent. We have to reflect upon its bearing on our present situation and its implications. Many admire and applaud human creativity, but few understand it, and few place it at the centre of their understanding. The contention here is that the creative act is central, not exceptional, and that it is the most important clue to being ourselves at this point in history.

## The eclipse of creativity

For more than three centuries, we have paid honour to the achievements of human greatness without acknowledging their foundations in the human person. The success of critical philosophy's interpretation of modern science led to a world view of detachment and objectivism. Our personal importance in the process of knowing was downgraded and the human element became fragmented or lost. The two main streams of philosophy in the modern period, rationalism and empiricism, were both distortions of human understanding as it actually is, and they helped to construct an outlook that has threatened the existence of human life itself. Dividing the self into parts, separating body and mind, the whole was lost. Beyond philosophy, this disintegration was continued as each branch of science tried to define humanity as a psychological self, an economic self, a sociological self or a biological self. More disastrously, the loss of our sense of humanity was a loss of our commitment to seek the truth, even though this might be an infinite task. So from the problem of knowing there came the problem of being and of doing, and we became adrift in a vast cosmos without a sense of identity and purpose.

This eclipse of the creative nature of the person can be traced and illustrated in four ways: in science, in philosophy, in art and in politics. The dogma of objectivism began with and was modelled after the mechanism of Galileo and of Newton. Before Galileo, there was still an awareness of the anthropocentrism of reason, but this reason was thought to be in harmony with the rational order of the universe. Copernicus, Bruno and Kepler believed in beauty as a scientific standard and sought a rational theory of celestial movements that would meet this standard. In Galileo, we see the transitional figure in the movement of scientific detachment. In many ways he was also a Pythagorean, a believer in the beauty of the universe and its harmony between mathematical number and physical structure. We know of his great use of 'thought-experiments' or theoretical imagination rather than the later-emphasized 'sense experiments' or laboratory tests. Still, Galileo influenced the future, and a part of his approach became the norm when his mathematical approach to science was reduced to what can be measured and quantified. This doctrine, known as the distinction between primary qualities (shape, size, quantity and motion) and secondary qualities (colour, sound, smell), and enunciated by Galileo, became a foundation for the separation and elevation of the objective over the subjective.

When Newton formulated the laws of gravitation, the effect crystallized the new mathematical view of reality. Nature was seen to be a mechanical phenomenon explainable in terms of mathematics. The human person was banished from the world of nature except as an effect of the forces of nature, an entity to be understood as atoms in motion. The implications of this view are still being worked out in the present, as human beings are studied as stimulus–response mechanisms, cybernetic systems and biochemical organisms; and these studies view their subjects as completely reducible to physics and chemistry without remainder. The strategic consequence of this scientific development is the denial of the intrinsic freedom of the human person. In each view, human behaviour is the result of collocations of atoms and their interactions. The knowledge of each person is thus truer the more it approximates the standard of mechanistic scientific measurement. The credit for knowing and discovery in this view goes to the method, and leads to the mistaken view that great scientific feats are made by following rules and formulas exactly. Accordingly, once we can simulate completely the human brain in a computer, we shall have the ideal scientific explorer.

Movements in philosophy took the new scientific advances seriously and reflected their objectivism, leading to a series of views that separated the knower and the known and reduced our knowledge to forms of positivism. This history led in our century to two disparate but related philosophies: linguistic and existential. The linguistic development was a result of the loss of ultimacy in the objectivist type of knowing derived from science. Linguistic philosophy saw the impossibility, by the scientific view it held, of inquiring into the metaphysical nature of things. Instead of trying to find out about the noumenal, about ultimate causes and reasons, this philosophy became analytic, examining the nature of our words and sentences as they contribute to meaning. While it began with the hope of making knowledge and language exact, linguistic philosophy in its later stages moved from the restrictive boundaries of the objectivist ideal in science to an appreciation of the richness and abundance of meaning in language that is beyond the exact. Nearly coincident with the growth of linguistic philosophy was existentialism, which also had roots in the late nineteenth century. Existentialism was also a response to the objectivism of the scientific outlook, but it took an opposite course, attacking the value of objectivity and reclaiming the realm of the subjective. Sartre's thesis that 'man makes himself' is a direct refutation of the notion that we are the mere consequence of deterministic forces. Existentialism is in many ways a reaffirmation of human freedom. Still, this freedom is arbitrary and absurd. The human person is free to create, but this person is alone in a universe bereft of truth, of ultimate bearings.

The displacement of the human person by a more objectivist style is also seen in modern art. In an intensely innovative period, this art has represented in its own way a temper in which the human being is subjected to the ideas of a world view influenced by science. The Expressionist type of art and its successors particularly show a quality of the scientific outlook, although it is far more interesting than most scientific perspectives. The art of the 'good old days' was representational and subject-centred. The artist showed his or her talent by discovering beauty and portraying it in a subject that others could easily recognize. In the modern period, the Impressionists began a departure from this tradition by turning their attention away from the subject to the perception of light experienced by the artist. As E.H. Gombrich has pointed out so clearly, 'By calling the portrait of his mother "Arrangement in grey and black" Whistler flaunted his conviction that to an artist any subject is the opportunity of studying the balance of colour and design'.[3] This shift of focus from the subject to the execution of the subject shows a style of depersonalization that became known as 'abstract'. Rather than abstract, however, it was more accurately a way of art that was persuaded

---

[3] *The Story of Art*, Phaidon, London, 1972, p. 459.

that what matters in art is not the subject but the solutions to problems of form. Paradoxically, this turn towards form and de-emphasis of subject has led to the appreciation of beauty formerly neglected as common, and even ugly subjects have found a significance. This aspect of modern art discloses a return to creativity because it shows that even the attempt to move away from our personal canons of beauty is guided by a human imagination extending beyond the surface into depths that can move and inform us. Still, the overall impact of modern art has been one of despair and a sense of abandonment. In its own distinctive way, it has seemed to depict the human subject unconfident and uncertain of its place in the scheme of things.

This style in painting is also similar to a type of music developed by John Cage. Here, too, the usual standards of what the listener would consider music are ignored in favour of investigating the possibilities of new forms, whether they are conventionally musical or not. Cage's music is sometimes called 'chance' music because it replaces familiar form with the accidental hearing provided by the listener or the sound that occurs in the period of the performance. His famous piano concerto where the audience assembles, the pianist comes and takes his place at the keyboard but never plays the keys, then the pianist leaves in a formal way, presents not a joke but an intriguing challenge to the concept and structure of music. In its own creative way, this experiment seems to suggest an emptiness and meaninglessness. The human being, once secure in a universe of meaning, is now dared to establish meaning arbitrarily.

In the realm of politics, the disappearance of the creative person is seen in the instances of authoritarianism that deny grounds for dissent, not merely on the basis of power but in the belief in the absoluteness of their ideology. Perhaps one of the most blatant examples of this phenomenon was in Stalinist Russia, where the belief in the scientific objectivity of Marxism allowed its critics no grounds for dissent because one could not disagree with science. While this form is less obvious now, it has its analogies in other political phenomena that occur regularly. One is the distrust of the personal judgment of persons unless it can be grounded in some objective evidence. An instance of this was seen when Daniel Ellsberg in America released the Pentagon Papers, documents classified as secret. The papers exposed the decision-making that had led to the deeper involvement of the United States in the Vietnam War. Ellsberg's declared purpose in this action was to hasten the end of the war. Many people had difficulty accepting his stance of wanting to disclose the truth. Even liberal critics of the Vietnam War impugned the motive of Ellsberg's being concerned for the truth and suggested more plausible explanations, such as his being a publicity-seeker or a peculiar person. Such interpretations indicate how the politics of a democracy is also weakened by the difficulty of believing in a person's doing a noble thing truly for the sake of right.

The extent to which the creative powers of the person shaping his search for truth is distorted by the separation of the objective and the subjective is pervasive. As noticed in this brief survey, this separation cannot really be done. Even in forms that seemingly deny the centrality and importance of the person, there is present to the observer the personally imaginative and personally creative feat. What we have begun to realize and to establish, giving new freedom to humanity, is why this is so.

## Science and creativity

The place where the dethronement of the creative powers of the person began was in science; and it is here that the restoration of our understanding of these most distinctive human qualities is also being recovered. As we briefly indicated, the outlook that has shaped the modern world with a view of objectivism and detachment is the consequence of a mistaken view of scientific discovery. Studies in the philosophy of science are increasingly showing that this model of strict detachment and precise formulation are not at the heart of making great scientific discoveries. Science does utilize careful controls, observable experiments and public evaluation, but these conditions in themselves are secondary to the creative imagination which employs the standards of science.

Changes in the philosophy of science are themselves indicators of aspects of creativity in science that are now being recovered. One of these is the admission that there is no exact scientific method leading to discoveries.[4] Scientific ideas and theories are not derived directly from observed data, but they are 'conjured up' to account for the data. Hypotheses and theories are guesses trying to establish relations between accumulated observations. Without the contribution of the creative person, scientific discoveries would not occur.

The role of guessing in scientific discovery points to a second evidence of the role of the creative imagination in science, namely the importance of interpretation. N.R. Hanson showed that all data are

---

[4] Carl G. Hempel, *Philosophy of Natural Science*, Prentice Hall, Inglewood Cliffs, N.J. 1966, pp. 14–15.

'theory laden'.[5] There is no such thing as neutral or uninterpreted data. Scientists approach the data of science from a network of views that led to their collection, and they appraise them from the standpoints of background, training and interests. Their appraisals and judgments are a part of the theories they hold and use as tools for viewing the material they gather. Hence, the problems chosen for study and the evaluation of their results function within the theoretical framework in which they work. Again, the role of personal judgment is paramount.

This role of theory in handling data leads to a third area, stressing the inventive role of personal community. Scientists are aided in their search by the background and community of science. Many useless repetitions of other people's results and wasted attempts are avoided by the guidance of the scientific community. Working from the community's sense of values and knowledge, they are better prepared for what to imagine and seek. This communal sense of knowing is more convivial and implicit than formal and explicit. It is a major part in the seeding of the intuition that grows into scientific fruition; the number of scientific breakthroughs at centres of science is related to this feature. Greatness in science follows the example and art of the major figures, as much as it does mere technical and precise treatment of their work. Watson, in his account of the discovery of the structure of DNA, made this point by observing that one of the ways Linus Pauling helped him was Pauling's example of using common sense rather than trying to make things complicated. 'Pauling', says Watson, 'never got anywhere by seeking out messes'.[6]

The most profound and far-reaching grasp of the creative nature of knowing in science, and in general, is given in the recent work of Michael Polanyi.[7] Polanyi pioneered in going beyond a criticism of scientific objectivism to showing a holistic epistemology as the only one that can adequately account for our creative feats of knowing and that is, in fact, necessary to understand our vocation as human beings. His work is a major foundation for the understanding of what it means to be human. For the remainder of this essay, I wish to show some of the most relevant points of Polanyi's theory of knowledge and then to develop, in particular, his understanding of intuition.

---

[5]  *Patterns of Discovery*, Cambridge University Press, Cambridge, 1958.
[6]  *The Double Helix*, p. 38.
[7]  See Richard Gelwick, *The Way of Discovery, An Introduction to the Thought of Michael Polanyi*, Oxford University Press, New York, 1977.

### Knowing and being

Polanyi's theory moves from a specific basis in the structure of knowledge to a general view of our place in the universe. The starting point is found in a clue from the Gestalt psychology of Wolfgang Köhler. This psychology was primarily concerned with perception, and held that the whole or total quality of an image is perceived rather than perceiving parts and then building them into whole images. Furthermore, Gestalt psychology claimed that the whole or configuration is more than the sum of its parts. Polanyi made a radical departure, however, by seeing that the processes of Gestalt were not based upon strict mechanical laws of internal equilibrations but were actually the actions of shaping by the personal powers of the individual. In this way, he was going far beyond what Gestalt psychology had been willing to see, namely that their own work pointed to a revolutionary way of understanding knowing that broke with the mechanistic approach of the past. To follow through the implications of Gestalt meant that perceptual knowledge was the result of our active participation in our knowing.

To explain this alternative view of knowing, Polanyi began to develop a concept of the way we know that showed how we attained the greatest truths of science and also shared centrally in this as creative persons. Much of the motivation and insight for this enormous task came from his own experience as a physical chemist facing the violent disturbances in Europe during this century.

One of the fundamental principles he found was that in all knowing there are two types of awareness—a subsidiary and a focal—that are linked together by the person. These two types of awareness helped to account for both the phenomenon of Gestalt and the mistaken ideal of objectivism. Whenever we know, there is a focal target—a problem or an object—to which we attend. We have the feeling of being at a distance from this focal target, which gives us the idea of separation or detachment. Actually, the focal awareness is an indwelling and an integration of particulars into a pattern that we seek to understand or recognize. For example, we see the face of a friend in terms of the totality of its characteristic parts integrated into a coherent whole. If we for a moment change our focus to some singular feature of the face, we lose the whole. These processes of integration which focus on the whole person or some isolated feature are not actually detached but ones that we indwell and rely upon in order to be focally aware.

Here, the second type of awareness, subsidiary awareness, comes into purview. To see a face as a whole, or even a detail of it, we depend upon myriad clues assimilated into ourselves, and we rely upon them as parts of a coherent reality to which we attend. This side of knowing reveals then that the focal target is not really detached but only seems so, as we attend away from the clues to their joint significance. That we can move from looking at wholes to parts and then back again to wholes suggests the interrelation of comprehension and of analysis, of subject and object, knower and known.

Such a concept of knowing also shows how knowing is a skill, something that can be learned and done by connoisseurship but not by formal rules. To know is an action of bringing the clues of our background and preparation, subsidiary awareness, to bear upon problems or facts. The way we do this can be guided but it is finally a matter of each individual's capacities to rely upon her subsidiary awareness in order to make sense out of the focal concern. The example of learning to ride a bicycle is a strong illustration of this skill-aspect of knowing. She may know a great deal about the physics of gravitation, motion and levers, have expert coaching and still not be able to ride. Unless she can indwell the principles comprehensively, along with the observation of other riders, and let this be the subsidiary background, she will falter. Even if beginning to ride, she starts to think focally of the principles instead of attending to the whole performance of which they are a part, she will lose her balance.

From the skill of routine learning to the art of making scientific discoveries, it is, in principle, only a short step. A scientist engaged in the solution of a problem is involved in skilful knowing. Her powers of thought are concentrated upon interesting and promising clues. She relies upon them in order to attend to her problem. Her role is crucial, for it is the way she arranges or rearranges clues into patterns that offers the discovery. Therefore, Polanyi observed that it is not surprising that Einstein's revolutionary theories were attained in a manner comparable to learning to see in a new way with inverted spectacles.[8]

Polanyi named his new concept 'tacit knowing', placing the emphasis upon the large role of the subsidiary particulars borne and integrated by the person. These integrations are 'tacit' because they function implicitly to make possible what is known explicitly. The tacit dimension calls attention to his discovery of an essential domain in the knowing process that directly refutes the ideal of objectivism.

Further elaboration of tacit knowing led to new ways of designating

[8] Michael Polanyi, 'The Creative Imagination', *Chemical and Engineering News*, 44, April (1966), p. 86.

the achievements of knowing.[9] Basic to these distinctions is the realization that Polanyi has shown that knowing is a unitary act, not a dividing between subject and object. The terminology he devised helps to refer to our knowledge without falling into the dichotomous connotations of earlier discourse. For example, the brain-mind distinction has led to 'the ghost in the machine' criticism of Gilbert Ryle. This critique presumes to have reduced the mind to being the term for the intelligent manifestations of operations of the brain. With Polanyi, however, the terms 'brain' and 'mind' have a significant connection and difference.[10] The brain serves subsidiarily the purpose of integrating, which is different from the mere neural operations of the brain. If you observe the brain in the act of knowing, you will, of course, see its neural pathways but you will not see its ideas. What is occurring is that our focal awareness is on the sensory mechanisms. If we attend to the mind of a person, these aspects will have to become subsidiary, not focal. Then we shall view the person as having a mind by subordinating the operations of the person's brain to a more comprehensive achievement, meaning. Knowing then has a 'semantic' aspect, but it is an aspect because meaning cannot be separated from the functional structure that underlies it.

Another distinction made by Polanyi throws additional light on the brain-mind problem. It is sometimes thought that we are in a disjunctive situation having to choose between either brain or mind. By viewing knowing as Polanyi does, this choice is not forced. We have instead the possibility of recognizing the brain's contribution by seeing it in the integration of pattern. We have indicated above that the mind is signified by meaning, which is not reducible to its particulars—brain operations—without loss of the mind itself. The other side of this is that the mind cannot be without the subsidiaries that contribute to its comprehensive performance. Present in the semantic aspect of mind are also the integrated clues of the body, including the brain. The clues held in the neural network appear as a coherent pattern of the mind. The clues from subsidiaries integrated into pattern are the 'phenomenal' aspect, which is to say that brain operations appear in the pattern to which they contribute.

Polanyi is not particularly concerned with the brain-mind problem, but with the objectivist ideal of knowledge, which contributes to this problem. To continue on the brain-mind problem is then a matter of example, not the chief thrust of Polanyi's epistemology. Using this

---

[9]    Michael Polanyi, *The Tacit Dimension*, Doubleday, New York, 1966, Chapter 1.
[10]   Michael Polanyi, *Personal Knowledge*, University of Chicago Press, 1958, p. 372.

example, we can see how Polanyi's third designation of tacit knowing indicates that what we know through the union of subsidiary and focal awareness leads to knowledge of reality. When we rely upon clues we are responsive to the stimuli of reality that produce these suggestions. Such reliance implies that the semantic and the phenomenal aspects are also ontological. The meaning and the pattern have a bearing, not only upon the knower but also upon reality itself. In short, what is called objective is an aspect of reality that we have contacted by indwelling our subsidiary awareness. The mind, therefore, is real. The mind is a comprehensive entity existing at a level above the subsidiary operations of the brain on which it depends.

When this ontological aspect is put in its fuller significance, it indicates how knowing has a 'universal intent'. The aim of our integrations is to make sense out of internalized clues that bear upon structures of being beyond us. Coherence, pattern and meaning are achieved in order that we may have knowledge of reality. Our intellectual passions serve the truth—difficult and hazardous to attain —that is known only by participation and involvement. For such reasons, our deepest and greatest knowledge must be called 'personal knowledge'. The objective pole of knowing that is found and shared with others is our way to truth. But the objective pole is the correlate of the subjective, and we cannot have one without the other.

Tacit knowing, then, is about the human capacity for learning routinely from what is already around us as knowledge and is also about what is yet to be discovered. Its structure admits that knowing is a risk, but it also shows that knowing is counted real and true by us when it gives meaning and pattern that others can also share. Most importantly, it shows the responsibility and opportunity for the human person not only to indwell the received knowledge of the world but also to employ it as the foundation for further inquiry into truth. Truth is not found by giving up our personal involvement, but by recognizing our inherent involvement in all knowing and by accepting responsibility for it.

Existential as this might seem in the emphasis upon the subjective and the person in knowing, tacit knowing is unlike existentialism because it stresses the role of community and tradition. We do not begin, according to Polanyi, from ground zero and make the world or our own truth. We begin within the social lore and wisdom of our society. From it we gain the standards that help us to become seekers of truth. The society does not have all the truth; it has our present understanding of it. We make our way by accepting and criticizing standards from the past and by pursuing them further. Truth and reality are not possessions but inexhaustible ranges that leave open indeterminate and promising possibilities.

One of the consequences of the mistaken objectivist ideal, particularly promulgated during the Enlightenment and effective since, is the distrust of tradition. Tradition is one of the vital bearers of those transcendent standards that guide our lives. Our greatest truths are symbolized and embodied in our civilization and cannot be made completely explicit, yet they are passed on as we participate in the institutions of our society.

Tradition and its role in nurturing the pursuit of truth is one of the features of tacit knowing. It is illustrated in the work of science, which progresses partly by its adherence to a tradition fostered and administered by the scientific community. Scientific conscience and ideals are developed by the example and tacit influence of the scientific community along with its explicit teachings. It is in such a community that the subsidiary awareness of scientists is trained and prepared for the task of advancing the knowledge they receive. The destruction or abandonment of tradition and community would be the ending of our basis for growth.

Tacit knowing upholds, then, two important features of the communal and traditional nature of knowing. First, it explains how we use tradition to indwell and form the background for the problems to which we attend. Secondly, it explains how we pursue truth as a possibility greater than we can articulate at any moment. Our knowledge of truth is partly tacit. 'We know more than we can tell.'[11] Knowledge of truth is a comprehensive integration of the bearing of subsidiary particulars on reality, and these particulars always contain possibilities we have not yet articulated or explored.

The tacit character of knowing also brings to our attention the biological foundations of knowing. Polanyi's epistemology is exceptional in placing the understanding of knowing within the perspective of evolution. It has already been indicated that knowing is an achievement—that is, a feat of integrating particulars into wholes that bear meaningfully on reality. It has also been suggested that there are levels within the structure of knowing, in the example of the brain-mind problem. Examination of the levels of tacit knowing shows it to be an extension of the evolutionary picture of human emergence.

[11]    *The Tacit Dimension*, p. 4.

Observing the panorama of living things, Polanyi finds throughout the forms of life, from amoeba up to humans, an heuristic impulse, a seeking and finding, a setting and satisfying of standards intrinsic to the organism itself. At each level of life there is an activity of adjustment to the larger reality of which it is a part. Survival depends in part on the organism's capacity to interpret and relate to the world around it. Here is a rudimentary beginning of the universal intent that appears in the human person.

Besides the heuristic ingredient in living things there is also a development, along with complexity, of the powers of learning and knowing. The points where these anthropomorphisms become precisely actual are difficult to specify, as evolutionary development happens slowly and by degrees. 'Knowing', 'learning', 'universal intent' and 'standards' are obviously anthropomorphic, yet these intellectual capacities are prefigured throughout the evolutionary story. Our powers of reading, engineering and invention can clearly be seen in higher animals. They can observe correlations between signs and events, thus read; they can contrive means for ends, thus engineer; and they can reorganize previous learning to meet new problems, thus invent. Our chief and immense advantage is our capacity to use language for storing information and pondering on problems.

When seen from this angle, tacit knowing fits well into the evolutionary knowledge we have. In the two types of awareness, we have the functional structure by which one level relies upon another for its achievement. This principle can be seen either biologically or epistemologically. We can understand how the development of the central nervous system laid down conditions that allowed for a more stable and effective exploration of the environment by the higher organisms. We also notice the opportunities and hazards that this level added as creatures increasingly became interpreters and less instinctual beings. We can also understand how the growth of knowledge lays down conditions that also make more stable and possible far-reaching explorations of reality. Proportionately, the hazards are greater as we build here, but it is the logic of our being.

The idea of tacit knowing culminates in Polanyi's vision of a society of explorers. The creative challenge stands at the centre of knowing. The structure of knowing is such that we are meant to indwell the world in order to rise to continuing levels of understanding. Knowing from his perspective is not accidental but the attainment of a long series of purposeful possibilities, from primeval incandescent gases to human beings. Each stage was fraught with danger and possibility of mishap, yet centres of knowing have evolved by the attraction of reality. George Wald was, I think, near to the insight of Polanyi when he said in his address on 'The Origins of Life' at the centennial celebration of the National Academy of Sciences:

> Judging from our experience upon this planet, such a history, that beings with elementary particles, leads perhaps toward a strange and moving end: a creature that knows, a science-making animal, that turns back upon the process that generated him and attempts to understand it. Without his like the universe could be, but not be known, and that is a poor thing . . . Surely this is a great part of our dignity as man, that we can know, and that through us matter can know itself.[12]

Still, Polanyi goes beyond Wald in pointing up the creative dimension of knowing as well as the distinctiveness of it. It is not because we are unique as knowers but because we are knowers who know each other and thereby participate in the unfolding of reality that we are unique. The meaning of being human is clearer as we focus on this aspect of knowing.

### Creativity and intuition

The leap of the creative imagination to a new discovery or insight is frequently called intuition, but intuition is regarded as the acquisition of truths or knowledge we cannot account for. The consequence of this view is to reduce the burden of creativity on all of us and to leave it to chance. By this ordinary definition of intuition we are left regarding it as obscure and mysterious, and we concentrate our heuristic efforts on the familiar objectivist model of hypothesis and experimentation. Once we see how tacit knowing illuminates the nature of intuition and of discovery in science, we are freed and impelled to consider the creative possibilities of all human knowers.

Poincaré outlined some of the main features of intuition or scientific discovery in his well-known stages of preparation, incubation and illumination. In these stages, he pointed to some of the important elements, namely the requirement of background and of training for the competency to approach a problem and its solution; also, a period of play and experimentation that allows for loosening and reordering of our understanding; and finally, a moment of spontaneous insight when the solution is recognized. Throughout his discussion, the movement from problem to solution is understood to be a tacit process that we cannot make explicit. To these stages, tacit knowing adds

[12] *Proceedings of the National Academy of Sciences in the USA*, 52, August (1964), pp. 609–10.

clarification and places an obligation on all human beings to accept their creative potential.

Viewed from tacit knowing, scientific discovery is an interplay of two principal elements, intuition and imagination.[13] Discovery follows the structure of tacit knowing with subsidiary awareness embodying clues that guide us to the integrations of our focal awareness. Intuition and imagination are aspects of the interplay of subsidiary and of focal awareness, as we shall see.

By intuition, Polanyi does not mean the supreme and immediate knowledge of Leibnitz, Spinoza or Husserl. Instead, Polanyi sees intuition as a guiding of imagination throughout a discovery process, and intuition can be identified and seen at different stages. For Polanyi, this intuition has a basic characteristic which is 'a skill for guessing with a reasonable chance of guessing right; a skill guided by an innate sensibility to coherence, improved by schooling.'[14]

This intuitive skill is observed by Polanyi to be operating in ways that can be designated as 'anticipatory', 'strategic', 'questing' and 'final'. In each of these there is present our reliance upon clues that suggest and prompt us, even though we cannot make their sense completely known. They are true instances of 'knowing more than we can tell'.

Discovery begins with what is called 'anticipatory intuition'. This point is crucial, for it is the directing of our energies and attention towards a task of understanding. Such intuition is only the preliminary sensing of a hidden truth that must await further efforts and steps before the finding of it. It is at this point that one of the most important differences between great and ordinary science lies: the ability to sense a hidden but promising problem. Anticipatory intuition is marked by its being the stage where our human desire for understanding becomes attached to dim but interesting aspects of reality. This stage is the choice of a problem. A problem itself is intuitive or skilful guessing or foreknowledge of a hidden coherence. Anticipatory intuition directs us to problems, but most of the clues remain in our subsidiary awareness and they appear semantically, phenomenally and ontologically in our focal awareness only as promises of future coherence.

Once discovery begins with anticipatory intuition, the second major element begins to play its part. This element is the imagination. Guided by the clues from our intuition from our subsidiary awareness, the imagination proposes ideas to try to understand the hints from

[13] 'The Creative Imagination', pp. 86–91.
[14] *Ibid.*, p. 89.

the intuition. The imagination is called by Polanyi the 'thoughts of things that are not present, or not yet present—or perhaps never to be present'.[15] But the imagination does not work statically. It is dynamically directed by two other forms of intuition, strategic and questing.

Before discussing the other stages of intuition, let us pause to summarize. We have defined intuition as a skill for guessing with a reasonable chance of guessing right. We can distinguish imagination from intuition by calling imagination the integrator and proposer— the integrator and proposer of ideas and possibilities for the searching activity of the intuition that has foreknowledge of a future coherence. We can state that the relation between intuition and imagination is dynamic, one of interplay. Put in this way, we can see more clearly the basic structure that would apply to discovery.

A brief example may help us further. Polanyi shows the interaction of intuition and imagination and their place in scientific discovery by the use of an analogy. Suppose you are asleep at home one night, and then you are awakened by a loud noise. The noise is a clue in your subsidiary awareness, and it is not yet clearly identified. You arise and begin to ask 'Was it the wind, a burglar?' At this stage, the imagination is proposing ideas to the intuition. The solution to the problem proceeds as your intuition and imagination continue to interact, guiding you with further clues that lead to ideas that lead to verification that satisfies the original seeking of our subsidiary awareness. The subsidiary awareness has served to give clues that lead to the focal awareness of a problem and of possibilities until it is resolved.

The process of scientific discovery and other great human achievement is, of course, more arduous and more lengthy. For this reason, Polanyi's other forms of intuition show the continuing interaction with imagination. The form that follows anticipatory intuition, which senses a problem, is 'strategic intuition'.[16] Strategic intuition guides the imagination in choosing worthy problems and guessing paths for their exploration. Without this form of intuition, anticipatory intuition could point out many problems, but it could not guide the person about which problem to choose. Much waste of time and resources would occur if strategic intuition did not help to guide the imagination in estimating the chance of discovery. By relying upon strategic intuition, the person is informed of the possibilities of approaching coherence

15 *Ibid.*
16 *Ibid.*

and discovery. Throughout a discovery process there are many points where decisions about alternatives have to be made, and here the strategic skill for guessing, with a reasonable chance of guessing right, is always crucial.

The third form of intuition, 'questing intuition', also plays a decisive role.[17] It is the basis for determination and perseverance that keeps the discovery process going. The accounts of scientific discouragement and struggle, of years of plodding and of difficulty before the break through are famous. It is here that questing intuition plays its vital part. Throughout an inquiry there is a guiding sense of what the scientist is seeking even though he or she is not able to state it. It is the continuing feeling of a potential coherence that lies within grasp if the scientist can just find the way. As the search progresses or falls backwards, it is this intuition which steadies the pursuit and gives a constant aim and purpose.

The last form of intuition discerned by Polanyi is 'final intuition'.[18] Final intuition is nearer to what Poincaré called illumination. It is the last stage and the point where the intuition claims to have made a discovery. The intuition is now at the point where it may be proved to be true or mistaken.

This survey of the forms of intuition—anticipatory, strategic, questing and final—clearly represents a dynamic structure of tacit knowing. It shows how throughout an inquiry there is interaction between our subsidiary awareness and our focal awareness that accounts for our sensing hidden coherence and our integrating these clues into imaginative proposals for exploration. Discovery and intuition definitely remain partly unaccountable experiences, yet they are less mysterious. The role of the tacit domain is now seen and, rather than being mere chance and unexplainable, is itself a form of awareness that we recognize.

## Knowers and standards

We began our discussion with human creativity represented in art and science. The claim was made that it is in creativity our essence is seen. In the two given examples, of Michelangelo's Sistine Chapel and the discovery of the structure of DNA, many elements were present; and to a few we have given our attention. Foremost has been the understanding and appreciation of the personal power of the

[17] *Ibid.*, p. 88.
[18] Michael Polanyi, *Knowing and Being*, ed. Marjorie Grene, University of Chicago Press, Chicago, 1969, p. 202.

human being for seeking the truth and stating his or her findings. We have seen that it is by a bodily knowing, through which we indwell clues subsidiarily and integrate them into focal awareness, that the clues become knowledge. Such knowing is possible because of an evolutionary heritage that progressed from rudimentary seeking and finding to the amazing achievements of human beings. There is a profound sense in which we know ourselves as we behold these extraordinary feats of creativity. Works of art and discoveries of science thrill and overwhelm us, from the most naive to the most sophisticated person, as they intimate 'that is us, that is who we are meant to be'. This reading of ourselves into and identifying with the works of others is our final point in what it means to be human. This avowal and participation in the greatness of others shows that human creativity is social and that it is a calling to unlimited ranges of reality.

There is in the admiration of the individual achievement a proper tendency to give credit to the unusual powers of the particular person, yet this tendency is distorting when it makes absolute the loneliness of the brilliant. As the structure of tacit knowing has indicated, and especially the work of the intuition, we are able to know by our dependence upon the tradition, background and schooling which fill our subsidiary awareness with clues. The custom of speaking of the knower really needs to be corrected to a deeper sensitivity that we all know, because we are knowers together.

Such a sensitivity is more than gratitude; it is ontologically appropriate. When we speak of knowers, we are truer to the structure of our being and to the logic of evolution. While we acclaim the outstanding human achievement of the individual, we need to observe that it is by the standards of universal intent that it is possible. These standards are like stars that guide us. They are not of our own making but they belong to our universe of an immense journey. The individual pioneer is beckoned forward by standards that are shared. When his or her discovery becomes known, we are able to greet it because we were going in that direction, too.

Such a view of knowing reveals that knowing is 'I–Thou', in a sense deeper than this concept is sometimes used.[19] When we claim to know, we expect that another person can and will acknowledge that we know. This mutual exchange of ideas and information assumes a framework that allows that we know each other as persons who can know. The presence of such a framework is itself a manifestation

[19]   Michael Polanyi, *Personal Knowledge*, University of Chicago Press, Chicago, 1958, p. 346.

of the structure of being, a structure that leads to persons who know persons. To acknowledge the knowing of others is really an acknowledgement between persons. This fact is itself one reason why an impersonal knowledge is a mistaken view.

Once again the structure of tacit knowing is exemplified, for the 'I–Thou' nature of knowing is made possible by acts of indwelling based upon subsidiary and focal awareness. To know someone else as a person involves self-knowledge that accredits them as being like us. To know another person as a 'Thou' instead of as an 'It' is to affirm and be open to an active centre of being that thinks, feels and seeks. We know such an active centre by its having an unspecifiable and deep character like our own. If the other person were an 'It', this person would be more specifiable and determinate. When we know another person as a 'Thou', we encounter a richness and a freedom that is surprising and fascinating. We do not know in advance exactly who this person will turn out to be, but we expect that in some way she or he will reach out to a firmament of standards we share, and we realize that we may be influenced by her or his being.

There is a definite difference between knowing inanimate things, living things and human persons, that culminates in the knowing of the 'Thou'. Knowing inanimate things is indwelling the subsidiary clues and forming them into focal integrations that tell us of passive entities—objects that are mainly acted upon. Knowing living things is indwelling the subsidiary clues and integrating them into beings that function—ones that are in this sense active towards a purpose such as growth, and the success of this purpose is decisive for the ongoing of that being. At this point, they anticipate personhood because we recognize in these beings an element akin to ourselves, the problem of success and failure. Knowing a person is much more. In this indwelling, our clues form to tell us of another centre of action that, like us, not only struggles between success and failure but also has to determine what these standards are. Thus, we meet in a situation of exploration.

The movement from knowing inanimate objects to knowing persons is a movement of degrees of indwelling and of ranges of focal awareness. To know a rock is to know something that is definite like ourselves, but we cannot share our freedom with it because we do not receive from it clues of freedom that we can indwell. To know a plant or an animal is to know something functioning like ourselves, but our sharing is limited because the clues from its functions limit our indwelling to mainly simple tasks—physical growth, food processing, reproduction and survival. To know a person is to know an active centre of thought like ourselves, which seeks to know the standards to live by. Here we receive clues of another subject facing an infinite range of choices and whose existence, like our own, is tied to his or her capacity for selecting among the infinite the ones that are true. So from our self-knowledge we recognize with hope our companions, seeking and finding their way. As like beings who share with us the potential choices of myriad relations to reality, we hope to know with them.

The choice of human direction, the course of human history, is a 'Thou' choice. Our destiny lies in the standards we have collectively set for ourselves. These standards, nevertheless, are not pure invention. They are the comprehensive integrations of experience that human beings have formed through their indwelling the structures of being. As human beings have known, they have modified and deepened their understanding of these structures.

Is such knowledge true? Tacit knowing implies it is true to the extent that it is an opening for an increasing understanding of the coherence and ranges of reality. Recall that discoveries are made in searches prompted by intuitions of reality. We send out our imagination deliberately to find proposals to satisfy our intuitive sense of a hidden but present reality. When the discovery is finally made, our inquiry comes to a rest but we are in a new position. In the course of our inquiry, we have indwelled and accepted clues that have led us to a new understanding. These findings change us and place us in a new potentiality for further explorations.

Once more, let us return to our opening examples of human creativity. Both speak of standards of beauty. Michelangelo portrays in the human being an affinity with the divine. We are partly encouraged in this view by the anthropomorphism of the figures. It is a human-like deity that reaches out and creates the person. We enjoy this portrayal because it confirms our own experience of having within us powers that are creative. We also notice in Watson's accounts of the research on DNA his respect for the creative process that is guided by the concept of a molecule being 'pretty'. These examples tell us that creativity and beauty go together, but what is beauty?

Beauty seems to be one of the marks of the depth of reality. It is like and probably a part of what we have been calling patterns and coherence in reality. It is knowable yet it is inexhaustible. As we approach it at one point, we are only prepared to see it in new and continuing ways.

Another feature stands out in these two examples of human greatness. The story Watson tells is one of involvement and work with others, without which the discovery could not have been made. The picture of Michelangelo's creation of Adam heightens this dimension. As the human Adam is faced with the moment of his creation, he is faced with a 'Thou', a divine person. Such a presentation reminds us of the Biblical theme that the human being is created in the image of God. If we put both examples together, we may have an understanding of what it is to be human in our world today. When we behold in another person his or her acts of creativity, we know the divine within us. We are human to the extent that we can know this infinite potential and accept it as our calling.

# Essay 9

## Roger Poole*

Ra, Khepri and Shu, Geb, Nut and Osiris; Zeus, Poseidon, Hephaestus, Hermes, Ares and Apollo, with Hera, Athene, Artemis, Hestia, Aphrodite and Demeter; Dagda, Lug and Nuada; Ymir, Audumla and Buri, Odin, Vili and Ve; Byelobog, Chernobog and Svarog, Domovoi, Dvorovoi and Bannik; Mithra, Hvare-Khshaeta and Mah, with Anahita, Tishtriya and Apo; Indra, Mitra and Varuna, with Agni, Soma and Savitar; Surya, Ushas and Puchan, with Prajapati, Prihaspati and Aditi; Ama-Tsu-Kami, Kuni-Tsu-Kami and Yomi-Tsu-Kuni; Izanagi, Izanami and Awa, with Susanoo, Amaterasu and O-Kuni-Nushi.

Just a few of the names of the divine invented by man. Sacred figures, demons, helpers, donors and begetters, spirits, monitors and protectors.

The sheer range and variety of the gods and demons invented by human beings through the ages is astonishing, but even more so is the constant reference made by these many gods and demons to recurrent, one might even say permanent, feelings in the heart of the human being. This mass of outer forms covers over a few very simple feelings.

It seems that there is an analogy, in the religious world, with the theory of language developed by Noam Chomsky. Chomsky advanced the idea that human beings are endowed at birth with a linguistic

* For Edith Weston and for John Perkins, with thanks for all they have taught me.

'competence', and that this competence allows children born into a language to create, freely, an infinite number of new sentences within their inherited language.

This competence is a form of freedom. Sentences that have never been uttered or thought before can be put together in a chain of correctly used linguistic units, such that a brand new meaning is correctly picked up by another member of that language group. Chomsky allowed himself to be astonished by the sheer prodigality of originality that language–users show.

He also advanced the theory that the 'surface structures' of any given language are related to, and emerge from, certain 'deep structures' in that language, and even hinted at the daring hypothesis that the 'deep structures' of all languages might be related to each other. It looked like a distinct possibility that 'deep structures' themselves related to the kinds of original meaning and silence which the phenomenologist Maurice Merleau-Ponty called 'primordial'.

It seems to me that, just as men and women are born with this native linguistic 'competence', so they are born with what I am going to call 'religious competence'. Between the plethora of gods and demons cited above, and certain 'deep structures' of religious sentiment in human beings throughout ages of time, there is a relationship analogous to the one suggested by Chomsky in the matter of language. The many forms of deity are 'surface structures' which relate to 'deep structures' of feeling.

The 'deep structures' of feeling do not find it easy to find expression for themselves. Some of the forms of deity invented by human beings are grotesque, some are cruel and terrible. Others can be sublime, and many of them are beautiful.

Chomsky is not alone in seeing that the ability to create new strings of meaning in a language is itself a form of freedom. George Steiner, in his recent book *After Babel*, has linked the freedom that is the condition of language production, to the freedom from oppression, repetition and abuse which newly-created language alone offers. In inventing and maintaining a multiplicity of tongues, human beings erect barriers against spiritual apathy. Language is freedom. Or put another way, the ability to create freely in language is itself an innate ability to protect and maintain freedom.

In inventing language, men and women create the sacred, and, in inventing the sacred, they constantly preserve a flow of freedom, called words. The early stages of divinity always have something to do with the bequeathing or the exchanging of words, formulae or messages.

Words and gods are interchangeable. Who speaks words, speaks religiously. Who speaks religiously is forced to use words.

'What it means to be human'? Men and women have a need for religious experience. They need it, they lust after it, they want to have it. It is like food, air, heat and motion. It is a necessity of life. There is no culture known to me that does not have its form of religion. Wherever people find themselves, in whatever extreme of heat or cold, of blazing sun or endless ice, they will invent stories of gods and demons. Sometimes indeed, it seems as if the need for religious sentiment and structure actually precedes the need for food, housing or survival. The religious need can take hold of its victims and shake them till they die.

I am suggesting that 'religious competence' is something human beings are born with, just as they are born with faculties that process space and faculties that process time. The need for religious experience is, like any other need, a matter that it is perilous to ignore. Religious competence that is denied or disallowed will turn against itself and emerge in some other form.

The analysis of religion founded by Malinowski and his colleagues of the functionalist persuasion is all too partial, though it undoubtedly contains an aspect of truth. Human beings do invent gods for explaining the world more satisfactorily, or for controlling it to some extent. But this is only part of the answer. Human beings also invent gods because they have to, because they are numinously inclined towards doing so.

The human being has a need to think religiously. It is natural to him, whether amid a merciless blue sky he is staring up at a sun that seems intent on incinerating him, or whether he is stranded alone in the humming birches of a Scandinavian forest, to project over the scene some divine thinking. Man brings this divine thinking into being, because he cannot help it. He produces it as naturally as he breathes. The sun which glitters so dangerously up there, that is surely some sort of pressure on the world, some force which will have its way with us below. The forest which heaves with the gusts of an oncoming storm, certainly contains those who will help escape, and those who will do their best to prevent it. These thoughts occur naturally. Recently, walking at night along the shores of a frozen Canadian lake, in a darkness so absolute that light was almost an abstract memory, and in a silence so great that it nearly bruised the ears, I could easily have believed in every totem of the Hurons. To pitch camp here, next to this huge immobile lump of ice, to attempt to sleep through this profound night, was indeed to enter into relation with spirits which, between now and morning, would decide my fate.

That this feeling may not be perfectly improper I shall try to suggest, by recalling a story told of Bertrand Russell. In later life, walking in Wales, the great rationalist and humanist came to the top of a hill and stared down over a bay. So great was the beauty of what he saw, he recounts, that he had to grab hold of a gatepost to prevent himself from having a religious experience.

These feelings of religious presence seem to 'lie in wait' for the sceptic and the cynic. Observing people walking round the recent massive exhibition of Turner's gyrating canvases in London, I could not help but notice many of them trying hard to prevent themselves from having religious experiences. They did not always make a very convincing job of it. The same phenomenon I have observed in the cool subterranean oval rooms where Monet's vast *Water Lilies* are on permanent exhibition in Paris. It is interesting to watch people coming into the rooms, girded and shielded from religious perception by constant abrasion in the streets, and suddenly to have to participate in an emotion so intense that they are quite unprepared to stave it off. Certain kinds of competence one is born with one neglects to put to any good use. But that does not mean to say that the competence is lost, and there are moments when it is suddenly recalled in discomfiture.

But in our time, the religious competence is being denied and derided. The practical effect of Malinowskian functionalism has been to disseminate the conviction that if a religious phenomenon can be reduced to an explanation at the level of utility or control, then the specifically 'religious' component in the religious phenomenon can be discounted, and finally ignored. But it is quite possible to accept the truth of what the functionalist wants to point out—that religious thinking has a function and practical aims in view—without in any way concurring with this shearing-away of the spiritual dimension of religious activity. Behaviourism, positivism, sociobiology, ethology and many other pseudo-sciences have all added their weight to the functionalist position, until today it is not respectable at all to admit to religious awareness or experience. And this progressive denigration of a faculty that is as natural to us as eating or sleeping explains an immense amount of things not usually connected with talk about religion at all.

Perhaps the best way to approach this theme of repression is through the phenomenon of absence. The absence of religious meaning is made present through the manifold forms of communal despair of the sixties and seventies. The religious need or competence pullulates silently, emerging in horrible or grotesque forms. Behind the various forms of cultural and political self-expression that take the human body as their medium and sign, there is a repressed religious competence, abused, irritated, derided, desperate and vicious. It will out, yet it is denied access to conscious acceptance. So it cowers, terrified yet malevolent. So great has been the force of derision at the expense of religious sentiment, that religious sentiment itself has become an element in its own anti-expressivity. By this I mean that although the desire for religious experience shows plainly through hash and Castaneda and long overland journeys to India, it is not ackowledged as a legitimate need. It is merely regarded as eccentricity. That the sentient part of the Western world has had to embrace firstly the politics and then the religions of the East, is a clear indicator that the West is not allowing the religious competence to flower.

I choose that metaphor carefully. The immediate rejoinder suggests itself: Why should it be assumed that the West has any duty to let religious competence (supposing there to be any such thing) flower? I suppose that an appeal to simple self-interest would seem, in our day, undemocratic. So, let me suggest that the phenomenon of absence makes itself felt most plainly on those occasions when, obviously, some form of religious activity is plainly called for. And I instance Christmas and Easter.

These two occasions are experienced, so far as I can observe, as phenomena of absence in the modern Western bourgeois family. Obviously something is meant and implied by all this fuss, and yet nothing transpires. The effort to stave off the necessity of acknowledging some form of religious meaning in the seasons of Christmas and Easter is great, and each parent has to meet the demand as best as he or she can. The main aim is to get through the two religious seasons, or at least the key days of those seasons, without acting in any way that is overtly absurd, or that offends in any way the private beliefs of the parents. No help is offered from any communal wisdom. Each family suffers its dilemma separately, behind closed doors, and largely without uttering a word of the difficulty of the problem. The problem is, how to get through the day (given as highly significant) without in any way attributing significance to it.

At Christmas time, amid all the bustle and fun, the presents and the tree and the turkey, what should one actually *do* at 11 o'clock on Christmas morning? Take the children to church on a once-a-year spree, and try to face the thing out, hoping that there will be enough others there to cover up a refusal to participate in singing the hymns? Or sit it out at home, ignoring the Christmas services coming out of the telly and the scenes of rapturous exchange from St Peter's in Rome, between the Pope and his half a million wildly excited pilgrims from every corner of the world? And what will the children make of this double-standard event, a religious occasion without religion, a church festival without church, a sense of momentous happenings without any corresponding events?

The same thing occurs at Easter, but it is even worse then, for the presents and the tree are not there to cover up the emptiness at the centre. True, there are chocolate eggs and chocolate bunnies, but no kid is taken in by them. And anyway it only takes three minutes to eat a chocolate bunny.

What does one as a parent *do* with the children for the rest of Easter day? How does one overcome the sense of an occasion violated, a meaning denied, a possibility refused?

Parents are in a desperate mess over this. Intuitively, obscurely, they feel that children need religion ('what it means to be human' is obviously to have some kind of need like that) and yet they cannot in all conscience endorse what goes on in church, convinced rationalist–empiricist–behaviourist–reductivists as they are. So they shuffle and equivocate. They *have* to, so to speak, because they are intelligent as the world is intelligent in our time, and believe, as the Royal Society did in the late seventeenth century, that science has chased all the hobgoblins and fairies, the gods and demons, out of our minds and hearts.

So it may have, but it has not also made a tidy job of it by depriving the human being of his religious competence. If science had indeed done that, then it would have as much cause to congratulate itself as a surgeon who has just made an absolutely clean removal of a cancer. But science has bungled the job. The competence remains.

The competence, driven underground by fifteen years of modern childhood, will reappear somewhere along the road, mutated, odd, distorted in drugs, sex and violence. Or it may emerge as a tremendous longing for the spiritual dimension to existence, a longing all the more desperate in that it cannot pronounce its own name. For the necessary words have been subtly subtracted from common usage. This tremendous longing will, in our time, be mute.

However, this play of absences does allow for the intermittent flash of some sort of divine information. In recent years, there have emerged a string of persons so strikingly authentic in their action in the world, that the world has accorded them that grudging recognition which is only accorded when the usual expressions of distrust and accusations of inauthenticity have proved impotent against their spell. I think of such people as Martin Luther King, Mother Teresa of Calcutta, Solzhenitsyn. Figures of a slightly older date have re-emerged as figures filled with significance for today: Kierkegaard, Tolstoy, Bonhoeffer, Simone Weil. These are people whose connection to the divine is so authentic and so obviously a matter of total integrity that irony cannot touch them. I think, as an excellent example of the kind of irony I mean, of Lionel Trilling's brilliant study *Sincerity and Authenticity*. In this book, he shows how the modern European sensibility has become progressively more incapable of genuine authenticity. In the gentlest way possible he indicates that, at least in the field of literature, those who took themselves to be the most self-transparently authentic writers and thinkers were in fact only offering modifications of stances taken by their own predecessors, and with every modification comes a dilution of purity. Harold Bloom has followed a similarly deflating itinerary in his book *The Anxiety of Influence*. It would appear there that no modern poet since Milton has spoken, except in a crippled subservience to his 'precursor'. These theorists of irony warn us not to take our own utterances too seriously. They remind us to have a proper sense of doubt in the face of our most brilliant insights and our most authentic thoughts. And they also, invoking the subversions of Nietzsche, Freud and some others, remind us how much of our moral utterance is a matter of posturing.

But these incisive studies of irony and inauthenticity and hidden debt cannot touch the figure of what I call the 'indirect communicator'. I borrow the term from Kierkegaard, who meant something very precise and personal with it, and I borrow it in order to extend its range of reference. Figures like Bonhoeffer, Solzhenitsyn and the others have a way of imposing upon a sceptical, or even a frankly disbelieving, acquaintance the fact that they are beyond the reach of irony, and, being beyond the reach of irony, are unassailable by merely human criteria of sane or well-bethought action. Mad they may be, but even the sceptic has to admit that they are mad in a kind of disconcerting and reassuring way. The death of Martin Luther King is not a fit subject for irony. The jokers and the slappers on the back fall silent. For once, it is *their* words that sound inauthentic, when they attempt their usual levelling observations.

What quality is it that the 'indirect communicator' possesses which is capable, in life and in death, of wringing from a resolutely secular world this latter-day acknowledgement of something that transcends secularity? For a split second, the act of the indirect communicator falls athwart the expectations of his audience. There is no explaining it. Doubt supervenes, and with this doubt an openness to reconsider things that may have been relegated to dead certainty long ago. The indirect communicator forces attention, by disappointing expectation. Let me instance the case of Dietrich Bonhoeffer.

Dietrich Bonhoeffer was arrested by the Gestapo in 1943, and was held for eighteen months at the Tegel Prison in Berlin. Later he was moved to close confinement in the Prinz Albert Strasse prison, and in 1945 he was moved to Buchenwald, thence to Schönberg, and hanged at Flossenbürg. His connection with the plot on Hitler's life was very tenuous and very naive. He died, more than anything else, because of his own religious convictions and the actions to which they led him.

The details of Bonhoeffer's life in prison can be gathered from Eberhard Bethge's biography. But some things stand out as decidedly peculiar. Many of the warders, for instance, Bethge assures us, 'tried to arrange the rota of duties so that they were allotted to that section of the corridor where Bonhoeffer's cell was . . . There were several requests, even from a sargent-major, to be allowed to be photographed with this prisoner in the courtyard . . . When the sirens howled and the bomber squadrons seemed to take their course directly over Tegel, those in the section got as close as possible to Bonhoeffer, who seemed to remain so calm.'[1]

I wonder what strange quality it was that made these guards and warders of the Gestapo wish to be near Dietrich Bonhoeffer when the bombs were falling. Something, perhaps, that had been resolutely denied them in the strict indoctrination of their youth hesitantly recurred to them, at some lost subliminal level. Something that their lives had been systematically denied, suddenly recurred to them as a possibility. Some form of courage, which their indoctrination had separated them from, was briefly re-seen in the presence of Bonhoeffer in the prison.

And what did Bonhoeffer do in Tegel? He sat and wrote letters, read, kept quiet. He tried to persuade the guards to stop persecuting prisoners who were receiving particularly rough treatment. He was active only in that sense.

---

[1]  E. Bethge, *Dietrich Bonhoeffer,* Collins, London, 1970, pp. 750–1.

Yet the effect on his co-prisoners, on his guards, on the prison staff, was profound. The beginning of a poem he wrote in Tegel shows us how he appeared to the others in the prison at that time:

### Who am I?

Who am I? They often tell me
I would step from my cell's confinement
calmly, cheerfully, firmly,
like a squire from his country-house.

Who am I? They often tell me
I would speak to my warders
freely and friendly and clearly,
as though it were mine to command.

Who am I? They also tell me
I would bear the days of misfortune
equably, smilingly, proudly,
like one accustomed to win.[2]

This is, so to speak, one 'half' of the communication achievement in the 'indirect communicator': the public half, the half deliberately emitted to create a certain impression. The other 'half' of the communication is the hidden half, the half which takes place in ethical subjectivity, and, in Bonhoeffer's case, in terror. The poem continues:

Am I then really all that which other men tell of?
Or am I only what I myself know of myself,
restless and longing and sick, like a bird in a cage,
struggling for breath, as though hands were compressing my throat,
yearning for colours, for flowers, for the voices of birds,
thirsting for words of kindness, for neighbourliness,
trembling with anger at despotisms and petty humiliation,
tossing in expectation of great events,
powerlessly trembling for friends at an infinite distance,
weary and empty at praying, at thinking, at making,
faint, and ready to say farewell to it all?[3]

It is in my view the clash between the outer and the inner 'halves' or 'sides' of his communication which gives to the presence of the 'indirect communicator' its profoundly unsettling quality. The observer sees one 'string' of actions, or visual impressions, and checks these out against some other, indefinable quality, which he also senses to be present in the object of his observation. The first series of

[2]   D. Bonhoeffer, *Letters and Papers from Prison*, enlarged edition, SCM Press, London, 1971, p. 347.
[3]   *Op. cit.*, p. 348.

impressions do not 'click' with the second string of impressions. In some strange way, the actions of the indirect communicator fail to 'endorse' themselves at the level of a unified statement. Indeed, they subtly contradict themselves. There is a kind of 'gap' or discontinuity between the public stance and what is intuited to be the inner reality. And in the distance deliberately held by the 'indirect communicator' between the outer string of evidences and the intuited inner string of evidences consists, it seems to me, the powerfully hindering and upsetting force of his communication. It is the very split in the nature of the sign the indirect communicator emits which makes it impossible for the observer or the recipient to respond in a simple, naive or unified way. He is suddenly exposed to doubt, and it is moreover a doubt that he has to settle for himself and in his own way. This is why Kierkegaard, who was the first to become explicitly aware of the inner mechanism of the indirect communication, used to refer to it as a process which set the *observer* into existential movement. Far from being able to assimilate something simple, something 'objective', something ready-made, something immediately deployable as good advice in the commonsense world of everyday *praxis*, the observer of the indirect communication is suddenly drawn into a movement taking place within himself. He is beginning to grasp the problem as the indirect communicator sees it, but the replies he makes to that problem have (inevitably) to be his own. There is no ready-made 'objective' counter the observer can simply take over from the indirect communicator. He has been set in motion by what he has seen, or rather by the subtle cracks and fissures in the cohesion of what he has seen, and from now on the problem has become his own. The effect of the indirect communication is to set the *observer* into motion, into subjective ethical process. Subjectivity thus becomes truth. Truth is in motion, and the observer has to take up his own stance to what he finds has begun to go on inside him.

How does the poem by Bonhoeffer weave together the two strands of his own communication?

Who am I? This or the other?
Am I one person today, and tomorrow another?
Am I both at once? A hypocrite before others,
and before myself a contemptibly woebegone weakling?
Or is something within me still like a beaten army,
fleeing in disorder from victory already achieved?[4]

---

[4]  *Op. cit.*, p. 348.

It is clear from this that Bonhoeffer is quite *aware* that a problem exists, that the two 'strands' or 'halves' of his communication conflict in some way that throws doubt on the 'authenticity' (to pick up Trilling's concept) of his own communication. So he suggests to himself first of all that he *alternates* his communication's two halves in time; then that he holds to both parts *at once*; and finally that he does not *understand* that the negative side is already a positive side, an achieved victory. But none of these three solutions to the split communication really satisfies him. So he throws his whole weight into one final massive couplet of resolution from outside:

> Who am I? They mock me, these lonely questions of mine.
> Whoever I am, Thou knowest, O God, I am Thine.

It seems that, even in despair, the German mind cannot write anything that does not have a powerfully consistent logical structure. This poem, though one doubtless gets only a faint view of it from the translation, is one of the most perfect I know, from a formal point of view, ranking with the most refined architecture of George Herbert. It engages centrally with the problem of what the split, or 'indirect' communication, is, and attempts to resolve the problem through the very form of the poem itself. The major opposition of the inner and outer 'sides' of the sign is queried by three possible conceptual instruments, and these are all rejected for a fourth, which is resolutely imported from outside.

One observer of Bonhoeffer in the very last months of his life has a specially privileged place in any analysis of the Bonhoefferian sign, because of the totally sceptical nature of his mind and the frank contempt he entertained for any form of religious or emotional humbug and slackness; and that is Captain Payne Best. His book, *The Venlo Incident*, is one of the unknown classics of the last World War. It makes furiously good reading. Best is one of those heroes who only exist in Biggles books. Best was a high ranking Intelligence officer captured by the Nazis at the very beginning of the war in Holland. He was driven to Berlin for questioning with a sack over his head. When he arrived, he refused to be questioned until he had his monocle returned to him and had been offered a sandwich and a strong whisky. Later on, Best was kept as a 'prestige' prisoner, with many other illustrious personages, with whose lives Hitler planned to buy his personal safety at the end of the war if things went too badly wrong. During these long years of imprisonment, Best decided to run the prison on his own lines. He reported brutality shown by camp personnel to the Commandant. He took a good deal of pleasure in being politely rude to Reichsführer Himmler when he visited the prison on an official occasion. At Christmas, the Commandant, who had grown to rely on Captain Best for information and advice, brought him a cake, a Christmas tree and two bottles of wine for the festive season.

But it is not Best's classical cool nerves and unflappable courage which counts in our consideration of the effect Bonhoeffer had upon him, but rather his emotional and intellectual temper. He was a rationalist of the most pure kind. He had nothing but contempt for the Nazis, and viewed all Germans with amused or hostile indifference as basically good children who had been led astray by an evil schoolmaster. He did not hate the Germans, for Stoic reasons. He held to a view that all men were the same, and only varied from time to time in adventitious ways. He therefore waited for the bad dream of the Third Reich to pass away with all other such evanescent phenomena, and when he found himself in a bus with dozens of other 'prestige' prisoners in Bavaria, within miles of the advancing American front, he quickly resumed the command that was natural to him, and ran the hotel in which the prisoners and their guards were stranded, until such time as he could hand over to the appropriate superior officer.

It is his attitude to Bonhoeffer which is so striking and interesting. He had obviously never met anyone like Bonhoeffer before, and was conscious that, in some way he could not define to himself, the man was unique. Nor indeed is it in the few lines he devotes to a summary of Bonhoeffer's religious authenticity that the main tribute from Best is to be found, but in the entire description of him, from the moment when he first sees Bonhoeffer to the moment when Bonhoeffer is taken off to be hanged on April 8, 1945.

I refer the reader to Best's book for the latticework of observation and recognition the atheist Best found himself bringing to bear upon the Christian Bonhoeffer. As Best tells it, the story seems one of a growing consciousness that the disparate acts of Bonhoeffer, which Best observed, added up in effect to a sum greater than the parts of his indirect 'discourse'. Best finds his attention being claimed in a different way from the way he usually expected to observe his fellow men. He finds himself fascinated by Bonhoeffer, watching him with the kind of attention one might bring to a crossword puzzle.

The few words in which he sums up his impressions give no clue to the richness of the observations that scatter the pages. But he writes

'Bonhoeffer was all humility and sweetness; he always seemed to diffuse an atmosphere of happiness, of joy in every smallest event in life, and of deep gratitude for the mere fact that he was alive . . . He was one of the very few men I have ever met to whom his God was real and ever close to him.'[5] And Bethge quotes a personal letter from Best to his family to this effect: 'In fact my feeling was far stronger than these words imply. He was, without exception, the finest and most lovable man I have ever met.'

Coming from Captain Payne Best, this is a tribute indeed—one of the most rare. For temperamentally Best was closed to this sort of lived sign. He mentions most of his fellows in Sachsenhausen or in Buchenwald only with contempt or amused and hostile indifference. He was obviously a proud and supercilious man, with no patience for shows of excessive moral virtue or self-righteousness in a situation that, according to his view of things, should never have arisen in the first place.

It may be that Best respected Bonhoeffer as he did because he believed that Bonhoeffer was the only man he had met, during his years of imprisonment, who had transcended fear as totally as Best himself had done. If he believed this, he was wrong, as we know from the poem *Who am I?* and the *Letters and Papers from Prison* as a whole. I do not know whether Best ever felt fear. If it is possible for a human being not to feel fear at all, then Best must be one of those few who escaped it. And Bonhoeffer, due to the immense theological and personal travail of the year in Tegel and Prinz Albert Strasse, must also have appeared to have transcended fear. Best believed, probably, that he and Pastor Bonhoeffer had happened to meet in some privileged area of the spirit, in which equals could recognize each other. The acknowledgement Best accords Bonhoeffer is that of an officer and a gentleman. It is not patronizing, nor is it stinted. It is sincere, and its most striking characteristic is that through it Best testifies to the existence of a power of which he professes to have no knowledge or experience whatsoever, and of which he had previously doubted the very existence.

Partly the subtle indirection that Bonhoeffer 'brought off' must have been due to the nature of the theological reflection he was experiencing during his year in Tegel. With the realization, developed in the theology of that year, that God belongs to the centre and not to the periphery of existence, he had managed to transcend not only his own

---

[5]  E. Bethge, *Dietrich Bonhoeffer*, p. 823.

fear but his fear on behalf of his family. The vision of Christ in the hands of the Gestapo had led Bonhoeffer to consider every man who suffers as occupying the body of Christ. What spiritual force it was that overtook him in that cell we cannot name. In fact names are useless here. But something convinced him that in the situation of total destitution and abject terror there is a spiritual aid which can come to consciousness as being itself central to that destitution and that terror, and which can wipe out fear even in a situation that is itself terrifying.

This spiritual force, whatever its nature, belonged to the mystery, or the alchemy of Bonhoeffer's deliberately split sign. It endowed his mere presence with a peculiar quality all of those around him felt, even if they could neither understand nor sympathize with his theological convictions. It was something which itself banished fear, even under air-raid conditions. Nameless and emanating from an obscure point of origin, it was a lived reality which issued out into public space as a peculiarly potent kind of indirect communication —a communication which was largely wordless and unspoken, and which bore directly on the unspoken and hidden aspects of the consciousness of those around him, influencing them in ways which they could not name but only acknowledge.

The openness to religious impressionability is then an enduring feature of what it means to be human, even when, and especially when, religious convictions have been relegated to the rubbish heap at some earlier point in life. There is no one, I think, who can by an act of will refuse to be moved by religious experience, just as there is no one who can by an act of will refuse to be moved by human beauty or the beauty of bay and headland, water and cloud. These refusals are quickly made redundant by the force of response which lies in every one. There is a sense too, in which the convinced atheist is far nearer to religious experience than the indifferent. I think of the passionate atheism of the poems of Ted Hughes in *Crow*. Time after time, God is indicted, prosecuted, convicted. Crow flies off cachinnating to himself at God's incompetence, God's mediocrity, God's helplessness, God's cruelty, God's indifference. Time after time, through the poem, we scent the direct presence of an actual disappointment in God, as a lover who finds his loved one less than he had thought her. The atheism of Hughes, like indirect communication, has this power to awake in the reader the sense of the split sign, the self-negated affirmation. In trying to see the crevice in what appears to be an unbroken series of indications, we are ourselves trying to puzzle out why it is that Hughes is so disappointed. Perhaps we had forgotten what the sharp pang of disappointment felt like. The atheist restores it to the reader.

But necessarily indirect communication begins and ends in the human body. The body is capable, being placed in a certain situation, of so acting that it sets up a sharp series of oppositions to what normally goes on or is accepted in that particular political or social space. The body can reinforce a social convention, or it can, by deploying against expectation, itself throw that convention into question. The body used dialectically—as Kierkegaard used it, for instance—is itself an instrument of criticism which has as its aim to throw the moral expectations prevalent in that society into sharper relief.[6]

It is the body as presence which is so powerful. The body can be distinctly perceived as a presence when it acts in a privileged space, which it manages to set up itself by dialectically confronting the expectations and suppositions of a certain political arena. This is ethical space. In ethical space, religious phenomena stand out with peculiar and striking insistence; they assault the unprepared and disturb the convinced.

It is interesting in this connection to note an amazing and unpredictable turn in the avant-garde of French philosophy. Traditionally Marxist and socialist, the French Left has suddenly thrown up a set of 'new philosophers' whose common point of concern is the abuse of human rights in Russia and China and elsewhere in the world where Stalinism still reigns.

The very existence of this movement, springing from the main tradition of the twentieth century French Left, is surprising enough. But what gives even more food for thought is the fact that it is the life and work of a single embodied individual—Alexander Solzhenitsyn—which binds the members of this dissident strain together. The appearance of *The Gulag Archipelago* finally shocked even the theoreticians of the French Left into a recognition of what communism, as practised in Soviet Russia, in fact is. The theoretical importance of Solzhenitsyn's massive work took a long time in emerging. For Solzhenitsyn describes the plight of any individual caught in that impersonal system so minutely and so accurately that every reader has to find some sort of answer to the questions, about what it means

---

[6]   I have attempted some illustrations of this principle in my book *Towards Deep Subjectivity*, Allen Lane, London, Harper and Row, New York, 1972. Two further studies of the phenomenon of indirect communication await publication.

to be human, that it poses. The two massive volumes, documented, researched and supported throughout with such humane scrupulousness, presented a tremendous challenge to the unexamined assumptions of the humanist Left.

*Time* for September 5, 1977, had a long study of the 'new philosophers' in Paris. Bernard-Henri Levy is quoted as saying: 'We are realizing that the 20th century's great invention may prove to be the concentration camp, which is generalized murder for reasons of state. Mine is not a theory of sadness, but rather a recognition that one cannot institutionalize happiness.' André Glucksmann says 'If there is one thing new it is to be found in Solzhenitsyn. It is not the revelation of the concentration camps, because we already knew about those. Rather it is Solzhenitsyn's teaching on how to resist the *gulag*, how to perceive it from inside the system.'

'If there is one thing new, it is to be found in Solzhenitsyn.' That is the genuinely unexpected position. It must surely have something to do with the fact that Solzhenitsyn's own career has been so striking. Like Bonhoeffer, he has had an opportunity to 'double' his own communication. His life in the Gulag makes sense in terms of his novels, and his novels in turn throw into relief the physical and continued existence of the Gulag. The sudden and violent expulsion from Russia, the arrival in Germany, being pursued by reporters, the flight to Sweden and to the United States, the outright denunciation of American foreign policy in crisply argued television interviews; all this made Solzhenitsyn's physical appearance on the Western political scene so much more dialectically charged. He managed to disappoint the hopes of all his supporters in the West, who were dismayed when they found themselves the butt of his scorn; and in turning the tables in this abrupt fashion, Solzhenitsyn deliberately made his own central contention about the corruption of Russia the more biting. It was not (it became clear through the constant vision of that mournful form and melancholic face on Western television screens) that Solzhenitsyn wished to enjoy the fruits of a free and prosperous Western environment. No. He despised that, if anything, more than he despised the party bosses in the Kremlin. Utterly determined to negate the hopes of all his Western fans, Solzhenitsyn turned on them savagely and berated them for intellectual sloth and emotional cowardice. Never has any man used the dialectical possibilities inherent in a sudden deportation from East to West with such shattering lack of compromise.

The fact that the disaffected French Marxists see their common rallying point in Solzhenitsyn is a tribute to the immense authority with which he manipulates his communication. The hidden or inner 'side' to his communication takes its start from certain deeply held beliefs, which Solzhenitsyn rarely spells out. But it was there in *The Gulag Archipelago* for anyone who was looking for it, in the most disturbing chapter of all, that called 'The Bluecaps':

> So let the reader who expects this book to be a political exposé slam its covers shut right now.
>
> If only it were all so simple! If only there were evil people somewhere insidiously committing evil deeds, and it were necessary only to separate them from the rest of us and destroy them. But the line dividing good and evil cuts through the heart of every human being. And who is willing to destroy a piece of his own heart?
>
> During the life of any heart this line keeps changing place; sometimes it is squeezed one way by exuberant evil and sometimes it shifts to allow enough space for good to flourish. One and the same human being is, at various ages, under various circumstances, a totally different human being. At times he is close to being a devil, at times to sainthood. But his name doesn't change, and to that name we ascribe the whole lot, good and evil.
>
> Socrates taught us: *Know thyself!*
>
> Confronted by the pit into which we were about to toss those who have done us harm, we halt stricken dumb: it is after all only because of the way things worked out that they were the executioners and we weren't.[7]

It is because Solzhenitsyn has a sufficiently profound understanding of what he is considering *not* to make the simple damning indictment the reader of the *Gulag* feels so often tempted to make, that he has had such a powerful, indirect and religious effect on the French new philosophers. For their 'recognition' of him is indeed a further proof of the fact that religious competence is incapable of being repressed, that it keeps on surging back and back and recreating the world in the light of its own understanding. The *Time* article cites Jean-Paul Dollé as saying: 'We are in a very Socratic period. From bistro to bistro, people are asking all the important questions of life. What good is a nuclear breeder reactor? What is a woman's true identity?' That reference to Socrates picks up the other one, in Solzhenitsyn's own text. What good is it to condemn evil in others, when one doesn't realize its potential for harm in oneself? This metaphysical realization is itself part of a renascent religious competence in action: that is why the new philosophers in France are not interested in condemning an existing structure in political terms, but are delving down to where the evil lies, in human hearts. The evil that is visible everywhere in the world.

⁷  A. Solzhenitsyn, *The Gulag Archipelago*, Collins, London, 1974, p. 168.

Solzhenitsyn's own text cited above is in the major tradition of Russian realist fiction, and its moral profundity makes one think of the passage in Dostoevsky where Father Zossima goes down on his knees to Ivan, recognizing his evil and the suffering that awaits him because of it. Solzhenitsyn's adept use of the ambiguities present and potent in the heart of all men has triggered off a recognition in the French 'new philosophers' that the phenomenon of evil is too big for any one social or political philosophy to contain and to explain satisfactorily, that one needs a deeper kind of understanding of human beings. It does not seem to me at all likely that the new philosophy in France will end us as a religious philosophy, but that does not affect the fact that it is a profoundly religious man who has forced them, by his sheer honesty alone, to look again at a half century of political self-deception, and to condemn Marxism and Stalinism as unworthy to lead us into any decent future.

It is in the body that the sign begins and ends. The body is the outward and visible form of a reality which the body expresses. It is interesting in this respect that it is precisely on the question of the embodiment of Christ that the most contemporary theology has run into thick controversy. And behind the bodies of Dietrich Bonhoeffer, of Mother Teresa of Calcutta, and of Alexander Solzhenitsyn, we have intermittently seen the body of Christ. Mother Teresa, in her talks with Malcolm Muggeridge, makes the point explicitly:

> 'Also side by side with the spiritual training, they (the Sisters) have to go to the slums. Slum work and this meeting with the people is a part of the noviciate training. This is something special to us as a congregation because as a rule novices do not go out, but to be able to understand the meaning of our fourth vow, which promises that we give our whole hearted free service to the poorest of the poor—to Christ in his distressing disguise. Because of this it is necessary that they come face to face with the reality, so as to be able to understand what their life is going to be, when they will have taken their vows and when they will have to meet Christ twenty-four hours a day in the poorest of the poor in the slums.'[8]

Just as the body and figure of Christ hover behind the figure of a Bonhoeffer or of a Solzhenitsyn, so does that body hover in and inhere in the body of 'the poorest of the poor—Christ in his distressing disguise', as Mother Teresa puts it. She is certainly drawing forth one of the meanings of Matthew 25, 35-40:

> 35 For I was an hungred, and ye gave me meat: I was thirsty, and ye gave me drink: I was a stranger, and ye took me in:

---

[8]  M. Muggeridge, *Something Beautiful for God*, Collins, London, 1972, p. 97.

36 Naked, and ye clothed me: I was sick, and ye visited me: I was in prison, and ye came unto me.

40 . . . Verily I say unto you, Inasmuch as ye have done *it* unto one of the least of these my brethren, ye have done *it* unto me.

Mother Teresa has picked out the affinity between the body of Christ and the body of the distressed in contemporary Calcutta. She does not see the body of the leper, the abandoned child or the old man left to die in the gutter, she sees the presence of embodied Christ, directly. This act of transformation is possible only because of the mutual embodiment of Christ and leper: the human form.

It is highly significant, in this connection, that contemporary theology should have chosen to engage fully with the problem of the incarnation of Christ. A recent collection of essays that has caused much controversy, *The Myth of God Incarnate*, proposes that the belief that Christ was God, the Second Person of the Trinity, made Man, is not necessarily an authentic part of Christian doctrine. Professor John Hick, the editor of the collection, sets the tone when he proposes the following:

> That Jesus was God the Son incarnate is not literally true, since it has no literal meaning, but it is an application to Jesus of a mythical concept whose function is analogous to that of the notion of divine sonship ascribed in the ancient world to a king.[9]

Since much rests on the concept of what a 'myth' is, Professor Hick says explicitly:

> The idea of divine incarnation is a mythological idea. And I am using the term 'myth' in the following sense: a myth is a story which is told but which is not literally true, or an idea or image which is applied to someone or something but which does not literally apply, but which invites a particular attitude in its hearers.[10]

This definition of 'myth' seems to me indistinguishable from a definition of 'a lie'. And there is a sense in which the whole discussion in *The Myth of God Incarnate* takes place at an enormous distance from observed incarnation of any sort. The term that contributors to the collection choose to centre on is the very term to which they give in fact no weight or value at all: incarnation precisely. But when Mother Teresa, who spends her life studying incarnation, says with breathtaking simplicity that the poorest of the poor are 'Christ in his

⁹  J. Hick, *The Myth of God Incarnate*, S.C.M. Press, London, 1977, p. 178.
¹⁰  *Op. cit.*, p. 178.

distressing disguise', she perceives in the wretched incarnations before her, directly, the divine presence itself. For her, God Incarnate is not a myth, but a daily reality.

*The Myth of God Incarnate* called forth, within the year, an angry volume of contention and rebuttal, *The Truth of God Incarnate.*[11] Although the contributors to this volume have chosen to maintain the thornier of the two possible contentions, they write with point and wit. Michael Green, the editor of the collection, traces the presence of attributions of divinity to the body of Christ in the writings of St Paul; and, for me, one of the pleasures of following this debate has been to be sent back to read and ponder the enormously charged language about the body which St Paul uses to describe Christ and Christians in the world. Like Blake, St Paul sees not so much with the eye as through it. Everything is charged to the highest degree with incarnation, which is itself spiritual substance straining to transcend the limitations of its physical form. Thus Paul, observing Christ in the world, observes spiritual substance in action. Thus the Christians to whom he writes, the backsliders, the weak of faith, the corrupt, the vacillating, St Paul rallies with enormously earthy and racy language which never leaves the image of the body for long. 'For God is my record, how greatly I long after you all in the bowels of Jesus Christ', he writes in Philippians 1,8. And he can carry out the rapid conceptual transitions between abstraction and presence with tremendous brio and gusto: '(I, Paul) Who now rejoice in my sufferings for you, and fill up that which is behind of the afflictions of Christ in my flesh for his body's sake, which is the church', as he writes in Colossians 1,24.

It is not surprising, then, that Professor Green leans very heavily on the language St Paul uses to describe Christ in the world. St Paul, in his use of language, attributes divinity directly to the body of Christ. And Professor Green cites, among other things, Colossians 2, 9: 'For in him dwelleth all the fulness of the Godhead bodily.'

The contributors to *The Truth of God Incarnate* may well be holding on to the least popular and the least palatable of the two possible contentions, but they remain rather cannily much nearer to the specificity of the incarnation of Christ. Professor Hick urged in his collection that

> It seems clear that we are being called today to attain a global religious vision which is aware of the unity of all mankind before God and which

[11]   M. Green, *The Truth of God Incarnate*, Hodder and Stoughton, London, 1977.

at the same time makes sense of the diversity of God's ways within the various streams of human life.[12]

For this reason, it seems eminently reasonable to Professor Hick to regard all religions as having roughly the same importance. 'We should gladly acknowledge that Ultimate Reality has affected human consciousness for its liberation or "salvation" in various ways within the Indian, the semitic, the Chinese, the African . . . forms of life.'[13]

With its happy reliance on that last Wittgensteinian formulation, this proposition seems to me to be indistinguishable from explicit pantheism. Provoked, no doubt, by passages like this throughout the Hick collection, Professor Green emphasizes that the real issue being debated is the one between specific Christianity and oceanic pantheism. He writes, for instance:

> There is a sense in which much that passes for Christianity today is not Christianity at all but a form of Hinduism . . . And once we lose sight of the particularity of Jesus and salvation through God become man in him, then our faith becomes just one more stream emptying itself in the sea of Hinduism. What survives may make Christian sounding noises, but it will no longer be Christianity. The nerve of the faith, God made manifest in the flesh, will have been cut.[14]

How the debate will develop one cannot yet say. But that the debate has chosen to centre just *here*, on the very incarnation of Christ and its divine or non-divine nature, is itself highly significant. The body is all we have, so to speak, to look at the divine in terms of.

But the question can be led far deeper than either of the two volumes have yet gone. For if the poorest of the poor are 'Christ in his distressing disguise', and the *Imitatio Christi* is the presence of Christ in his most sublime manner, what emerges from that is that it is through the body that we catch a glimpse of the divine at all. And it seems to me that the body is capable of creating divinity, of calling divinity into existence. It can be argued for centuries (and it has been) what form of divinity inhered in the physical mantle that the carpenter from Nazareth inhabited, and no answer will ever be susceptible of finality or proof. But no one ever doubts that what preached, walked, ate, and was finally nailed on to a cross was a human body. It is that body, very precisely, which creates the possibility that Jesus was in the divine, or in contact with the divine, or that he actually through his act called the divine into existence. It is human beings who do

[12] *The Myth of God Incarnate*, p. 180.
[13] *The Myth of God Incarnate*, p. 181.
[14] *The Truth of God Incarnate*, p. 115.

this. Christ's human or bodily nature is never in traditional theological debate thrown into question, but rather the divine element in that embodiment. I suggest that the question ought to be inverted. What was it in the body of Christ that allowed him to be perceived as divine at all?

For he was perceived as divine. Of that at least there is documentary evidence in the four gospels, the Acts, Revelation and the Letters of St Paul. Indeed, as Michael Green asserts with great vigour in *The Truth of God Incarnate*, St Paul's use of language explicitly makes the divine claim for the body of Christ as that body had been seen and listened to during its mission.

It is, however you regard it, undeniable that the physical membrane which the carpenter from Nazareth inhabited was attributed divinity by some who saw him, and some if not all who wrote about him or in his cause. *That* seems to me to be the interesting problem in the debate about the incarnation of Christ: not *whether or not* the divine inhabited a body of flesh and blood, but *in what way* it did. For bodies, like words, bring meaning into existence, and when body and word are suited to each other dialectically, a religious meaning too can be brought into existence. And that seems to me to be the most astonishing faculty of man, the most profoundly interesting quality in what it means to be human: that, through the use of and the perception of the human body, as it acts in social and political space, the divine itself can be called into being, and in a such a way, too, that belief is wrung, however unwillingly, from others.

There is religious competence. There is religious expertise in the management of the sign. But the most remarkable of all is something which has no name, but which could be called religious undeniability, the kind of feeling that Roman centurion must have had when, after watching the weather and certain other unusual phenomena which had occurred during the afternoon, he said 'Truly, this was the Son of God.'

But that feeling did not only happen once. It happens again and again. Suddenly, here and there, almost against one's will and certainly against one's better judgment, one catches glimpses of the divine, brought into being by the act of the human body.

# Essay 10

## David Holbrook

When we ask the question 'What is it to be human?' we are in fact raising the question of the nature of knowledge. There is today one unquestioned authority in the sphere of knowledge: science. But it seems that if we apply the procedures of science to the question of what it is to be human, we must end up with a very pessimistic and despairing answer. Everything is 'matter in motion' and nothing more, operating by chance and necessity; man's life is pointless and futile. So, science, a discipline for exploring the nature of the world out there, ends up for us as a metaphysic, even though it has no qualifications to do so. How do we escape this problem? Only by examining the nature of knowledge itself, and revising our approach to how and what we know, as I shall try to show.

Many people today feel trapped in what they believe to be an inescapable scientific view. This is based on reductionism. Reductionism is a procedure by which, for certain scientific purposes, everything is explained by being broken down into its parts and operations, so that living things are explained as 'nothing but' certain elements operating according to the laws of physics and chemistry. This is a perfectly valid and effective method; the fallacy is to suppose that everything can be understood in that way. The popular scientific view is also positivist: nothing exists that cannot be seen or measured. (We may recognize the fallacy in this whenever a scientist as a person relates to one of his family as a person rather than an aggregate of atoms, and recognizes such things as love and conscience as real.)

186

These approaches to reality are very much part of our Western philosophical tradition, and have been predominant since the Scientific Revolution of the seventeenth century, inspired by Gallileo, Newton and Descartes. No one wants to go back on this revolution; but what needs urgent re-examination is the 'model' of the human being, and the world it impresses upon us. The view of life it implies seems convincing because of the marvellous effectiveness of science. We hope that terrible scourges like cancer will eventually be conquered by microanalytical analysis of the mechanisms involved, and let us hope they are.

But there are other aspects of the world-view of science in this tradition that stand in the way of our understanding of truth in a more whole sense, as we shall see. For one thing, the view of the universe as a great machine operating by blind chance, in which man's moral being is without point, is in fact a modern myth developed by imaginative means and based on a misunderstanding of what science says, and of the nature of knowledge. Moreover, one component of this myth is our concept of ourselves as a kind of machine, in a universe which is a machine. This machine is to be understood as a machine, it evolved as a machine (as by selection of the more efficient parts of the mechanism) and we shall triumph over it as a machine. The subjective symbolism of this, in an industrial age, should be evident. I have even heard a scientist speak on the radio of the human being becoming able in the future to turn round a black hole, to extract energy from it. Such a fantasy —utterly unreal surely when one gathers that the postulated black hole is so dense even light cannot escape from it—is the kind of thing sometimes presented under the guise of science, exceeding the most impossible fantasies of the poet. Yet it is believed to be reasonable. It is obviously time to examine the subjective roots of scientific faith!

Since the universe presented to us by this kind of science has no place for human achievements, human culture, values, aspirations, creativity and spiritual yearnings, it seems to many that the only response is that of despair, futility and nihilism. Many desperate gestures in the world of today's culture originate in these feelings of powerlessness and pointlessness—even though they are really based on ignorance and misunderstanding. Thus, in the world of the arts in which one might expect human beings to be asserting a powerful sense of meaning, we have prostration. Francis Bacon the painter, for example, has said, 'I think that man now realizes he is an accident, that he is a completely futile being, that he has to play the game out without reason.'[1]

The assumed 'scientific' basis for such a statement becomes clearer when we read a critic like Anne Stevenson who declares that 'David Holbrook . . . must see himself as no more . . . than DNA's way of making more DNA'[2]—Crick and Watson having revealed that all life is composed of large molecules strung along a double helix, making up variants of DNA. According to this view, this is all we are; life can be reduced to chemistry, and because chemistry by its very nature can be reduced to physics, we can be reduced to nothing more than an expression of the laws of physics.[3] Only the smallest, invisible parts of things are allowed to be 'real'. This 'realism' is for the scientifically minded a defence against metaphysics; but, as we have seen, it becomes a metaphysic itself—and a very pessimistic and nihilistic one at that.

How do we begin to unravel this problem? First, perhaps, we need to remember ourselves. If mechanism were true, everything we do would be the 'product' of impersonal forces, of the laws of physics and chemistry, of biological drives, instincts, the impulse towards 'equilibrium', 'genetic coding' or genetic selfishness, aggression, sex, 'DNA' or 'social forces'. But we know that this is not so. For example, we are likely to jump up in a biology lesson and ask, as Viktor Frankl did when he was a young man, 'What meaning, then, does life have?'[4] If biology is reducible to chemistry and physics, what do we make of the statements 'Biology is reducible to physics' and 'Biology is not reducible to physics'? Obviously, when we turn to truth-statements, something else is operating other than natural laws. Both the reductionist and anti-reductionist exist, so they and their quest for truth cannot be the product of impersonal forces and natural laws.[5]

[1]  David Silvester, *Interviews with Francis Bacon*, Thames and Hudson, London, and Parthenon, New York, 1975, p. 28. Quotation taken from 'Ethics in Evolution' by Bernard Towers, a paper given at the Third Inter-Disciplinary Symposium on Philosophy and Medicine, University of Connecticut, December 1975.

[2]  Anne Stevenson, review of *Sylvia Plath: Poetry and Existence* by David Holbrook, 'A Matter of Life and Death', *Times Literary Supplement*, 12 November 1976, p. 1412.

[3]  F.H.C. Crick, *Of Molecules and Men*, University of Washington Press, Seattle, 1966.

[4]  Viktor Frankl, 'Reductionism and Nihilism' in *Beyond Reductionism: The Alpbach Symposium*, eds Arthur Koestler and John R. Smythies, Hutchinson, London, 1969, p. 399.

[5]  See 'Reducibility: Another Side Issue?' in *The Understanding of Nature: Essays in the Philosophy of Biology*, Marjorie Grene, D. Reidel Publishing Company, Dordrecht, Holland, and Boston, U.S.A., 1974.

There are, then, entities that operate to far more complex and autonomous dynamics, and the scientist's excitement and satisfaction with discoveries and hypotheses are themselves indications of the necessity to have a philosophy of life that is not the 'nothing but' reductivism of mechanism.*

When we turn to science, we in fact find that there are many points of view, and of these many are very much opposed to the reductivist or mechanistic viewpoint. Viktor Frankl's objections are perhaps now well known; but as an existentialist psychotherapist, it may be objected, he does not come to the problem from a strict scientific training. More impressive from that standpoint is the contribution to the Alpbach Symposium of Professor Paul A. Weiss, Emeritus Member and Professor, Rockefeller University, New York, who declared 'organisms are not just heaps of molecules. At least, I cannot bring myself to feel like one. Can you?'[6] Professor Weiss talked on the need for biology to enlarge its conceptual structure 'so as to be able not only to encompass living nature, but to fulfil the postulates raised by the realities of phenomena germane to living systems.'

What Professor Weiss is pointing to is the need for the multifarious complexity of life to be taken into account. There has, of course, always been an impulse in science to discover one unifying principle to all our knowledge; and to this end there have been a number of principles that have become combined into reductivism. Science is not allowed to tell us about the real world: instead of talking about thrushes or worms, we must talk about 'gene pools'. Science must tell us only about aggregates of phenomena, and about 'primary qualities' of which things are composed, their least parts. In everything we must find the 'atom', and our analysis must be particulate. Of course, as DNA analysis has shown, such particulate analysis can be most effective. Error creeps in, however, when such particulate analysis is extended over the whole field, rather than taken as a guide to how certain phenomena are produced. It is gradually dawning on scientists, not least in biology, that we cannot know the whole of Nature and cannot use the models that apply in one area to explain *everything*—as Anne Stevenson implies when she tells me I am simply DNA's way of making more DNA. Moreover, it is becoming clear that particulate analysis is not the one way to understand living systems.

---

* I am not, it should be noted, trying to revive vitalism or any other such mystical beliefs. There is nothing 'else' there besides matter.

[6] 'The Living System, determinism stratified' in *Beyond Reductionism: The Alpbach Symposium*, p. 42.

Many fallacies that pervade the Humanities and the Arts at the moment are, in fact, based on the ignorant application of a few scientific principles to our attitude to human nature. There is a misconception of the nineteenth century 'discovery' that 'nature is red in tooth and claw' as Tennyson put it. Then there is a widespread misunderstanding of the true meaning of 'the survival of the fittest' that is conceived of in terms simply of the physical prowess and aggressive tendencies of individual organisms.[7] In the title of the book *The Selfish Gene* (by Richard Dawkins, with a painting on the book jacket by Desmond Morris) we have an implication that our living world is 'the world of the gene machine' which is 'one of savage competition, ruthless exploitation, and deceit.' (from the blurb). Apparently, we 'are the only animals capable of seeing through the designs of the selfish genes and of rebelling against them'.[8] This brings us to the third naive assumption of the twentieth century, that because genetic mutations and recombinations that represent the 'pool' from which 'nature' selects are events based for the most part on chance, there can be no logic or order, no reason or significance to be discerned in evolution. All questions of 'higher beings' or progressive development towards 'higher states' of life, or teleological explanations which imply movement towards fulfilment or goal, are regarded, in the light of such assumptions, as being totally invalid. The only scientific metaphysic must be one of brutal, accidental and utterly purposeless existence.

The success of these nihilistic theories in attitudes to life at large is often attributed to the effects of Darwin's theories on belief. Perhaps, however, it was belief that was already declining—there was already

---

[7]    Bernard Towers, *op. cit.* Professor Towers is at the Department of Pediatrics and Anatomy, Center for the Health Sciences, University of California, Los Angeles.

[8]    Richard Dawkins, *The Selfish Gene*, Oxford University Press, 1976. The propaganda about this book put out by a university press may surely be questioned—because it brings university publishing down to the level of commercial gimmicks. The blurb, for example, tells us 'The world of the gene machine is one of savage competition . . . But what of the familiar examples of apparent altruism found throughout nature, from mothers who work themselves almost to death for their children, to small birds who risk their lives warning their flock of an approaching hawk? Richard Dawkins shows how they all result from the selfishness of genes, exploding the cosy view held for so long . . . ' etc. Such sensational nonsense is a falsification of science, because no such firm conclusions may be reached, for example, about human behaviour of such a complex kind as a mother's relationship with her children. This kind of disgraceful mumbo-jumbo for public consumption is a consequence of Desmond Morris's publishing success and the publicity methods used by his publisher; a university press ought surely not to capitulate to such vulgar distortion.

a depletion of faith, and the extrapolation of misunderstood scientific theories has rushed in to fill the gap, the *horror vacui*. As one critic points out, such theories as the 'survival of the fittest' are hypotheses put forward to explain such puzzling phenomena as the geographical distribution of plants and animals at various stages in certain areas, and the extinction of certain species and the survival of others. Such theories originally had no philosophical implications, but by degrees an orthodox evolutionary theory has developed that makes wider and wider claims about the nature and destiny of human beings, their being and becoming, and their position in the universe, and has become a philosophy.[9] Yet this philosophy of life lives with many self-contradictions. William Paley, in his *Natural Theology* (1802), argued that many complex organs were so beautifully designed and so perfectly adapted to the animal's need and environment, that they could only be the result of conscious design—design, therefore, by God. Evolutionary theory since has thrown Paley's watch-maker away: yet he (or He?) persists in 'scientific' form in many evolutionist arguments. For instance, in *Major Features of Evolution* G.G. Simpson said 'it is certain that if we can see any advantage whatever in a small variation (and sometimes even if we cannot), *selection sees more.*'[10] This endows a dynamic called 'selection' with foresight, so that it becomes God or watchmaker in disguise. And this kind of argument slips in often, as scientists are trying to account for developments. For instance, discussing the evolution of the human being in *Origins*, Dr Richard Leakey and Roger Lewin say 'The exigencies of life aloft must have given natural selection a particularly keen cutting edge, speeding along the process of evolving sophisticated mechanisms, such as an opposable thumb, for coping with the challenges of everyday life.'[11] Yet, in their own terms, 'what Darwin accomplished was to demonstrate how, through exceedingly gradual (passive) adaptations to the environment and through changes from generation to generation, a species may diversify or simply become better attuned to its world producing, ultimately, a creature which is different in form from its

---

[9]  Karl Stern, *The Flight From Woman*, Allen and Unwin, 1966, p. 289. See also E.W.F. Tomlin, 'Fallacies of Evolutionary Theory' in *The Encyclopaedia of Ignorance*, eds Ronald Duncan and Miranda Weston-Smith, Pergamon Press, 1977, p. 227.

[10]  G.G. Simpson, *Major Features of Evolution*, Columbia University Press, 1953, p. 271 (my italics). See also 'Two Evolutionary Theories', chapter VII in Marjorie Grene's *The Understanding of Nature*, p. 131.

[11]  Richard Leakey and Roger Lewin, *Origins, What New Discoveries Reveal About the Emergence of Our Species and Its Possible Future*, Macdonald and Janes, London, 1977, p. 41.

ancestor.'[12] But these processes can only operate by strictly passive or negative means, chance mutations coming into being and surviving or not surviving, as the case may be. Darwinian theory rejects the Lamarckian theory that, as it were, by continually stretching their necks towards food, giraffes could evolve a long neck. Thus it must be heretical surely to suggest that because primates went to live in the trees some kind of 'environmental pressure' would *generate* the opposable thumb. In millions and millions of years an opposable thumb might appear in one primate, and this might give an advantage which might persist through 'survival of the fittest'. But to suggest that such a complex and considerable change as the opposable thumb came into being—leapt forward, as it were, towards a new form— because so many primates without opposable thumbs fell down from the trees is absurd. Such fallacies are only possible because of a failure to look at forms, activities and processes, at morphology, in the 'category of life'.

Another important principle of Darwinism is that the theory of natural selection demands that organs are efficient at all stages of their evolutionary development; if they were not, their possessors would simply have become extinct.[13] This makes it very difficult to explain, for example, the origins of extremely complex organs such as the ear or the eye or feathers, which at the earlier stages of their growth might well not have contributed any advantages to the organism. In *Evolution Explained*, Peter Hutchinson delineates how the ear bones, the malleus, incus and stapes, could have been produced in successive organisms by the kind of random variation which is the crux of Darwinian evolutionary theory. But he does not answer the question as to why such complex developments should have taken place when they conferred no immediate advantage—certainly not one that might have enabled those with the new rudimentary ears to survive better than those without.

The truth, as Marjorie Grene makes plain, is that throughout evolutionary history there are evident leaps forward in development —photosynthesis, breathing and thinking, for example—for which orthodox Darwinian theory can provide no explanation.[14] Darwinian theory can explain minute particular developments such as the survival

---

[12]  *Ibid*, p. 30.

[13]  Peter Hutchinson, *Evolution Explained*, David and Charles, Newton Abbot, 1974, p. 160.

[14]  Marjorie Grene, *The Knower and the Known*, Faber and Faber, London, 1966, chapter 7 'The Faith of Darwinism', especially pp. 196ff.

of dark moths in sooty environments and so forth. But for the major developments in evolution it provides no answers; on the biggest issue of all, as to why there should be mice, birds, elephants and men *at all*, it can say nothing.

Yet evolutionary theory and the 'chance and necessity' principle have become today's unquestionable dogmas. As many have pointed out, from Viktor Frankl to Karl Stern, scientific method cannot even be applied to such questions as the origin of the world and life, the infinite variety of forms, the destiny of the human being, the presence of hate and corruption and their co-existence (as Stern says) in the world with love and beauty—whatever breath-taking results scientific method may have obtained in our analysis and control of the world. Scientists and philosophers of the strictly positivist school even deny the genuineness and validity of such problems—they are 'pseudo-problems', even though to you and me they are such burning questions that we cannot live unless we try to solve them.

The 'objectivity' towards which science strives cannot deal with them. As Stern says, the processes of being and becoming, because these are 'inward' questions, resist the objective analysis. Yet in the face of this predicament, we are asked to believe a 'scientific' picture of the world which has become a metaphysic, yet which is in truth absurd. Indeed, it is worse than absurd: it is really quite mad. Here I am not using the word 'mad' merely as a term of abuse. Psychoanalysts like Harry Guntrip have indicated there are schizoid elements in science,[15] while even Michael Polanyi has spoken of the 'pathology' of science.[16] Karl Stern accuses the view in 'science' of cosmogenesis of being 'crazy'. 'And I do not mean crazy in the sense of slangy invective, but rather in the technical meaning of psychotic.'[17] He characterises this world picture thus:

> At a certain moment of time the temperature of the Earth was such that it became most favourable for the aggregation of carbon atoms and oxygen with the nitrogen-hydrogen combination, and that from random occurences of large clusters molecules occured which were most favourably structured for the coming about of life, and from that point it went on through vast stretches of time, until through processes of natural selection, a being finally occured which is capable of choosing love over hate and justice over injustice,

[15]   Harry Guntrip, *Schizoid Phenomena, Object-relations and the Self*, Hogarth Press, 1968, passim.

[16]   Michael Polanyi, *Science, Faith and Society*, University of Chicago Press, 1946; *The Study of Man*, University of Chicago Press, 1958; *The Tacit Dimension*, Routledge, 1967.

[17]   *The Flight from Woman*, p. 290.

of writing poetry like that of Dante, composing music like that of Mozart and making drawings like that of Leonardo.

We do not have to go as far as this, says Stern: 'I have a certain number of years ago been a single cell, microscopically small, and now I sit at a desk writing. Millions of data from the cumulative sciences form a fearfully intricate net of causalities to tackle this mystery but *my being and becoming are not caught in that net*'[18]— but it is from imagining ourselves caught in this net we need to escape.

As Stern points out, the idea that all living things are random points of arrestation in a blind mechanism of physical occurrences, governed by pragmatic advantages, is the expression of the Cartesian objectification of living things. It is a product of a whole philosophical tradition that has found only geometry to be real, together with the atomistic micro-mechanistic explanation of life, so that the concept of 'wholeness' has been lost; and with wholeness, the recognition that in any living system the whole is more than the sum of its parts, not in any mathematical sense but in terms of the collective behaviour of highly complex living *systems*. No living system can really be understood apart from its whole ecological context, while important aspects of its existence, such as intentionality in lived time, are lost in mechanistic approaches.[19] Exploring the question 'What is Life?', Erwin Schrodinger came to the conclusion 'I . . . that is to say every conscious mind which has ever said or felt "I" . . . am the person, if any, who controls the "motion of the atoms" according to the laws of nature.'[20] George Wald, a Harvard biochemist and Nobel Laureate, put it another way when he said 'It would be a poor thing to be an atom in a universe without physicists. And physicists are made of atoms. A physicist is the atom's way of knowing about atoms.'[21]

And not only may we restore intentionality by putting human beings back into the picture, and the 'kind of consciousness' the higher animals have. Many scientists find the urge towards potentialities as yet unrealized a fundamental property of matter itself. David Layzer, for example, argues that matter when seen in 'duration' inevitably tends to arrange itself in groupings and hierarchies of increasing order, of increasing complexity, of increasing information. In an article in

[18]   *Ibid* (my italics).
[19]   See Weiss in *Beyond Reductionism: The Alpbach Symposium*.
[20]   Erwin Schrodinger, *What is Life? The Physical Aspect of the Living Cell*, Cambridge University Press, 1945.
[21]   George Wald, Introduction to *The Fitness of the Environment: An Inquiry into the Significance of the Properties of Matter*, new edition, L.J. Henderson; first published by Beacon Press, Boston, U.S.A., 1931.

the *Scientific American*[22] he writes 'The present moment always contains an element of genuine novelty and the future is never wholly predictable. Because biological processes also generate information and because consciousness enables us to experience those processes directly, the intuitive perception of the world as unfolding in time captures one of the most deep-seated properties of the universe.' Other philosophers have drawn attention to the problem of the dimension of time as it is missing from much mechanistic thinking: Professor Marjorie Grene and Maurice Merleau-Ponty, the French phenomenological thinker.[23]

The 'chance and necessity' concept of the universe and human beings in it, then, is extremely naive: if simple mechanism were true, and the environmental and genetic determinists were right, then the only appropriate response would be despair, nihilism and a sense of futility. But surely we should accept such a picture as the true one only if it squared with our ordinary everyday experience—and the abstract, micro-reductionist approach does not. Can we really believe, if we look at only the best achievements of human beings, and especially of science, that it is a profound truth that 'nature does *not* know best; that genetical evolution . . . is a story of waste, makeshift, compromise and blunder'?[24] If man is a waste and a blunder, how is it Peter Medawar can give a Reith Lecture over the marvellous system of wireless communication?

Sophisticated Darwinians like Konrad Lorenz assume without question that the origin and formation of species can be explained as a succession of fortuitous variations and mutations passing through the mesh of selection, as Professor E.F.W. Tomlin points out in an essay on 'Fallacies of Evolutionary Theory'.[25] But as Tomlin argues, there are many well-concealed assumptions in the theory, one being that negative elimination of unfavourable mutations is enough to explain the development of new forms. Evolution offers a single unified process: yet we are expected to believe that while the growth of each individual animal is an ordered process, the growth of a species can happen only by accident. While science everywhere displays order and coherence, and ontogenesis may be ordered, phylogenesis must remain

[22]  David Layzer, 'The Arrow of Time', *Scientific American*, 233, 6, 56–59, 1975.
[23]  Maurice Merleau-Ponty, *Phenomenology of Perception*, Routledge and Kegan Paul, London, 1962, 'Temporality', pp. 410ff. See also Marjorie Grene on Merleau-Ponty on Time, *The Knower and the Known*, chapter 9 'Time and Teleology'.
[24]  Peter B. Medawar, *The Future of Man*, Reith Lectures, 1959, Methuen, London.
[25]  E.W.F. Tomlin, 'Fallacies of Evolutionary Theory' in *The Encyclopaedia of Ignorance*, p. 227.

a chance matter of trial and error, yet with the negative dynamic assuming a positive role. And even in this we find a new watchmaker: 'selection is one of the great constructors of evolution. The other constructor is mutation.'[26] Any recognition of the dynamic of growth and development is described in some such terms as 'apparent purpose' —a term Dr Julien Huxley uses, as Tomlin points out, without defining it or saying why it is only 'apparent'.

Anything may be allowed, that is, except a recognition of what is clearly evident from normal observation: the impulse of life towards ever-developing multifarious forms, higher organization, and self-consciousness, the fact that 'life strives'. This principle is recognized by Michael Polanyi and Professor Marjorie Grene.[27] Polanyi writes 'the process must have been directed by an *orderly innovating principle,* the action of which could only have been *released* by the random effects of molecular agitations and photons coming from outside, and the operation of which could only have been *sustained* by a favourable environment.'[28] Teilhard de Chardin argued that if there were not built into matter (even in its simplest form) the possibility of combination and co-inherence with other matter, and further that if there not built into matter-in-time an inherent tendency to form increasingly complex systems by such advancing integration, then self-reflective consciousness as we know it in human beings would never have been possible.

Thus in many spheres of scientific and philosophical thought, human beings are striving towards a more adequate view of the evolutionary process and of our place in the universe. Tomlin argues that 'The entire microphysical world is now seen to come within the organic sphere, revealing a "line of continuity" between all individuals or being.'[29] All evolution is an 'interior' process, characterized by thematism (that is, the recognizable similarities in bone and other

---

[26] Konrad Lorenz, *On Aggression*, Methuen, London, 1966.

[27] Marjorie Grene, *Approaches to a Philosophical Biology*, Basic Books, New York, 1968, passim; Michael Polanyi and Harry Prosch, *Meaning*, University of Chicago Press, 1975. Polanyi somewhere draws a comparison between an elephant and a thunderstorm: the latter only seems self-supporting as a system; the elephant is autonomous in the way life is—life in this sense transcending physics and chemistry. Polanyi declares that anyone who cannot see the difference between an elephant and a thunderstorm could not easily be persuaded that 'life strives' and is thus different from other systems. See also, on such questions, W.H. Thorpe, *Animal Nature and Human Nature*, Methuen, London, 1974.

[28] Michael Polanyi, *Personal Knowledge*, Routledge, London, 1958, p. 386. The italics are those of E.W.F. Tomlin.

[29] E.W.F. Tomlin, *op. cit.*, p. 227.

structures). The present impasse in evolutionary thinking is because of the interpretation of biological facts in terms of out-of-date physical theory, and because of attempts to find one unifying principle to explain the whole of nature, especially in micro-reductionist and mechanistic terms. These may be false goals, but they are preserved by extraordinary fallacies, which are clung to with dogmatic fanaticism. A book which demonstrates this is Norman Macbeth's *Darwin Retried*.[30] He shows that scientists often cling to evolutionary theories that are clearly full of holes, because there is no other explanation. (As Macbeth points out, the lack of an alternative is no justification, for of course any explanation which does not hold water should be abandoned easily at once, by the very tenets of positivist science itself. This does not happen, however, over evolutionary theory.) Some evolutionary theories are simply tautologous, as is the fundamental belief in 'survival of the fittest'. (What is the fittest? That which survives.) We find this kind of argument even in the best books: I found an example in Dr Leakey's *Origins*: 'The keen selection pressures of this new ecological niche must have produced a basic stock that was superbly adapted to the new environment, for we have the highly successful primate order to prove it'.[31] Evolutionary theory may be an attempt to show how the 'highly successful primate order' came into being: but it does not demonstrate the accuracy of the hypothesis (of 'survival of the fittest') to point to that successful order's existence, because it is from this fact that one begins, in trying to explain how it came into being. Today, many of the opinions of evolutionists depend upon blind faith, as Professor Otto Frisch demonstrates, in his essay in the *Encyclopaedia of Ignorance*: discussing the development of feathers, he says 'Even if a very unlikely mutation caused a reptile to have offspring with feathers instead of scales, what good would that do, without muscles to move them and a brain rebuilt to control those muscles? *We can only guess* . . . Much about the process of evolution is still unknown; but I have no doubt that natural selection provides the justification for teleological answers.'[32] In such faith we have something akin to deference to Papal infallibility. As Tomlin says, Darwinism hardened into dogma, before it had been thoroughly analyzed. Norman Macbeth exposes the ridiculous consequences—yet the scientists still do not even blush, and certainly do not recant.

[30] Norman Macbeth, *Darwin Retried*, Garnstone Press, London, 1976.
[31] Richard Leakey and Roger Lewin, *op. cit.*, p. 41.
[32] Otto R. Frisch, 'Why', *The Encyclopaedia of Ignorance*, p. 3 (my italics).

Here an important chapter in writing about the philosophy of science is that on 'Order' in Michael Polanyi's last book, *Meaning*.[33] In this, he points out that although there have been teleological arguments about the nature of life, the modern mind has turned against these, in favour of mechanical explanations, combined with the metaphysical view that life is pointless and absurd. From this it is only a step towards a completely behaviouristic approach to psychology, in which it is possible to abandon all 'mentalistic' talk of purposes or aims or goals in the discussion of animal or human behaviour. A major influence here is the belief that micro-analysis as of 'DNA' demonstrates that all explanations other than the mechanical are absurd. But Polanyi, who was himself a distinguished chemist, points out that the operations of DNA cannot be the product of the laws of physics and chemistry: life transcends physics and chemistry. The 'code messages' which are a part of the DNA-RNA operation cannot be merely the product of physical forces, because these could only produce 'noise'. 'Codes' imply a message, and the message implies a hierarchical principle. This requires a recognition of processes and structures in life-stuff which cannot be understood as reductions to chemical and physical laws though there is nothing else there other than matter. It is rather that while DNA molecules obey physical laws, they also obey other laws. We cannot, for example, tell by chemical and physical analysis what is the function of certain human tools: much less likely, then, it is that we can tell how complex organisms function by a mere physical analysis. Moreover, we are only interested in the arrangements of the molecules because of the secret of their life-messages: Polanyi elsewhere uses the analogy of some stones arranged on a railway station to read 'Welcome to Wales'.[34] We are only interested in them because of their order— and the way they 'belong' to a human social and personal order in which language is used, to *mean*. We are not interested in the stones before they were arranged, nor in how they will lie about after the line is closed. But the arrangement, which forms the message, implies enormously complex meanings, relationships and dynamics in another dimension. When we come to the 'message' of DNA, it not only belongs to the processes of replication, and simple growth; it also becomes capable of modification under certain circumstances. Some organisms, for example, will 'press' certain cells into use in a quite different form, if there is a catastrophe. In embryonic growth, there

[33]   Michael Polanyi and Harry Prosch, *Meaning*, p. 163.
[34]   Michael Polanyi, *Personal Knowledge*.

are many different processes which develop at different times. As Crick himself writes, 'At the molecular level we understand some of the most fundamental developmental processes . . . But how an organism constructs a hand, with its thumb and forefingers, with all the bones, the muscles and the nerves, all assembled and correctly connected together, that we cannot explain . . . '[35]

To recognize these 'other' dimensions in which living organisms operate is to recognize order, to recognize that hierarchical order in living things which makes biology so very different from the physical sciences. And if we put man the scientist back into the picture, as part of the animal world and as a complex dynamic manifestation of matter, then we restore meaning to that world. Man and his culture become manifestations of the autonomous 'centricity' of all living things. As Polanyi says, 'We can now understand scientific enquiry as being a thrust of our mind towards a more and more meaningful integration of cues . . . living things, individually and in general, are also orientated toward meaning, and it is clear, from our immediately preceding chapters, that man's whole cultural framework, including his symbols, his language arts, his fine arts, his rites, his celebrations and his religions, constitutes a vast complex of efforts—on the whole successful—at achieving every kind of meaning.'[36] How different from the emphasis in today's culture!

Nothing could be more absurd, than the primary expression of nature's impulse towards meaning, man, using his science to declare the world meaningless and his existence absurd. Polanyi concludes that 'We might justifiably claim . . . that everything we know is *full* of meaning, is not absurd at all, although we can sometimes fail to grasp these meanings and fall into absurdities. In other words, meaning can be missed, since the emergence of life opens up the possibility of success but also, of course, the chance of failure.' The principle that 'life strives' also has the corollary that 'life can fail' —but in the dichotomy lies the generation of freedom, without which life is nothing. Polanyi concludes his chapter by saying that he and his co-author have tried to show that 'modern science cannot properly be understood to tell us that the world is meaningless and pointless, that it is absurd. The supposition that it is absurd is a modern myth, created imaginatively from the clues produced by a profound misunderstanding of what science and knowledge are and what they require, a misunderstanding spawned by positivistic left-overs in our thinking

[35]  F.H.C. Crick, 'Developmental Biology', *The Encyclopaedia of Ignorance*, p. 303.
[36]  Michael Polanyi and Harry Prosch, *Meaning*, pp. 178-9.

and by allegiance to the false ideal of objectivity from which we have been unable to shake ourselves quite free. These are the stoppages in our ears we must pull out if we are ever once more to experience the full range of meanings possible to man.'[37]

Polanyi's kind of emphasis is found in a whole area of what may be called 'philosophical anthropology'. Perhaps the best introduction to this field of study is Marjorie's Grene's *Approaches to a Philosophical Biology*. In this she, a disciple of Polanyi's, examines the work of a number of biologists in Europe and America whose approach is very different from the narrow reductionist one of British traditions. These include Adolf Portmann, Helmuth Plessner, F.J.J. Buytendijk, Erwin W. Strauss and Kurt Goldstein. These are, roughly speaking, in the European tradition to which such figures as Wilhelm Dilthey and Edmund Husserl belong. The emphasis is on man's place in the animal kingdom, but on his special dimension of culture and symbolism. We are biologically formed to be cultural animals, and our pattern of development is unique among mammals. Our consciousness, however, is a development of the 'kind of consciousness' found in the higher animals. But this emerges from forms of inter-relationship: 'communion is constitutive of the person'. Because of this primary element in his development, man is by nature a moral being. The rhythm of our growth is directed towards the emergence of a culture-dwelling animal, and this is expressed even in the structure of our anatomy: our upright posture, for example, is a manifestation of our stance towards the world, our openness to it and our responsibility towards it. A great deal of Professor Grene's book is devoted to a consideration of what kind of new approach to knowledge is required in biology and especially in the study of man, to encompass those elements of consciousness and meaning which appear primary to those with whom she is dealing. In this re-examination of the nature of knowledge, this book parallels her *The Knower and the Known*, which again is concerned to heal some of the inadequacies of the Newtonian-Cartesian tradition, which left us with a world in which man, his achievements and aspirations, had no place.

The mechanistic, matter-in-motion determined homunculus, which is the 'model' of man in positivist science, lacks all those characteristics which make life worth living. Chief among these is 'intentionality', a concept from Edmund Husserl—the creative movement towards the

---

[37]    *Ibid*, p. 181.

future. Husserl is a central figure in philosophical anthropology. His *Crisis of European Sciences* opens with the declaration that the objective sciences have lost sight of man, thus betraying the original *telos* of Greek philosophy, when it set out to find the whole truth of existence. Scientific objective truth is exclusively a matter of establishing what the world, the physical as well as the spiritual world, is in fact. 'But can the world, and human existence in it, truthfully have a meaning, if the sciences recognize as true only what is established in this fashion, and if history has nothing to teach us than that all the spiritual world, all the conditions of life, ideals, norms upon which man relies, form and dissolve themselves like fleeting waves, that it always was and ever will be so, that again and again reason must turn into nonsense, and well-being into misery? Can we console ourselves with that?'[38] Husserl asks us to be 'functionaries of mankind': 'The quite personal responsibility of our own true being as philosophers, our own inner personal vocation, bears within itself at the same time the responsibility for the true being of mankind.'[39] We must seek something to believe in: and this, too, is Polanyi's emphasis—indeed, Polanyi's importance is that he stresses that there is no reason why we should not find meanings which are more than mere 'sandcastles' to be swept away on the next tide of 'matter in motion'.[40]

In the work of Husserl there are developments that parallel those of Polanyi, then, and also those in the thought of Maurice Merleau-Ponty. In the area of 'reflective philosophy', in 'Continental philosophy', in existentialism and phenomenology, an immense revolution is going on, while in philosophical biology there is a quest for a new kind of science which can find and speak of living things— as the symposium *Against Reductionism* shows. At the moment, resistance is still strong, especially in Britain, which is the one blank spot in the spread of phenomenology, as Professor Herbert Spiegelberg registers.[41] However, interest is growing—in the kind of perspective indicated by Marjorie Grene:

> Whatever I succeed in knowing, it is *I* who achieve knowledge, I in my contingent, personal existence, I-in-situation. Such an 'I' is alive. 'Minding' as Ryle called it, is one form of living, and can be understood only as

[38]   Edmund Husserl, *The Crisis of European Sciences and Transcendental Phenomenology*, Northwestern University Press, Evanston, U.S.A., 1970, p. 7.
[39]   *Ibid*, p. 17.
[40]   *Meaning*, p. 162.
[41]   Herbert Spiegelberg, *The Phenomenological Movement*, Nijhoff, The Hague, 1965; *Phenomenology in Psychology and Psychiatry*, Northwestern University Press, 1972.

a species within that genus. But living, in turn, is one kind of natural being.[42]

There is never anything else other than persons knowing: human scientists seeking the truth. There is never any 'objective' body of 'real truth' to which we have to defer. So, the answer to the question 'What is it to be human?' requires an answer that concerns itself with new approaches to knowing, and in this a considerable conceptual reform is necessary.

The point has been made in various other spheres. It is made by Professor Ernst Cassirer, for example, in his *An Essay on Man*[43] in which he asks for man to be defined as the *animal symbolicum*. The natural sciences, he declares, have shown that they cannot give an adequate account of man. Only when we take into account man's cultural dimension, his symbols and meaning, can we begin to understand what it may be that unites all the multifarious findings about humanity which so far lack an organising principle. The same view is taken by Cassirer's disciple, Susanne Langer, and together they tackle Kant's fourth question, 'What is man?' She believes that symbolism is a primary need in man, as urgent in his life as the need for food.[44]

In psychiatry there is a parallel movement, towards rejecting the ideals of 'objective' science and natural scientistic approaches to man's inner life, in favour of subjective disciplines. Ernst Cassirer's work provides a starting point for Jan Foudraine, for instance, in his book *Not Made of Wood*.[45] Foudraine asks psychiatry to think of itself as a form of education for people with life-problems, rather than as a medical science which 'treats' 'patients'. Parallel points are made in psychology by Professor Liam Hudson in *The Cult of the Fact*[46], by the authors of *Training Tomorrow's Psychiatrist*[47], Maurice Edelstone and Thomas Lidz, and by Dr Peter Lomas, in his *True and False Self*[48] and other works.

The influence of psychoanalytical approaches to human meaning and symbolism is beginning to be felt in philosophy. Professor E.A. Burtt grasps the nettle firmly in his book *In Search of Philosophic Understanding*:

[42]   *The Knower and the Known*, p. 185.
[43]   Ernst Cassirer, *An Essay on Man*, Yale University Press, 1944.
[44]   Susanne Langer, *Philosophy in a New Key*, Harvard University Press, 1963.
[45]   Jan Foudraine, *Not Made of Wood*, Quarter Books, 1971.
[46]   Liam Hudson, *The Cult of the Fact*, Jonathan Cape, 1972.
[47]   Maurice Edelstone and Thomas Lidz, *Training Tomorrow's Psychiatrist*, Yale University Press, 1970.
[48]   Peter Lomas, *True and False Self*, Allen Lane, London, 1973.

The most provocative note in the findings I wish to share is the conviction that philosophy must come fully to terms with the psychoanalytical concept of the human mind.[49]

The crucial fact cannot be ignored that 'behind anyone's thinking there are unconscious motives, to be taken into account beside the desire for truth.' Professor Burtt links the disciplines of psychoanalysis with those of existentialism. Greek thought was basically a theory of *being*: during modern times it has been mainly a quest for *method*. Philosophy, in the existentialist tradition, has come again to explore the nature of being, and is seeking to cure the disastrous split between 'science' and philosophy as the exploration of the whole truth of man. And then Burtt takes the plunge into a sphere which is anathema to traditional established philosophy: love. Our key to understanding in this realm of being is the experience of love—a central theme in both psychoanalysis and existentialism. As a child, man's consuming need is to be loved, so that he can find his way from anxiety, frustration and anger in the presence of the harsh realities that surround him, to an acceptance of an adult role in the universe. This is the theme not only of religious existentialism but also of non-religious forms. Since Kierkegaard, existentialism has offered a chance to people, to embark on the quest for their own self-realization—and for a sense of meaning in their lives. So, as Burtt points out, these new developments in philosophy do not seek to offer an abstract system, so much as a mode of existence in which each individual pursues his own quest for philosophic understanding—a quest which will never come to an end. Of course in this, as many, including Burtt, are aware, the new movements in philosophy are closer to Eastern thought than the pragmatic, analytical thought traditions of the West.[50]

There is much more to say about the emerging new disciplines of thought in these spheres: other books to be invoked, for example, are Dr Roger Poole's *Towards Deep Subjectivity*[51] and Theodore Roszak's *Where the Waste Land Ends*.[52] Here I would like, in conclusion, to return to the problem of 'models' that are entrenched in our culture and opinion at large. How can we bring the scientists involved in dispute about the question 'What is it to be human?' into touch with the philosophical revolution? The urgency of this task is perhaps

[49]   E.A. Burtt, *In Search of Philosophic Understanding*, Allen and Unwin, 1967, p. xiv.
[50]   See also E.W.F. Tomlin, *Knowing and Being*, Faber, 1958.
[51]   Roger Poole, *Towards Deep Subjectivity*, Allen Lane, 1976.
[52]   Theodore Roszak, *Where the Waste Land Ends*, Faber, 1972.

clearly indicated by reading Dr Richard Leakey's *Origins*. It is an important book, because in it Leakey reveals the inadequacies of the 'scientific' view of man offered by such popular writers as Robert Ardrey, Desmond Morris and even Konrad Lorenz. There have, of course, been previous replies to the 'naked ape' myth, for example, *Naked Ape—or Homo Sapiens?* by Dr Bernard Towers and Professor John Lewis.[53] These authors accused Desmond Morris of being scientifically inaccurate in many ways. But Dr Leakey and his co-author base their rejection of the 'naked ape' myth on many years' study of the extremely ancient remains of hominids in the cradle of man's existence, Africa. What they find, briefly, is that there is no evidence in these remains that man is basically aggressive or brutal, by genetic endowment or instinct. On the contrary, every indication is that man evolved to his higher state because he is 'co-operation man'. The crushed skulls and so forth on which the present myths have been constructed came to be that way because of natural causes, the collapse of caves, or other phenomena, not by conflict at all.

Lorenz, one of the founders of modern ethology, actually wrote 'There is evidence that the first inventors of pebble tools—the African australopithecines—promptly used their weapons not only to kill game, but fellow members of their own species as well.'[54] The main burden of Lorenz's book was that 'the human species carries with it an inescapable legacy of territoriality and aggression, instincts which must be ventilated lest they spill over in ugly fashion'. In this approach to the nature of man's nature and existence, archeological evidence, says Dr Leakey, was brought to weave and form *'one of the most dangerously persuasive myths of our time: that man is incorrigibly belligerent; that war and violence are in our genes.'* As Leakey says, this view was assimilated with unseemly haste into a popular conventional wisdom—enhanced by the elegant prose of Desmond Morris and the work of Robert Ardrey. It may also be added that much of the impetus behind Desmond Morris's work was supplied by an efficient and enterprising publisher, who clothed the myth in suggestive covers and made *The Naked Ape* and other books part of the cultural barbarism of the time. (Towers and Lewis delineate the processes whereby this false myth was promoted by journalists and

[53]   Bernard Towers and John Lewis, *Naked Ape—or Homo Sapiens?*, Garnstone Press, London, 1969.
[54]   Konrad Lorenz, *On Aggression*. The other relevant works are Desmond Morris, *The Naked Ape*, Cape, London, 1967; Robert Ardrey, *African Genesis*, Collins, London, 1961; Robert Ardrey, *The Territorial Imperative*, Collins, London, 1967. Here the bibliography in Towers and Lewis is most useful.

others to whom the 'ruthless' parable appealed.) Ardrey is more easily disposed of, for his ignorance of science.

Dr Leakey and Roger Lewin reject this conventional 'wisdom' on three grounds. First, no theory of human nature can be so firmly proved. Secondly, much of the 'evidence' used to erect this theory is simply not relevant to human behaviour. Thirdly, such clues as there are from science suggest that man is essentially co-operative. To make these points is not to deny the existence of aggression as a human problem. But, as the authors show in the rest of their book, human nature and behaviour are so complex, that the simplifications of the 'aggression' and 'naked ape' myths are ridiculous. Our nearest relations in the animal world, for example, gorillas and chimpanzees, are non-territorial. And when it comes to human acts like cannibalism, these may be done not for reasons of aggression at all, but actually because of a symbolic need to establish a sense of continuity. In the animal kingdom, the management of conflict is largely through mock battles. But farther along the evolutionary path, carrying out the appropriate avoidance behaviour comes to depend more and more on learning, and in social animals the channel of learning is social education. And, as the pictures of babies at their mother's breasts imply in Leakey's book, an important element in human behaviour is *liebende Wirheit*—'loving communion', a concept that is of course pre-eminent in the new philosophical biology and existentialist philosophy of man.[55]

Aggression is no inbuilt element in the animal kingdom. Human beings are not innately disposed powerfully either to aggression or to peace. In the evolutionary picture, surely, an innate drive for killing individuals of one's own species would soon have wiped that species out. And then Dr Leakey makes an important statement:

> Humans, as we know, did not blunder up an evolutionary blind alley, a fate that innate, unrestrained aggressiveness would undoubtedly have produced.[56]

As I have suggested earlier, Dr Leakey remains very much within the orthodoxy of Darwinian evolutionary theory, and lives with the consequent fallacies. But in declaring that human beings did not blunder up an evolutionary alley he is, whether he recognizes it or not, pointing to order and organizing principles of some kind: the statement is not one which endorses the 'chance and necessity' view,

[55] See Marjorie Grene, *Approaches to a Philosophical Biology.*
[56] Richard Leakey and Roger Lewin, *op. cit.*, p. 213.

the view which Professor Tomlin and Karl Stern reject as insane. But he also by implication rejects the views of Lorenz and Co. as belonging essentially to that impossible view of the origin and nature of life and existence.

This is important, philosophically. As Stern points out, the 'ruthless', mechanistic, 'accident' view of the universe has schizoid characteristics. But so, too, does the 'instinctual aggression' model of man. In the terms of Harry Guntrip's analysis of schizoid attitudes, it seems clear that this model appeals because it gives a false strength to us, in our thinking. To think of ourselves as instinctually powerful, sexy and aggressive, enables us to avoid the deeper existential problems, of our 'emptiness', our weakness and our lack of a sense of meaning. This is why Darwinian 'survival of the fittest' theory has such an appeal, as has even the bleak 'matter in motion' view of the universe, and the 'naked ape' view of man. These myths, strangely enough, even though they imply that we 'don't count' (as Francis Bacon sees us) also involve us in such strong feelings of being ' abandoné' (to use Sartre's term) that we can find black solace for our feelings of emptiness and meaninglessness in desperate gestures, of hate, suicide, despair, or other forms of nihilism. They are a false solace for a sense of loss of meaning, and an escape from the pains and responsibilities of being human.

The pathology of science thus extends right through from the misinterpretation of scientific evidence, to the reliance on 'scientific determinism' in modern art. But as Leakey himself argues, the result is a deep impulse towards irresponsibility and avoidance of the real problems: 'There are many reasons why a youth may "spontaneously" smash a window or attack an old lady, but an inborn drive inherited from our animal origins is certainly not one of them . . . Urban problems will not be solved by pointing to supposed defects in our genes while ignoring real defects in social justice.'[57] 'Those who argue that war is in our genes not only are wrong, but they also *commit the crime of diverting attention from the real causes of war.*'[58]

Dr Leakey's is a deeply stimulating book, and it cannot be fully summarized here. His conclusions are marvellously positive: 'We are essentially cultural animals with the capacity to formulate many kinds of social structures; but a deep-seated biological urge towards co-operation, towards working as a group, provides a basic framework for those structures.'

[57]   *Ibid,* p. 223.
[58]   *Ibid* (my italics).

At the end Dr Leakey reverts to conventional evolutionary theory, and persists in attributing our origins to 'accident'. At the same time, however, he warns us that our future is in our own hands: our predicament cannot, therefore, be determined by any 'natural laws' or 'instincts' but is an aspect of our freedom. 'To have arrived on this earth as the product of biological accident, only to depart through human arrogance, would be the ultimate irony.'[59] This makes a valuable emphasis. But, of course, the problem becomes even more exacting if we see our development not as a mere 'accident' but as the product of a perpetual urge of matter, of the universe, to become conscious of itself. Polanyi points out that we bear the terrible burden of being the only creature to *know*, the sole responsibility for being the possessors of the universe's awareness of itself. It is a terrible responsibility. In the work of Fred Hoyle and Professor Wickramsinghe[60] we have the startling possibility indicated that life molecules came down to earth from outer space and did not 'begin' here, by accident or spontaneous generation. It could be that life is an eternal aspect of the cosmos, for ever and ever seeking a home in which to develop its potentialities, these leading on to higher forms of being, complexity, consciousness and awareness. Consciousness, declares Professor Tomlin, cannot be believed to have come into existence by accident.[61] To examine the dreadful but enthralling problems which now arise, in answer to the question 'What is it to be human?', we now need to marry the humanistic disciplines of a Dr Leakey (who is well aware of the nature of man as *animal symbolicum*)—that is, archaeology, palaeo-anthropology, primatology, anthropology and geology—with the new disciplines of philosophical anthropology—as in the work of those Marjorie Grene interprets for us, in phenomenology, psycho-analysis and the holistic studies of man and his meanings. In this, even poetry has its place, and the analysis of culture on phenomenological lines—that is, by the analysis of the meanings of consciousness. Important subjects of study include time, the 'antepredicative' or 'tacit' elements in knowing and perception, those which are below analytical explicitness, and the 'pull towards the future' to which Husserl pointed by speaking of 'intentionality'.

[59]    *Ibid*, p. 256.
[60]    Chandra Wickramsinghe, 'Where Life Begins?', *New Scientist*, 74, 1048, 21 April 1977; F. Hoyle and N.C. Wickramsinghe, 'Prebiotic Molecules and Interstellar Grain Clumps', *Nature*, 226, 5599, pp. 241-243, 17 March 1977; F. Hoyle and N.C. Wickramsinghe, 'Polysaccharides and Infrared Spectra of Galactic Sources', *Nature*, 268, 5621, pp. 610-612.
[61]    E.W.F. Tomlin, *Heythrop Journal*, July 1977.

Insofar as students of man's nature can escape from an inadequate approach which remains rooted in nineteenth century natural science, in physicalism, and positivism, and dare to encounter the baffling concepts and disciplines to which Marjorie Grene and others are pointing, we may look forward to a new and positive sense of man's role, his creative nature and his achievements, which could certainly have enormous implications for the Arts and Humanities.

# Essay 11

## Fay Zwicky

A twitchy sort of assignment, open invitation to pontificate, to stand revealed as a coy cross between Fromm and Muggeridge, bracingly pessimistic and ultimately tedious. Is it to be a series of cagey notes about identity, self-knowledge, alienation and related problems of humanistic ethics? A didactic P.R. project to hearten and do good? Or the coward's way out, parody? And what's a termite in the woodwork doing with a task usually assigned to pillars of the community?

Taking a deep breath then, I'll start by saying that being human to me means finding out again and again, at deeper and deeper levels, that what I thought I knew and understood I have failed to know or understand. I have learned that success turns to ashes in the mouth and stones in the belly; that some people really hate each other; that some people really hurt each other; that I did not really love those I believed I loved; that there is a price to be paid in full for the illusion called freedom; that real friendships are few; that there are many potentials unrealized; that toads are more often toads than princes; and that there are no miraculous people or events to come to the rescue when despair sets in.

As an over-achiever from way back, being human has come to mean learning to fail with whatever courage can be mustered and whatever grace, trying to escape the contamination of a success-ridden society while retaining hope and a craving for excellence. Setting goals which are free from the taint of society's definition of success while affirming one's capacity to care for and respect others, taking responsibility for one's own actions and developing awareness of their consequences. Fine sentiments, but how tenable in practice?

I can speak only from my own experience, with all the limitations and *hubris* that the professions of teacher and writer imply. I often find myself in conflict between the supposed freedoms of creativity and the constraints of the rational intellect which, taken together, may be said to represent the two chief ingredients of the creative process itself. If it is true that creativity is the outcome of a struggle between spontaneity and form, then I want to look at the possibility of reconciling what are often assumed to be two antithetical forces, and try to assess the relevance this reconciliation may bear on the matter of being 'human'.

For the poet, the struggle lies between the motive of the humanly perfect use of words and that of the aesthetically perfect use of words, seeking a solution in poetry to the problem of how to make words realize the human consciousness and the human consciousness fulfil the words. For the teacher, the conflict lies between the subtle illusion of being able to reclaim the lost, and the simultaneous awareness that your students are often wiser, less lost than you are yourself.

In a time of shaken belief and scepticism, when value-judgments are *verboten*, when experience (emphasizing action) is propounded at the expense of conceptual thought, the teacher turns tentatively to Goethe's aphorism: 'If we take man as he is, we make him worse; if we take him as he ought to be, we help him to become it.' Then the poet speaks out of the existential dichotomy: 'Who are you to suppose that you know what man "ought to be"? What right have you to risk playing God? Can you, an ordinary human being, afford to take such a risk? Are your motives as disinterested as you like to think? Why can't you just accept man (myself) as he is, things as they are, and let it go at that? Only a minority try to live up to ideals. Forget them and look after your own peace of mind instead of worrying about those existential questions which only arouse tensions and make life difficult for everybody.' And strictures about 'negative capability' and the danger to the artist of theoretical and moralistic structures hover disquietingly at the back of the mind.

But, in the typical impasse of those wary of religious constructs but equally unhappy about ethical relativism, I think there must be more to it, but what that 'more' is I'd be pressed to define in words. Viktor Frankl, concentration camp survivor, said 'Existence falters unless it is lived in terms of transcendence towards something beyond itself . . . man is responsible for the fulfilment of the specific meaning of his personal life. But he is also responsible *before* something, or *to* something, be it society, humanity, or his own conscience.' If you don't happen to believe in God, are you to be forever trapped in disunity?

The creative consciousness is always probing the conflict between a man's individual powers and the culture to which he belongs. There is always a battle between these powers and the culture that holds the individual within its confines. It is through the development of awareness of these powers that the human being's dimensions may be enlarged. If the poet is going to have anything of value to say, he is compelled to develop an awareness of the joys and dangers of over-assertive individualism. The poet's gift can then be seen as a force which has to be controlled with caution and humility. Paradoxically, it is a daemonic power by which the poet is more or less passively possessed, a power desirable but also potentially malevolent.

This ambivalence has bearing on what it means to be human because at a time when the margin of freedom is becoming blurred, pushed away from the concept of responsibility, it seems necessary for the artist to start looking at the degree of self-assertion it is permissible to take in a social context, to know the degree of personal freedom proportionate to social responsibility.

How is the poet to reconcile the growth of his individuality with the demands of the society in which he lives? Bertrand Russell, in his *History of Western Philosophy*, said 'Man is not a solitary animal, and so long as social life survives, self-realization cannot be the supreme principle of ethics.' And yet today we are constantly being told that because modern society 'has no future' it is foolish to give thought to anything beyond its immediate needs. Speaking of the need for 'love' and 'meaning', modern therapists seem content to define these merely as the fulfilment of patients' emotional requirements.

It is scarcely fashionable to encourage the subjects to subordinate their needs and interests to those of others, to some cause or concern beyond themselves. 'Love' as self-sacrifice, or 'meaning' as submission to a higher loyalty are dismissed as sublimation—oppressive to personal well-being and injurious to health. The overthrow of inhibition and the relentless celebration of the self are wrapped in the rhetoric of 'authenticity' elevated to the sublime cult of 'awareness'. The prevailing cry is to live for oneself, not for one's predecessors or one's children. And so we lose that valuable sense of historical continuity, the feeling of belonging to a succession of generations originating in the past and moving into the future. Our present remains uncorrected by the main history of human suffering.

The need for commitment, with the possibly tragic renunciation that this way of life dictates, must include relationships with other people. People become human only to the extent to which they become aware of themselves, affirm and assert themselves in relation to others. Self-seeking egotism—the prototype for the romantic protest—is remote from self-realization because it results in the alienation of others and the self. People need each other in order to be themselves, and I believe that those who succeed in realizing the greatest degree of independence and maturity are also those who have the closest relationships with others. When Yeats spoke of 'the terrible gift of immediacy' he knew what he was talking about. For to give freely of personal concerns, doubts, hesitations and despair is to become frighteningly vulnerable, and if, as a writer, your art becomes an instrument of despair, then your reader is also potentially vulnerable.

John Donne knew the tragic link between man and man that affirms the human condition:

> No man is an Iland, intire of it selfe; every man is a peece of the Continent, a part of the Maine; if a Clod bee washed away by the Sea, Europe is the lesse, as well as if a Mannor of thy friends or of theire owne were; any man's death diminishes me, because I am involved in Mankinde; and therefore never send to know for whom the bell tolls; it tolls for thee.

For the artist, this balancing of the tension between awareness of self as individual and as part of society is the most awkward and seemingly insoluble part of life and work.

How can this tension be resolved, if at all? Again, the question of responsibility. For the writer, I believe this involves developing the tragic sense which may serve, through the power to empathize with the sufferings of others, to reveal and warn about latent human cruelty. This power is linked with the preservation and awareness of a sense of evil. If a writer fails to be aware of his own complicity with evil, it's likely that he will also lack the compassion that might mitigate its effects which seems to be the *sine qua non* of what being 'human' means. The development and retention of the tragic view, a resistance to the atrophy of feeling in the face of affliction, and concern for truth through language seem to be measures of responsibility the writer may legitimately take.

What can the teacher do about developing the tragic awareness of experience? When D.H. Lawrence became a school teacher, he first began to experience what he called a 'living contact of men' and all that the phrase implies about pleasure and pain. He drew on this for some of the best of his poems, and I'm going to quote one of these in which Lawrence imaginatively and movingly defines those qualities which I believe to be essential in a teacher: the creative understanding of human nature, and a taste for excellence.

### The Best of School

The blinds are drawn because of the sun,
And the boys and the room in a colourless gloom
Of underwater float: bright ripples run
Across the walls as the blinds are blown
To let the sunlight in; and I,
As I sit on the shores of the class, alone,
Watch the boys in their summer blouses
As they write, their round heads busily bowed:
And one after another rouses
His face to look at me,
To ponder very quietly,
As seeing he does not see.
And then he turns again, with a little, glad
Thrill of his work he turns again from me,
Having found what he wanted, having got what was to be had.

And very sweet it is, while the sunlight waves
In the ripening morning to sit alone with the class
And feel the stream of awakening ripple and pass
From me to the boys, whose brightening souls it laves
For this little hour.

  This morning, sweet it is
To feel the lads' looks light on me,
Then back in a swift, bright flutter to work:
Each one darting away with his
Discovery, like birds that steal and flee
Touch after touch I feel on me
As their eyes glance at me for the grain
Of rigour they taste delightedly.

As tendrils reach out yearningly,
Slowly rotate till they touch the tree
That they cleave unto, and up which they climb
Up to their lives—so they to me.

I feel them cling and cleave to me
As vines going eagerly up; they twine
My life with other leaves, my time
Is hidden in theirs, their thrills are mine.[1]

[1] D.H. Lawrence, 'The Best of School' in *The Complete Poems of D.H. Lawrence,* William Heinemann, 1957.

The first thing that emerges from this poem for me is the similarity of the relationship between the teacher and his pupils to the ideal parent–child relationship. The intuitive sympathy he has with the growing spirits entrusted to him, the unpressured sense of help towards awareness with no strings attached. He is notably unsentimental about his charges. There's an empathic relationship in existence here— nothing impersonal or feelingless, no sense of matter-of-fact application to professional duty. Instead, a feeling of pulsating growth between teacher and pupil, a sense of spontaneity, joy and wonder, a responsiveness to a shared experience. And it is this experience of expressing one's individual identity in an integrated form in communion with others which shapes the teacher's area of responsibility.

Lawrence does not see the boys as extensions of his personality. There seems to be no urge to dominate or to possess. He retains his separate identity as they retain theirs, which is ideally what one would like to see happen in any parent–child relationship. He does not see himself as an infallible source of knowledge. He's not a law-giver or a statement-maker. He speaks of one of the boys as having 'found what he wanted, having got what was to be had.' He sees himself as a source of nourishment, and does not overestimate what there is to be had from him. This allowing of others to draw upon one's resources and capacities is rare, but teaching gives one many opportunities for learning and, at the risk of sounding pious, the human satisfactions gained from the lesson are incalculable.

To see the other person's reality as it exists, regardless of one's own interests, needs and fears is what the teacher aims to do, and nothing is harder to achieve. Because, to be able to do it means to feel very secure oneself, to have emerged from all those illusions of omniscience and omnipotence which one had as a child, and which are retained by most people well into adulthood. How many parents, for instance, experience the child's reaction in terms of his being obedient to *them*, of giving *them* pleasure, of being a credit to *them* and so on, instead of perceiving or even being interested in what the child feels for and by himself?

Similarly, how many teachers are capable of faith in each individual's potentialities as they *are*—not as the teacher feels they *ought* to be? The presence of this faith in the growth of potentiality defines the difference between education and manipulation. And it was Lawrence's intuition of this separateness and uniqueness, and of his own role in the process of growth, nurturer of young tendrils, that emerges so potently. This is part of what might be called the 'creative' aspect of the teacher's life, the intuitive art between adult and child in an area of trust that makes education a living process.

Something else important emerges from the poem, and that is the notion of work as discovery and excitement. Likening his pupils to birds, Lawrence speaks of the way in which they taste the 'grain of rigour' with joy. It is a tough grain, not easily digested—not finely ground pre-cooked pap.

When asked what was the proper end of man, Freud is said to have replied 'Lieben und arbeiten.' To love and to work. This ideal seems to be embodied in Lawrence's poem. The crux of a teacher's life lies in a conflict of a particular kind—the constant grappling with those emotional aspects involving problems of loving, and the intellectual aspects concerned with the setting and keeping of high standards. If this is the case, then it would seem natural that the teacher's first efforts will be aimed at reconciling these elements in himself before he can attempt their reconciliation in his students.

We have come to attach a certain importance to the notion of creativity, and this is seen in the unceasing attention paid to children's painting and poetry, and to the therapeutic uses of art. In some circles 'creative' does heavy duty as a term of universal approval meaning, more or less, 'good'. The word is now so much part of psychological and educational jargon that it covers just about everything from baking a loaf of brown bread to shaping an amiable relationship with one's mate. In other words, 'creativity' has received the imprimatur of the expert's approval. And like so many other virtues, it is as hard to denigrate as to say precisely what it means.

Much of what has been written on 'creativity' relies on the assumption that creative people are open, pliant and unconventional, and that the uncreative are inflexible, authoritarian and line-toeing. I suspect there is something not quite accurate about this assumption, especially since it goes along with the popular notion that the development of the rational critical intellect is in some way hostile to the creative temperament. Such emphasis is placed on the notion of creativity that the critical intellect is unthinkingly equated with the negative and the destructive. In the red corner you have art, creation, life; in the white corner you have criticism, annihilation and death. It is one of our more quirky modern heresies that art has been credited with virtually angelic powers, and word has got round to the consumer that the one thing you must not do when you come up against an angel is wrestle with him.

This is where the grain of rigour comes in, and its presence and my own pleasure in it make me question the idea that more conventional and structured educational practice stunts youthful creative impulses. By retracting the cutting edge that insecurity, competition and frustration may supply, the progressive dream of Utopian educators may come home to roost. For if people become autonomously adjusted to themselves and to each other, it is possible that the very springs of their intellectual and artistic productivity may be subtly suppressed. Happiness, in the sense of survival without pressure, may undermine the kind of effort which excellence demands.

Whether or not my apprehensions are justified, it is paradoxically plain that if educational institutions are more attractive places to be, students will be drawn a little closer to that 'rich emotional life' which is every teacher's wistful dream. And insofar as education systems encourage sympathetic teachers nurturing the creative impulse rather than subjecting their charges to ruthless authoritarian conditioning, one can only support the intent. But this does not preclude the belief that there can be neither true creativity nor true originality without a dedicated and persistent application to rigour, and a secure sense of the difference between what is of high standard and what is not. And here the roles of teacher and writer overlap, for this means specifically being able to distinguish between what is a truly valuable creative achievement and what is merely second- or third-rate in your own work as well as the work of others.

In order to make this kind of distinction you have to be responsive to what a writer is trying to say and why the writer wants to say it. You have to be familiar with all the tools available. And this means keeping a constant check on one's own intellectual and emotional equipment through the use of language and how it works. It means following up the varieties and nuances of meaning to which language has recourse, the connections and inferences, the conventions of the form within which a writer chooses to create, and how all these reflect the ideas and feelings of the writer. It means, in fact, very much what the establishment of personal relationships means—giving time and uncluttered attention to what the other person is saying. The key is language.

Auden said towards the end of his life 'As a poet, there is only one political duty, and that is to defend one's language from corruption. And that is particularly serious now. It's being so quickly corrupted. When it's corrupted, people lose faith in what they hear, and this leads to violence.' When the possibilities for communication break down, the bond between human beings is destroyed; aggression and violence surge. In our time of deep and insecure transition, the first thing to disintegrate is language and this crisis is affecting the arts and the intellect in profoundly troubling ways. When Melville's Billy Budd kills Claggart in a moment of rage and impotence, he has him say 'Could I have used my tongue I would not have struck him . . . I could say it only with a blow.' If language is the product of a deep-rooted web of potentiality for empathy between people, a shared structure, then its disintegration implies a breakdown in the social fabric. We hover at the edge of anarchy, and the craving for this stems from the despair and frustration of being unable either to communicate or love.

Platitude though it is, I see all the arts of language in eclipse to some extent because this is an age that communicates by images— more often than not images of violence. At universities and tertiary institutions generally, we now have a generation of students reared almost entirely within the span of the television era. They were the two-year-olds who saw ten thousand hours of television before they could read a single word. It's scarcely to be wondered at that the art that seems most akin to them is not literature but the film. Or that younger poets now write a kind of fragmented verse which presents carefully chosen images in carelessly chosen words. In our present culture, the book is no longer the pivotal point. It is still very much present and those who predict its demise never explain how we'll cope without it, even in the practical areas. But it surely can no longer be said to be at the centre of things.

If we add to this fact the information explosion, the claustrophobic accumulation of facts, the barrage of stimuli that calls for action, action and more action, it's not really surprising that teachers and writers feel a lack of confidence in their aims and values. In Australia, the poignant need to find a sense of identity seems to expose us perhaps more than elsewhere to the invasion of commercialism and the cold efficiency of the super-managers; and this puts an extra burden of awareness on teachers of the humanities of the commercial realities behind much contemporary culture. Australians don't have much confidence in their own standards. They tend to be cowed by the prestige of visiting 'experts' even though they may harbour reservations in private. And by being so intimidated they are often at the mercy of superficial trends of thought which include crass and disruptive approaches to education and literature. The price we pay for our kind of pragmatic culture is a heavy one. The most obvious form of this panic is our flight from the past: the anxiety to be up-to-date, to be shot of unfashionable ideas, to condemn everything unsatisfactory with the same formula—namely that it is too obsolete for the unimpeded movement towards the destined Utopia.

If we're at the mercy of experts and trendmongers who come and announce the end of the book with passionate conviction, and that everything should be handed over to film and television, we're in a very weak position as educators in the fullest sense of the word. For what happens to a society which doesn't want past work to survive? If the past isn't available, there's nothing against which we can measure the present, and all standards topple down the drain of contemporary 'relevance'.

The move to analyze trends, the scramble to get away from the texts which stand still and pursue the shooting stars of where-it's-at, is disquieting because it shows a readiness to abandon the search for standards. The person who recalls our attention to an important work is helping to stabilize our minds. The person who foretells the intellectual vogue of the week after next is assisting in their unsettlement.

And this is symptomatic of a deeper malaise—decisionlessness. Unless the human being is prepared to make decisions, even though they are not always right, personal power remains aimless and the social ethic unstable. According to Martin Buber, the inability to make decisions can be regarded as evil: 'Evil is the aimless whirl of human potentialities without which nothing can be achieved and by which, if they take no direction but remain trapped in themselves, everything goes awry.' In this sense, the mature human beings are those who make decisions that give purposeful direction to their potentialities and, within realistic limitations, take responsibility for their destiny rather than remaining at the mercy of 'fate' or 'what is happening out there'.

The unsettlement of minds is seen as something positive by those to whom the past is merely a dead weight, and tradition an obstructive nuisance. Like Huckleberry Finn with his 'I don't take no stock in dead people', the Australian does not see the future as emerging from the past, but as something shaped from the material of the present by an act of will which cannot function till it has been liberated from the past.

It's quite common to meet students, and young people generally, often remarkably lively and perceptive, who genuinely feel that the present age is so different from anything that went before that all the bridges have been dynamited, and that nothing of value can be handed down from the past. To these people, their own country a hundred years ago is a place more sterile, enigmatic and inhospitable than the Moon. As long as this view prevails, I fear that language, a literate populace and humanist values will stay out in the cold.

With the decline of language goes the death of conceptual thought without which there can be no communication between men. Konrad Lorenz said 'Culture can die even though men survive, and that's what threatens us today, because the growth, the expansion, of this immense body of cumulative knowledge requires brains, books and traditions. Culture is not something that soars over men's heads. It is man himself . . . Traditional languages take thousands of years to evolve. Language can be lost in a few generations. In our own day it is already becoming impoverished, and, as a result, so is the faculty for logical expression.'

If we're going to look at the question of present literacy, we have to cast about for a range, however minimal, of shared recognitions and values without which there can be neither a unified society nor the continuation of a 'lived' culture. And this is where I believe the teacher's responsibility comes in. When the spoken word becomes a mere sound, an unintelligible buzz, then not only does the ear go numb but also the mind and the heart.

If the skills of communication decline to the point where language does almost the opposite of that for which it was forged, words will cut off and isolate to cause more misunderstandings than they prevent. If the sin of the oversimplifier is to elevate the trivial, the sin of the overcomplicator is to squelch the magnificent or just pretend it isn't there. In the vocabulary of the 1970s there is an abundant language for fanaticism, but not much for ordinary quiet conviction. And there are almost no words left to express the concerns of honour, duty or piety.

All of us—from the admen with their doggerel to the tin-eared academics with their jargon—are victims as well as victimizers of the language we have inherited. It is the teacher's first concern, if he is to achieve that intuitive art, that area of trust between himself and his pupils, to try to assess the way in which words may be repaired, put back into shape, restored to accuracy and eloquence and made faithful again to the decrees of the mind and the heart.

The only source of optimism as far as I can see is the logic of necessity. No matter how casually or perversely we abuse language, we simply cannot live without it. People cannot survive on snorts and expletives. We crave definition of identity, and we cannot begin to understand what our lives mean until we have found words to define our bewilderment. Only by the most scrupulous attention to the tools of language can the teacher and writer hope to reconcile those emotional and intellectual complexities of communication that make the kind of creative comprehension one ideally posits as the goal of both professions.

We are taught to define our lives not by our debts and legacies but by our rights and opportunities. I have an idea that the order will have to be reversed. There is a whole way of being at home in the world that is best captured by the word 'reverence', which defines life by its debts—one is what one owes, what one acknowledges as a rightful debt or obligation, the taking of responsibility for others. And when Lawrence wrote of his students 'I feel them cling and cleave to me, As vines going eagerly up', he was saying something about the obligations as a teacher that go far beyond those professional duties laid down in the handbooks. He was talking about the passing on of human values, helping young people to shape and control for themselves the confusions and upheavals of their own development. And, having fallen systematically into all the traps outlined in the opening paragraph of this essay, this is as close as I can get to a definition of what being human means.

# Essay 12

## H.J. McCloskey*

**Summary**

1. In an introductory discussion the value attached to human existence by contrast with other animal and vegetable existence is noted. The questions are raised as to why this value is ascribed to human existence.

2. Biological and philosophical accounts of what it is to be human are noted and examined.

3. The concept of a perfect human being is examined in the light of descriptions and evaluations of certain human beings as imperfect human beings. The questions are raised as to whether the concept is a coherent one and, if so, how it is to be filled out; and if not a coherent one, what is the contrast with which we are operating when we speak of imbeciles, deformed persons, dwarfs and the like, as imperfect human beings.

4. The concept of a person is noted and contrasted with that of a human being. Persons do not constitute a natural species as do human beings. Much of the ascription of value to human beings is seen on analysis to be the ascription of value to them *qua* persons. However, value is also commonly attributed to human existence and to human self-development as such.

5. The value of humanness and of human self-development is examined. In particular, the question is raised as to whether the

* I am greatly indebted to Fr M. B. Ahern and Dr Robert Young for various critical and constructive comments concerning a draft of this paper.

221

content of morality is determined by the nature of human beings as such and, if not, what the nature of the connection is between what is good, admirable, right, obligatory, and human nature and human development.

6. Finally, it is argued that what is morally important and admirable in human self-development relates to man as a human person, this including reference to his humanity, but not to man simply as an animal. Certain avenues of self-development are open to man as a person which would not be open to non-human persons. These may have value but only as developments of the human person or for the intrinsic goods they bring into being, intrinsic goods such as pleasure, happiness, beauty, aesthetic excellence.

**Introductory**

To be human is to be something other than a god, a spirit, an animal, a plant or a mere physical object. To be a human being is to be a material, physical being but, notwithstanding what materialists have maintained, it is to be something more than a mere physical thing. It is to be an animal, but a special kind of animal, namely a rational animal. The rationality of the human being marks the human being off from other existing animals and, at the same time, shapes and modifies the human being's animal nature and determines how it is to be perfected. Man's mastery over other animals, his domestication of certain animals, has been achieved not by virtue of superior numbers nor through the possession of greater physical strength, but through his reason. If man is not the only rational animal—whether or not he is seen to be such depends on how much is written into the concept of rationality—he is, at least as far as can at present be determined, the most rational of all existing animals. On the other hand, to be human is to be less than divine, even though many thinkers have seen in man's possession of reason an element of the divine. Man is imperfect in very many respects: his rationality is very limited, his body is highly vulnerable and he is subject to deterioration and death through aging.

The view that to be human is to be something that is good, desirable, admirable and superior to being a mere animal, plant, thing, although something less than a god, is deeply ingrained in our thinking, being embodied in our language with the expressions, idioms, analogies which it contains. Thus, in spite of the persistent attempts of many theorists over the ages to portray man as essentially depraved, brutish, evil, as essentially a brutish animal, that is, to debunk him, the view that has persisted as the dominant view in our civilization is that embodied in our language: that, to be human is to be something good, superior, desirable, admirable, worthwhile. Thus we find that the word 'human' and words based on it, words such as 'humane', 'humanitarian', 'humanize', 'humanity', 'humanist' and the like, are pro-words. We wish to be seen to be humane men, humanitarians, men possessed of humanity, men who seek to humanize those in need of being humanized. It is true that, like words such as liberty and democracy, humanist is a word which has been appropriated even by those who reject ethical theories of the kinds originally called humanist. Thus we encounter talk of 'new humanism', 'real humanism' and the like, because the label 'humanist' is seen as one that is worth coveting, worth appropriating. By contrast, with some few exceptions and exceptional uses, words relating to animals are commonly con–words when they are applied to human beings and to human behaviour. Thus to be an animal, a beast, a brute, is to be something that it is undesirable that any man should be, it is to be a bad man, and this because animals, beasts, brutes are generally seen to be lesser, inferior kinds of beings. We use specific animal names, such as dog, mongrel, fox, rabbit, snake, slug, wolf, jackal and many others, as epithets of disparagement, usually relating a characteristic of the animal to the person to which the word is applied. Bird names are also commonly used as terms of derogation, such that to be described as a jackass, a peacock, a hen, a galah, a pigeon, a vulture, a crow or the like, is to be insulted or disparaged as one who is not what a man or woman ought to be. (It is relevant here that women having graduated from being crows to broads have come more recently to be referred to as birds, a usage which is both derogatory and patronizing, which it would not be if birds were as highly valued as human beings.) In a similar way, existence as a human being is seen to be much more valuable and worthwhile than existence as a member of the vegetable kingdom. We view with dread and horror the possibility of ourselves or any other human being becoming like a mere vegetable, a 'human cabbage' or such like. This is seen to be a mere step away from becoming a mere thing; and as perhaps worse than becoming a thing, for to become a mere physical object is to die, to become a corpse. When human beings die and become mere things we commonly, although not always, mourn and regret the loss of a valued existence; when a human being comes to have a vegetable-like existence, many of us see it as something worse than death. In general, we attach a very high value and a special kind of value to human existence, by contrast with the value attached to mere things, even valuable things such as computers, machines, jewels and beautiful objects. We sometimes seek to indicate the distinctive character of this value by calling it worth, although this is not the most apt characterization —worth relating more obviously to moral worth.

It is also, of course, true that we sometimes praise persons by reference to animals and animal traits. Thus we speak of some human beings as being as brave as a lion, as loyal and faithful as a dog, as clever as a monkey, and so on. However, when we so speak, we commonly are anthropomorphizing. Certainly, we seem not to be valuing animal existence as such, as something to be copied *in toto* by human beings. By contrast, like parents of young children, animal lovers rejoice in discovering new human traits in those they love, the power of speech and communication, a sense of humour, affection, gratitude, loyalty, and most of all, rationality in any of its other forms. The more human-like an animal such as a dog, cat, ape, dolphin, horse, is seen to be, the more it is valued, in this sense of value. (The horse, bull or dog may be valued in terms of hundreds of thousands of dollars even if not at all human-like, but this is to be valued and valuable in a different sense of value.) Paralleling this, those human beings, especially human infants, who lack specific human capacities, traits or organs, or who are more akin to non-human animals than are naturally formed and gifted human beings are commonly less valued. Regret is felt at their lack of natural human qualities, and sympathy is generally felt for them and those on whom they are dependent.

Probably few persons would wish to dispute these observations about how we human beings value human existence *vis-a-vis* divine, mere animal, vegetable, and mere physical, material existence. However, many would wish to examine our grounds for so valuing human existence as a very superior kind of existence, and to question whether we are justified in so valuing it. Here it might well be asked whether it is the case—as some theistic moral philosophers and, more recently, some ecological ethicists have argued—that our commonly accepted value judgments rest on an uncritical acceptance of a human-centred ethic; that we value what is human not because human existence really is intrinsically valuable and more valuable than all except divine existence, existence as a god, but simply because it is human; that ape-beings would value ape-existence, pigeons pigeon existence, and so on. Is there really something important and valuable about human existence, about being a human being, as distinct from being another kind of animal, or a mere plant or simply an inanimate thing?

These questions can best be answered by examining more fully what it is to be a human being.

## What it is to be human

The biologist explains human beings (man) as belonging to the subphylum Vertebrata, the class Mammalia, the order Primates, the suborder Anthropoidea, the family Hominidae, and genus *Homo* and the species *Homo sapiens*. This is not particularly illuminating to the non-biologist. More illuminating is the statement given by L. A. Borradaile. Borradaile writes:

> Man is related to a group of tailless, half-erect monkeys which includes the gibbons, chimpanzee, gorilla, and orang-utan. From these he differs far more strikingly by his mental attributes than by his physical features, but the following points are of interest. Man walks perfectly upright. His legs are longer than those of the great apes, and the great toe is not opposable. He is less hairy. He has a better command over his voice. His brain is twice the size of the gorilla, which in this respect approaches him most nearly, and his cerebral convolutions are more complex than those of the great apes. The cranial part of his skull is correspondingly enlarged. When the face looks forwards, the foramen magnum opens downwards, instead of more or less backwards, as in most other mammals. The dental formula is $\frac{2, 1, 2, 3}{2, 1, 2, 3}$ which is that of the great apes, but the small size of the canines and the absence of a gap between them and the incisors are peculiar to man. The chin and the projection of the nasal bones to support the nose are also human features.
>
> The essential facts of human morphology may be summed up as follows: Man is metazoan, triploblastic, chordate, vertebrate, pentadactyle, mammalian, eutherian primate.[1]

Whilst some biologists might quarrel with details—or rather with the way the facts are reported by Borradaile, for example J. Lewis and B. Towers have recently noted in *Naked Ape or Homo Sapiens?* that man 'has a larger number of hairs per unit area than do other primates or indeed mammals generally'[2]—few would wish to question the substantial points made by Borradaile. This then is man as seen by the biologist. Yet such an account does little to explain the basis of the value attributed to being human by human beings, other than by pointing to man's brain development and, by implication, to his likely greater rationality by contrast with that of other animals. What is important about such an account, for the purposes of this paper, is that it suggests that human beings constitute a distinct natural sort or kind, a sort that is clearly separable and distinct from other natural sorts.

[1]  *A Manual of Elementary Zoology*, O.U.P., Oxford, 1928, 6th edition, pp. 519–520.
[2]  *Naked Ape or Homo Sapiens?*, Garnstone Press, London, 1969, p. 36.

There has been a great deal of discussion between nominalists and realists concerning whether there are fixed, immutable species; whether or not the theory of evolution tells against the view that what exists is cut off sharply into distinct species. I suggest that for the purposes of this paper it is unnecessary to probe these issues, as what is important now, as things stand at present, is that human beings as a group can clearly be marked off from other species. (It is also evidently the case that other classifications in which the species *Homo sapiens* does not figure are possible.) If a species were to develop that resembled human beings in most although not all these attributes, we should have greater difficulty in marking off human beings from non-humans; and we may even find it more illuminating and useful to develop new concepts and classificatory systems to replace the concepts and classificatory systems in terms of which we speak of human beings, of man. However, at the present time, given the attributes of man and of other beings, man is distinct from other species and no serious problems of classification arise. We can readily identify who is a human being biologically either in terms of the physical attributes noted above, or in terms of chromosomes, or in terms of both. The problem of whether there are real essences, real, unchanging, permanent, sharply cut-off natural kinds, is therefore one which need not concern us, philosophically interesting though this question may be in its own right. The biologist can successfully and clearly mark off for us the human from the non-human animals.

Yet, when we successfully identify an animal as a human being, using the biologist's criteria, we have gained very little knowledge concerning the nature of the human animal by reference to which we can base and explain the widely accepted valuation of human existence. We gain that knowledge by determining what attributes are associated with these biological attributes. It is with the concept of man, of a human being, with which the ordinary person and not the biologist operates that we are concerned. The biologist points to the physical characteristics of man. The ordinary person, like the philosopher of man, is concerned with other, seemingly more basic, less tangible, less directly observable properties of man.

**Man as a rational animal**   From the time of Plato and Aristotle, a vast number of philosophers have sought to base their philosophies of man on the perception that man is a rational animal, that his good consists in his perfection as such, the good man, he who is good as man, being he who is excellent or perfected as a rational, human animal. Even philosophers such as J.S. Mill who explicitly reject an approach to ethics in terms of a consideration of human nature and of what is necessary to perfect it, and who seek instead to defend other seemingly opposed ethical theories (such as utilitarianism in its various forms), see the admirable man as being the man who develops his potentialities, where his potentialities rest in his rational, animal nature. It would therefore seem *prima facie* at least important that we determine what man is.

Is man a rational animal? Does the claim that man is a rational animal involve an acceptance of a view about real natures and real essences?

Clearly, many who have advanced this account of man have believed in the existence of real essences. However, contrary to commonly made claims, such philosophers need not have committed themselves to the distinct view that all biological men are rational animals. The natural, paradigm man was seen to be a rational animal. Those who were not were seen not to be perfect as men. This is one way, and a plausible way, of accommodating all the biological species of man under the definition of man as a rational animal. It would seem to be a much more satisfactory mode of argument than that adopted by other philosophers who have modified the concept of rational, and contended that all biological men, mental defectives of all kinds, those with undeveloped and damaged brains, are really rational, because potentially rational in rather curious senses of rational and potentially. All that need be claimed by one who advances this definition as a definition is that what distinguishes a being as a human being, as a man, what makes him to be such, is that he is a rational animal, where the kind of animal he is, his physical animal attributes, are those noted by the biologist. Provided that this claim is tidied up and filled out along these lines, and provided that it is clearly understood that this is what is being claimed—that is, that the paradigm man is one who is this kind of rational animal—little exception can be taken to the claim, even though it is true that more needs to be said by elucidating what is meant by rational.

Rationality covers a wide range of activities and capacities: the capacity to conceptualize, to engage in inferences, to enter into creative imaginative activities, to experience feelings and emotions in certain ways as appropriate responses to the experience of certain kinds of things, to choose, prefer, decide, determine one's actions, accept or reject ends or goals of actions, to make and act on the basis of moral judgments, and the like. Thus rationality admits of degrees. Those who are rational may be rational in some and only some of these ways. Some non-human animals are clearly rational in some of these ways; some to a degree may be rational in all these ways. Thus, when it is claimed that man is a rational animal, it is being claimed that man, paradigm man, is rational in all these ways, although not necessarily perfectly so but markedly more so than any other animal. That man need not be the only rational animal—that he is such is simply a contingent, not a necessary truth—means that the much neglected second part of the definition is equally important with the first part. Man is a rational animal, but he is also a specific kind of animal. A rational ass, a rational parrot or a rational dolphin would not be human beings, men. Inquiries into whether or not dolphins are rational animals are not inquiries into whether dolphins are human beings.

Man is a unique kind of animal. Philosophers from time immemorial have sought to mark off precisely what kind of animal man is, in terms of strange definitions such as: 'Man is a featherless biped'; 'Man is the only animal that laughs'; 'Man is a/the naked ape'. Clearly, such definitions will not do. What is required is the full biologist's definition of the detailed kind given by Borradaile. Other rational, featherless, laughing, naked, two-legged animals need not be men. If and in so far as morality involves perfection of human nature, to that extent it is ethically important to determine precisely what man's animal nature is, and what is required for its perfection. Different perfections, different excellences relate to different animal natures. Thus skills in flying are excellences of birds; physical development of man's body as the kind of body it is—the acquisition of skills in walking, running, climbing, jumping and the like—are excellences of man. The same skills in other animals, such as horses, emus, elephants, fleas, gorillas, fish, need not be excellences for them, and this because their animal natures and constitutions are different from those of men. Thus if dolphins prove to be rational animals, the perfected rational animal, the dolphin, would be possessed of very different excellences—excellences in swimming, jumping out of water and the like—that the rational animal, man, when fully developed, would not possess.

Thus, to be a human being is to be a certain, specific kind of rational animal, with a certain kind of body, possessed of certain specific potentialities. An imperfect human being will possess these attributes —some or all—imperfectly or not at all. What of the perfect human being? Must the perfect human being possess all human excellences, potentially or actually?

### The concept of the perfect human being

Although we speak in a very facile way of beings who are imperfect as human beings—for example, of those who are born seriously mentally or physically impaired—there are problems in developing a concept of a perfect human being if we seek to specify in any detail what the mental and physical attributes of such a human being are. The difficulties here are reflected in difficulties concerning what count as imperfections. To be born without arms and legs or with an undeveloped or damaged brain is to be an imperfect human being. So, too, in respect of faculties such as lack of sight, hearing, taste, etc. A human being who is a perfectly proportioned man except that he is only 65 cm tall is deemed to be an imperfect human being. Yet when we approach the question positively and consider what are the attributes of a perfect human being, we are less confident, and clear answers elude us. Is the perfect human being 1.8, 2 or 2.1 metres tall? Does the perfect human being have the capacities of the best Olympians? Can all these different capacities physically be combined? Intellectually, is the perfect human being one who is possessed of the highest intelligence, the greatest creative, imaginative genius in music, mathematics, philosophy, all the sciences and all the crafts, of which human beings are capable? Or is a man a perfect human being if he simply lacks all defects and imperfections? If so, how do we determine what are defects and imperfections other than by reference to a concept of an ideal, perfect human being? Historically, the perfect physical human being has been seen to be one who, within certain physical sizes and with no limits of colour of skin, eyes or hair other perhaps than that he not be albino, is perfectly proportioned, where aesthetic criteria have been employed in determining what are perfect proportions. Those who fall outside the size-range may be seen to be perfect dwarfs or perfect giants but not as perfect human beings. There is even less determinableness in respect of intellectual attributes. With many other things—perfect tomatoes, horses, steers—we use economic, utilitarian, aesthetic criteria to fill out the concept. This is not what is sought by those who seek to fill out a concept of a perfect human being. I suggest that the reasonable conclusion to draw here is either that the concept is not a coherent one, or that it is a poly-concept, a grouping of overlapping concepts from which we select what is appropriate to our purposes. If I am right in this, then the important practical conclusion to be drawn is that when developing theories about self-perfection of human beings, we should look not only or mainly to some abstract conception of human perfection but also to perfection of specific human natures, perfection of particular human beings. Even here, as we shall see, there is a large area of indeterminacy as to what constitutes perfection of the nature.

A perfect X need not be something that is perfect or excellent in general. This would be as true of human beings if we could fill out the concept of a perfect human being as it is elsewhere; a perfect human animal need not be a perfect animal, nor need it be perfect or excellent unqualified. Thus, if we accept the theory of evolution, it is reasonable to believe that other higher, superior animals, superior to man, will evolve. Their animal natures may be superior or inferior to the nature of man as an animal. Their superiority may be because of their possession of greater rationality than man. Whatever be the basis of their superiority, it is clear that their perfections will differ from the perfections of man. Thus if it were to be found that dolphins are highly rational, moral animals, it may become reasonable to believe that a super-dolphin-type rational animal may evolve which surpasses man in excellence and whose nature when self-perfected surpasses that of man's self-perfection. Whether or not the superior animal that develops be a dolphin- or ape-type animal, it is clear from the limitations inherent in man's rational as well as in his animal nature, that a superior being is a possibility. Man's reason is limited; he is highly fallible; his creative capacities are very limited; his feelings get in the way of his intellectual judgments; he has limited control over his desires. An animal that lacked these imperfections would be a superior animal, and not simply in respect of potentiality to survive. What this amounts to is that although human beings are persons, superior persons can be envisaged, such that they need not be human beings. This leads me to look at the concept of a person and to contrast it with that of a human being.

### The concept of a person
A person need not be a biological human being. Persons, logically, may have different kinds of physical bodies, bodies which are organisms and bodies which are inanimate substances. It is arguable that persons may exist as purely spiritual beings, as immortal souls, angels, gods, God. Persons are to be characterized by reference to rationality, actual or potential, rationality which involves at least the capacity for informed choice. A being may be rational in a lesser sense, in the sense of being capable of minimal communication, and hence of some conceptualization and inference; however, unless it were

simply an imperfect instance of a species, of which the more perfect members can reason, communicate and think in an informed way and generally be managers of their own lives, we should not call it a person. Even so, it would not strictly be a person, and in so far as it was accorded the title person it would be an honorary title.[3]

There are some problems in respect of the notions of a perfect person or of being perfect as a person, although fewer problems than with the concepts of perfect human being, perfect as a human being. To be a person all that need be possessed by a being is rationality in the sense of rationality I have indicated. Animality is not essential. A person that is also an animal is not superior *qua* person to one who has, say, a mechanical body. On the other hand, animal traits may impose limitations on a person such that a non-animal person may be a superior kind of person. Thus limitations on a person's freedom of choice which are imposed by desires that are physically based, desires such as uncontrollable hunger and thirst, seem to be imperfections in a person. Here two points need to be made. First, we deem emotional capacity and sympathy to be excellences of persons, all persons. A person who could not feel love, compassion, sympathy, concern for others and the like, would be deemed an imperfect, emotionally stunted person. A full person is capable of experiencing feelings, emotions, is possessed of imaginative creativity in respect of feelings. An unfeeling, and unimaginative, unfeeling person is a lesser person. Desires and emotions are obviously closely linked. Secondly, we can distinguish from the concept of person the more specific concept of a human person. We deem a being a lesser human person if he lacks natural human desires and feelings—where the feelings are specifically human feelings, and desires such as sexual love and desire, courage and fear, self-control and desires in general. A human being who, with aging loses many human physically based desires, becomes a lesser human person but not less of a person.

That it is the human being *qua* person or *qua* human person that we most value will be argued more fully later. Here, to underline the difference between the human being seen *qua* thing or animal and valued as a person, we need only to consider those behaviour modification methods which commend themselves to us as acceptable and those which are not. Hurtful methods such as aversion therapy may be acceptable if they render a human being a full person: shock treatment if a human 'cabbage' becomes a person; whereas leucotomy

---

[3]  For a fuller discussion of the concept of a person, see H. J. McCloskey, 'The Right to Life', *Mind*, LXXXIV, 1975, pp. 403–425.

seems morally outrageous because it so impairs the human being as a person, although perhaps very little as an animal.

## Humanness as valuable

Many philosophers, including myself, have sought to follow Kant in suggesting that the value of human existence, existence as a human being, is to be found in the fact that human beings are persons, human persons. All those human beings that possess worth are persons. To be a good man is to be good as a person because it is man's being a person that is the source of his worth and excellence. Why else does man have such value and worth by contrast with brute beasts?

However, there are difficulties in the way of embracing this view. Ordinary moral thinking very decisively rejects it in some respects and in respect of some implications at least. Even Kant felt the need to acknowledge the moral insight implicit in commonsense morality, that there is moral value in man's development of his specifically human capacities and not simply those he possesses as a person. We accept as being full persons, beings who are imperfect as human beings— persons such as spastics, those born without limbs, those who become paralyzed such as paraplegics and quadraplegics. Such beings need not be imperfect as persons; they are imperfect as human beings and they are significantly less valued as such, so much so that P. Foot bases her opposition to active euthanasia in part on the dangers arising from the widespread nature of this kind of valuation.[4] The person who ascribes all worth and value to persons can consistently attach less value to such modes of existence only in so far as such imperfections are also imperfections of the beings as persons. Typically they are not such. Yet none of us would have any doubt about which mode of existence we should prefer, that as an imperfect human being or that as one without such imperfections, whether or not the imperfections carried over to our persons and whether or not they exposed us to greater pain and suffering.

Very many philosophers, including Kant and Mill, have attached value to human self-development. Yet the philosopher who seeks to derive all values and all duties from the duty to respect persons can attribute value to self-development, mental and physical, only in so far as it relates to the person as a person. Mental, intellectual, moral development is commonly self-development of the person as a person. However, man's physical self-development need not be such. Argument

---

[4]   P. Foot, 'Euthanasia', *Philosophy and Public Affairs*, 8, 1977, pp. 85–112.

would be needed to show that the considerable value so commonly ascribed to man's physical self-development is because of its being seen as part of man's self-development as a person. Physical excellences seem very commonly to be valued and prized by many people for their own sakes and not simply as aspects of the development of the human person as a person. This seems to be how those who advance the self-developed life as the good life or as an element in the good life see man's development of his physical capacities.

This is how our uncritical moral intuitions suggest that value is to be located. However, if we look more closely and critically at the nature of human self-development, where it is not to be valued as development of the person *qua* person, there are evident problems. The very considerable value attached to human self-development throughout the history of moral philosophy and, more especially, in the writings of the political philosophers of liberalism is in need of careful justification and argument that has been notably absent. To explain: Much of the value of the self-development of human beings *qua* human beings, and *qua* specific human beings with particular unique natures, can be explained in terms of intrinsic goods—such as rationality, knowledge, beauty, aesthetic excellence, happiness, pleasure—which are involved in or result from self-development. However, these are values enjoyed by human beings *qua* persons, whereas value is attributed to human self-development as specifically human self-development as distinct from development of the human person. This is most evidently true of human physical self-development. There pleasure, beauty and aesthetic excellence may enter into the common evaluations of physical self-development but they are not the core basis of such evaluations. The problem, then, is whether human self-development really possesses the value that is so commonly attributed to it, even when the value is not to be explained in terms of such intrinsic goods; and, if so, what is the nature and basis of this value. This problem arises both at the species level, in respect of development of human nature, and at the level of specific human beings and the development of specific human natures.

I propose at once to put aside as unsatisfactory one mode of seeking to account for the goodness of human existence and human self-development, namely that based on explaining 'good' as meaning 'good as'. Clearly, it is true that in one important sense of 'good'—that in terms of 'good' meaning 'good as', to be good as a human being—a human being must develop or perfect his human traits. This is a tautological truth, if 'good as' is used as it commonly is, to mean good or excellent of a kind. However, ethically, this would seem not to be a primary nor a central use of 'good'. In terms of such a sense of good, a good X, be it a human being, a dog, a tapeworm, a cancer cell, a torturer, a liar or a forger, need not be good; it need be possessed of no intrinsic value, and could be intrinsically evil. Thus, unless additional argument (additional to the mere reference to the use of 'good' to mean 'good as') is advanced, nothing of importance can be derived from the fact that a fully self-developed man is a good man in the sense of good as a man.

Yet there is a persistence about the belief that to engage in a self-developing life is to do something that has value, and much greater value than to live a life of pleasurable idleness, and further, that in so being self-developing, men will fulfil most or even all their duties.

Attempts to relate human self-development and value range from the radical contention that there is a necessary connection between all that is of value and human nature and human self-development, to the more modest claim that it is simply a coincidence that human self-development is valuable and dictates what is obligatory, with views such as that self-development of man has intrinsic value and/or is part of morality although not the only thing of value, not the whole of morality occurring in between. The latter views involve an acknowledgment that there may be conflicts between the claims of self-development and other goods and duties.

Obviously, very different concepts of self-development, of the development of potentiality into actuality, are involved in these various claims. Some conceptions of self-development are to be explicated in terms of a teleological, purposive unfolding of the potential into the actual, where the purpose is inherent in the actual. Others have seen self-development as consisting in a more literal making of the potential actual. Others again see self-development as consisting in any kind of self-making, any kind at all of the realization of possibilities inherent in our nature. Clearly, not all such kinds of self-developments are equally morally desirable, valuable, equally the source of what is valuable.

**Self-development viewed teleologically**  In terms of this kind of view, to be fully human is to realize the ends or purposes inherent in human nature. This is the account given in the Thomistic theory of natural law. That theory is developed as part of a theistic metaphysic. Without such a background metaphysic, it is hard to see why human nature should be viewed as having inherent purposes or ends which are always and only such that the realization of them is always good (or at least, *prima facie*, intrinsically good). If there were indeed innate, inbuilt purposes, there is no reason why they should always be such as to be valuable, morally good to realize, unless some wholly perfect creator and designer so planned them. (Evolutionary selection would relate only to survival and not necessarily to intrinsic value.) The alternative possibility, that this is a remarkable, contingent fact, could not be accepted without strong evidence that it is so. Thus, in assessing this view we are involved in determining whether there are such inbuilt ends inherent in human nature, whether they are wholly good and, more basically, whether (as some have claimed) they are more than good, being our very standards of goodness.

Against such a view, I suggest that what a superficial examination of human nature suggests to be the case—that our basic desires have ends that are intrinsically neither good nor bad, but which may be instrumentally either good or bad—is confirmed by a closer scrutiny of the facts. Thus the desires for food, drink, for sexual activity, pleasure, to reproduce, like our powers of reason, imagination, may be directed at good or bad ends. Their inbuilt purposes, keeping the human being alive, securing the reproduction of the species or being, acquisition of knowledge, etc., may be good or bad depending on the context and the consequences. Many have argued that there is an innate aggressive drive, that its purpose cannot be wholly good. I am inclined to see aggression as relating to other drives, drives for food, sex, security, rather than as a drive that is *sui generis*. However, whether I am right or whether it is a distinct drive, the same general point holds, namely that it is the end to which such a drive is put, not the drive itself, that is good or bad.

**Self-development viewed non-teleologically as the development of potentiality into actuality**    In one sense, whatever is a possible development for a human being *qua* human being is a human potential. On this view, to say that all development of potentiality into actuality is of value is to say that all that human nature makes possible is valuable. Thus human beings have the capacity to learn to walk, run, jump, learn a language, several languages, to engage in inferences, to predict the future, to plan and organize their lives on the basis of value judgments, and hence to control, check, organize their desires and feelings. Equally, human beings have the capacity to lie, cheat, torture, murder, destroy. Their mental and physical attributes as human beings are involved in both kinds of activities. The former are deemed to be valuable, the latter to be evil. Hence if all are described as self-developments, not all self-development can be judged to be valuable. Yet one is not being less human in engaging in the latter than in the former kinds of activities.

If the concept of self-development is to be justifiably restricted to the former kinds of activities (and yet to escape the difficulties of the teleological theory) some notion of potentiality is needed according to which the former activities can be described as the actualization of potentialities, whilst the latter activities are simply the making real of possibilities, not actualizing potentialities. The relevant concept of potentiality with which we operate here is that of natural development. It is natural for the acorn to develop into an oak, the human egg into a human adult, etc. Even if it comes to be possible to engage in manipulation of acorns and human eggs such that we can cause the acorn to produce an elm, a human egg a fish-like animal, etc., it remains true that the acorn is potentially an oak, the human egg potentially a human being. The sense is that this is the natural mode of development, how they will develop if not subjected to disturbing influences and biologically uncongenial environments. There are obvious problems in the way of spelling out the details of this account of 'potential' and of 'disturbing influences' and 'biologically un-congenial environments', but I suggest that the kind of account offered here is clear enough. It provides a basis for distinguishing a merely possible development from the development that is an actualization of a potentiality without reference to a concept of potentiality which is explicable only in terms of inbuilt purposes or ends of the Thomistic kind.

Let us ignore the problems involved in spelling out and justifying such a concept of the potential, and consider whether, if it proves to be a meaningful, coherent one, it would be true that the self-development of the human being in this sense of self-development, would always be of value, and possibly even be the basis or source of all that is of value.

Such human self-development may be of value either because all development of potential into actual is of value, whether it be of man, mammals, sheep, dogs, cats, etc., (in which case the claim that human development is the source of all value would not stand), or because human development and only development of human potentialities is of value. I suggest we can dismiss without lengthy discussion the former thesis that development of the potentialities of any X into actuality is valuable, whether X be a species, a particular member of a species or a feature of a member of a species. There is no evident reason for attributing value to the development of a hookworm from its egg, of a tumour from its initial cancer cell, of a carbunkle, etc. To prevent an egg of a member of a species developing into an adult seems to be *prima facie* evil, if evil at all, only if the egg is one of a special kind of species. Even then, as is evident from the debate about the morality of abortion, there are problems in claiming even this. To prevent all the eggs of a species—for example, hookworms, malaria, etc.—from developing some or all of their potentialities so that we stunt their developments or even render the species extinct, seems not to be evil, if there is no value in the full development of the species or in the existence of the species, and if the stunted development or extinction of the species involves no suffering or other evils. This would appear to be the case with the species I have mentioned—they being causes of evils, which in themselves possess no intrinsic value. What then is so special about human development, including human self-development?

Much human development in this sense of development has value for its being the development of a person which realizes intrinsic goods such as rationality, knowledge, beauty, aesthetic excellence, happiness, pleasure. However, not all human self-development has value on this account. Consider normal growth from infant to adult. Is there value in the increasing height, emergence of sexual organs and sexual capacities, and the like? Is the development of long-sightedness which comes with age something of value? I suggest that it is when the idea of the development becomes that of self-development that we are most prone to attribute value. This suggests that it is the creative activity of the self, the human person—not simply the development of the human animal—that has value. Whether or not this is so may best be assessed by considering physical development in the human being, and comparing it with similar development in animals.

Physical development of the human body has figured prominently in the ethical writings of many philosophers, from Plato and Aristotle to the present day. Not to realize one's physical potentialities is very commonly seen to be (as in the case of the idle English aristocrat of yesteryear) if not a moral fault at least an imperfection that is perhaps indicative of a moral character flaw. Yet when one reflects on the matter, it is hard to see what this value is, wherein it lies, other than in the aesthetic appeal of skills and movements. We admire a fit and well-developed animal, a cat, dog, tiger, dolphin, horse, but in so far as we attribute value to such development, it is typically aesthetic value. *Qua* development, there seems to be no intrinsic value.

It is human self-development, not simply human development, that is so commonly valued, and this seemingly because the element of rational self-activity introduces various intrinsic goods, including rationality, pleasure, happiness and knowledge into the situation. Where this is not so, no value is evident—for example, as with the physical developments, skills and the like, which involve little or no rationality, that is to say, no real development of the human person as a person and which may even retard or stunt the development of the human person, as with the swimming skills achieved by children who reach Olympic standards.

It is perhaps significant, therefore, that when we talk of valuable self-development of human beings, we so commonly move from talk about the species to talk about particular members of the species and their self-development as human persons. This further allows acknowledgment of the fact that different self-developments of individual human persons have different values according to the intrinsic goods they involve or bring into being, and the development of them as persons that is realized. The self-development of the moron is seen to have less value than the self-development of the genius, both because fewer intrinsic goods are realized and because the development of the person *qua* person is a less valuable one; yet both the moron and the genius may be fully developed as human beings.

Various of these considerations bring out why it is that the whole of morality cannot be derived from or encompassed in the narrow confines of human development. Much human development has no moral significance. Much human self-development also has little or no intrinsic value, whilst other self-developments of the human animal may stunt the development of the human person; other self-developments again are compatible with gross immorality, with the development of rationality and knowledge for use to harm and destroy other human beings, and to derive pleasure and even happiness from the same. Equally, much that is demanded by morality is antithetical to human development, including self-development. Self-sacrifice—of one's life or simply of avenues of possible development—may be, and indeed often is, morally obligatory. It is true that on occasion, and in a deeper sense of self-development, self-sacrifice may be a kind of self-development, as, for example, in the case of maternal self-sacrifice or with some work beyond the call of duty by a dedicated teacher, doctor, researcher; but more commonly, self-sacrifice is contrary to self-development. This is evidently so when a mother sacrifices her interests, her overall development, her life, for her children; when the soldier dies to save his mates; when the passerby goes to the aid of children being swept out to sea and continues his rescue work until he too perishes. Motherhood is only one aspect of the human being who is a mother; her human development demands much more than development simply as a mother. So too with the teacher, doctor, researcher, soldier. Further, self-sacrifice, even the sacrifice of one's life, may be morally obligatory. Similarly, other duties —such as those of fidelity, justice, promotion of good and prevention of evil (including animal pain), respect for persons—are more basic than and distinct from any duty of human beings to be self-developing (even though respect for one's own person does involve self-development of one's own person and of one's humanity in one's person); and all may involve some self-sacrifice in terms of self-development of the human being. In brief: A person who determined his morality solely in terms of what is dictated by his development as a human being, no matter how development is explained—unless it is defined circularly in terms of doing what is morally obligatory—would often act immorally, callously and without honour, integrity, justice or regard for other persons. Similarly, to seek to reduce all valuation to valuation in terms of human self-development and development generally, would be to value what has no value and even what has negative value, and to ignore the value and negative value of much that has no relation to man, things such as natural beauty and animal pain.

## Personness, worth and value

Thus I suggest that what we properly value and admire in respect of human development, apart from those features which result in intrinsic goods such as pleasure or beauty or which have other aesthetic appeal, are certain kinds of guided self-developments, developments of the human person by human persons, rather than simply developments of the human being as the human animal. Spontaneous development, such as the natural growth of the body, teeth, hair, etc., as we have seen, is valued only if it is useful or if it involves the emergence of beauty, rationality or some other evident intrinsic good. It is morally desirable, rationally planned self-development that is of value. Mill was clearly right when he commended human self-development as a good, to liken it and its value to the creative activity involved in the production of art and its value, for in each case it is only good creative activity that is of value. Creative activity such as that involved in planning a cruel murder, or a more efficient method of torture, has no value.

The point of importance to which I now wish to draw attention is that such morally desirable, rational self-development of the human being is development of the human being *qua* human person. This is of significance for a number of reasons. First, whilst it is clear that to be a person and to develop as a person are important to morality —all immorality is a kind of irrationality and abdication of one's personness—yet, for the reasons noted in the previous section, they cannot constitute the whole of morality. We cannot even relate the whole of morality to persons by reference to the duty to respect persons, as is evident from the fact of the moral relevance of pain in animals. Secondly, it is important because it is not simply man's personness that is relevant to his morality; his being a *human* person is also relevant. Certain actions appear to be obligatory or right or admirable because they relate to the nature of human persons as such; man's humanness shapes and determines how the person who is human is to develop himself as a person. Thus, if dolphins prove to be persons, dolphin-person self-developments will involve different things from those which human-person self-developments involve, such that what is deemed right and admirable by way of the self-development of a human-person may be deemed not to be so in respect of the dolphin-person; and *vice versa*. Thus, certain intellectual avenues of self-development of human persons via poetry, music or mathematics may be open to the human person and not to a dolphin person, whilst highly rationally developed water-skills may play an important part in the self-developments of dolphin-persons. My third point relates to the conclusion that should be drawn concerning the value of human existence, of being a human being rather than a member of some other animal species. I suggest that if other animals such as dolphins prove to be full persons, or if some other person–type animals evolve, person–traits would come even more evidently to be valued more than mere human traits, and that this would either force scientists to develop a new classificatory system in which persons became a species, or it would lead the ordinary person to make less use of the conceptual framework provided by the biological scientist and to operate more explicitly and more commonly with the concept of a person as a species concept. When such a new conceptual framework came to be generally adopted as the basic one within society, thinkers would come to discuss not 'What it means to be human', but 'What it means to be a person'.

# Essay 13

## Xavier Herbert

Obviously, the chief difference between the behaviour of humans and of other animals is the human capacity for both those opposites— conscious individualism and deliberate identification with others. Gregarious animals, mammalian at any rate, herd not through sheer instinct but from fear, since the most powerful predators live in comparative solitariness, while the naturally gregarious adapt easily to being alone when taken out of the herd into what might be called the protective custody of Man.

Thus herding is something acquired, learnt. The calf, the kid, the foal, is born into dependance on its dam for succour, and grows into dependance for protection and development to maturity on its brethren. Here identification with others would be largely a simple matter of familiar sensuary perception. Hence the gregarious creature is weakly individualistic, while the solitary feels kinship only under periodic urges of mating and maternity.

Man has the choice of either of the conditions, or both. Of course the choice is intellectual, no matter how muddled it may be and mostly is. Since the rational concept of Being is that oneself is the centre of the Universe (which ceases to be when oneself does), sharp awareness of individuality is necessary for perception of the reality of one's existence—*which is that one is unique in Creation*. But essential to rational existence is acceptance of the premise that all other creatures are similarly unique. Acceptance of this means Identification. Fulsome acceptance means Love.

The capacity to love is peculiarly human, and primarily intellectual. Without doubt, the first law was *Thou shalt not kill thy brother in the Rut.* The Rutting Battle is the periodic expenditure of all animal energy, the very climax of animal existence, its result nothing more or less than the survival of species. But Man, from the time he was able to bring thumb and fingers into opposition and so become the Manipulator who has all but mastered the Earth that spawned him out of chaos, wanted more than survival. He must have that mastery. Hence he must learn to control the impulses for which Nature equipped him solely to meet her own so wondrously subtle yet in finality so muddled ends.

It was a simple thing for sons to overthrow ageing sires in order to father the next generation. What taxed to the limit was the battle royal to determine which son was to succeed, since it is the nature of things that son must excel sire if the species is to survive. Our ancient ancestors, concentrated on serving Man's purpose instead of Nature's, settled the matter with invention of the Sororate—*You take my sister, I'll take yours*—the basis of all primitive systems of wife-allotment.

But what inclined Man to the change? It was the capacity to identify, to love. No matter how weak in its beginnings, it developed as that wonderful trick of manipulation, making survival easier; it released nervous energy for perspicacity beyond the limits of the senses. The young males, fraternizing in the play that eventually would bring them to ferocious vying in the rut and subsequent complete antagonism, perceived that their brethren were like themselves, images of themselves, identicals for whom to feel concern.

Next step in sublimation of wasteful instinctual urges was to spare the Old Man, surely out of developing *kindness* in the first place, but leading to greater intellectual *awareness* as the sire's superior humanness, advanced through his outliving much of the grosser urges of his prime, were put to use to guide otherwise callow youth. Thus was established Patriarchy, and so Coded Law.

So we have another human peculiarity, besides that of the capacity for identification with others: Awareness. Let us call these two things —Kindness and Awareness—Virtues, since a virtue is no mere state of oddity but an excellence, and human excellence only, as the word declares from its root: *Vir*, a man.

There is a third virtue, the paramount one: Courage. But leave it for the moment. I am moved to recall how first I was struck by the idea that the faculty for manipulation is what brought our species down from the trees, and how I impressed it on the most unlikely bunch of pupils, hopefully to the permanent benefit of their humanity.

It was at the end of the Pacific War—1945. I, along with a khaki mob, back from active service, was drafted to a General Details Depot, in Melbourne, for sorting out in the process of demobilization—of necessity a wearying business, because militarism is efficient only in destruction, never reconstruction. As our superiors could not bear to see us idle, especially when we were about to escape from their dominion, between the detailing parades they would find us futile and unpleasant occupations, commonest of which was to wear out still more leather by marching round the outer suburbs. As a sergeant of infantry, invariably was I picked as both victim and victimizer in this form of infliction. Hard enough as it was on the men, many of whom had been footslogging more or less futilely for five years and more, most growing from boyhood into manhood in the process, it was worse for me as one who had grown up to believe that all men are free and equal (which of course they are not under military discipline) but was regarded as another of those worst of military monsters, the men called Tigers—'Animals with a lot of stripes'—Sergeants.

Well, quickly I discovered that I could avoid the misery of aimless exertion and useless bullying by taking my platoons the short distance to the Melbourne Zoo, admittance to which was free for men in uniform. Naturally, the chief attraction was our poor relations in the Monkey House, where I made a success of these excursions from the very start by saying of a huge chimpanzee who greeted us with nasty barking that, given a tunic with three stripes, he would pass for a whole lot of characters we had come to be acquainted with in our campaigning. But I had to do better than that to hold them for the necessary hour or so, else some were likely to sneak off, go into town, get picked up by provosts and lay the blame on me. If not marching them, at least I had to be what was called 'ear-bashing' them.

I got my cue from observing how really stupid the great apes are, for all their seeming human-like cleverness. Sometimes we were there to see the tea-parties put on for the entertainment of visitors, when the creatures, chimpanzees and orang-outangs, appeared to behave with intelligent purpose to begin with, only to break down before long in exhibitions of sheer idiocy which, while it caused the onlookers much amusement, was really pathetic as demonstrating the utter ineptitude of non-humans put to aping humans. I would quote from Nietzsche (to ears deaf to me): 'What is the Ape to Man? A jest, a thing of shame.'

But more revealing was the behaviour at ordinary meals, of fruit and bread and milk. The milk was served in tin quart-pots from which they would drink in the manner of humans, grasping the handle but invariably failing to recognize the fact that there was a limit to the quantity. Having drained the pot, wanting more, they would raise it to lips again, and yet again, sometimes banging the vessel on the floor in what looked like exasperation but more likely was only a reflex of gustatory need. Some would go to the length of looking in the pot, but without realization because they would try to drink again. A paw might be thrust in, and licked when drawn out. In such acts there would be the appearance of concentrated attention, with rumpling of low brows, focussing of vision—but only momentary. Then the eyes would glance round, seeming to see things as a large whole, instead of in inspectionable parts—so different from the analytical staring of humans.

Then there was the manner in which they dealt with the sacking they had for wrapping themselves against the cold. Rugged up, they would take a piece of the stuff and examine momentarily, as if attracted by the warp and weft, but only to give up with a look of profound stupidity—unless there was a tear, when they would proceed to enlarge it, but mostly without looking at what they were doing, staring out at the audience so that one thought of it as an act of dominance display, which is natural to such creatures. Usually they would finish up stuffing it into their mouths.

But most interesting and significant was the manner of manipulation of the sacking. Although they could tear it with ease, they could do so only to a point, using the fingers of the hands, not the thumbs, after which it would be necessary to use the thumbs to gather the material for another go, which of course they were unable to do. Likewise, for all their strength, they seemed unable to start a tear. Observing this, I was reminded of what I had learnt of the purely human faculty for bringing thumb into opposition with fingers and pointed it out to my men, seizing their interest by adding 'At least Sgt Whooziss (naming a particularly nasty staff-sergeant back at G.D.D.) can do better than that—if only tearing paper in the latrine.'

Always I laced my ear-bashing with a lot of droll patter, but perhaps unnecessarily, because out of the several hundred men I dealt with in this way, not one did I find who did not show some interest in what soon I was deliberately preaching, namely the wondrous thing it is to be human, and the great responsibility one has to be as human as possible—humanness being a matter of degree, something added to the gift of being born with the faculty for it, added by oneself in learning the rules of humanity. I would say 'We have all become somewhat cynical about humanity through seeing so little of it of late. It took us all six months to become soldiers, which is to become nearly as stupid as apes. It will take us another six months to become human again. No . . . I take back what I said about become stupid as apes. Even Sgt Whooziss, for all his behaving like a boss ape, is like that only because he was not taught to be truly human. It will take him more like six years to become human . . . if he tries hard. But these poor relations of ours here . . . it would take them all of six hundred millenia . . . six hundred thousand years!'

Now to that third virtue: Courage. It is not peculiarly human, because it is shared by all creatures as equipment for survival. But it is a virtue only in humans, because in the lower animals it is almost entirely reaction to glandular stimulus, while in humans the reflex is more or less intelligently controlled—the more controlled the greater its quality as virtue. It takes far more courage to control an impulse to hit someone than to do the job, to exploit a fellow than to co-operate with him, to assume power than to give equality.

Our courage is no mere capacity to best a predator, a rival, a victim, but to challenge Creation to reveal its secrets so that we may make order out of what seems to our tidy minds chaotic muddle. I have said I believe it was this capacity which caused us to make that first tremendous effort to change prehensile forepaws into tools, by striving for that all-abiding advantage, manipulation. And so we have gone on with the striving, largely against our own animality—until we are so close to the status of demi-gods that it is easy to envisage our venturing forth into the depths of the Universe, to meet that force we cannot help but think of as a Creator, on *our own terms*.

Therefore, to be truly human means to be *aware* of one's uniqueness as an individual. But since our achievements in uniqueness are valueless unless contributing primarily to the progress of our species towards its as yet inconceivable high destiny, we must be *kind*. And to progress we must be for ever *courageous*, since that means constantly to be getting rid of those things which have become safe and cosy and static through familiarity, for ever facing the danger and discomfort of new realities.

So Courage, Kindness, Awareness. We all have to learn them, learning from the cradle to the grave—not by rote, but by intelligent application, always doubting the back-dragging ape in us, but ever trusting that wonder of the Universe as we know it, our Human

Intelligence. It isn't easy to be truly human. It never has been easy. But inevitably each generation becomes more human than the last. Look back in history for the proof. Take a look at the apes to see how far we've come, and take heart for the distance we still have to go.

'What is the Ape to Man? A jest, a thing of shame. So shall man be to Superman.'

# Details of Contributors

**Christian Bay** is a professor of political science in the Department of Political Economy of the University of Toronto. With a degree in law and a Ph.D. in political science from the University of Oslo, he has for the last two decades been teaching in North America: at Michigan State University, the University of California in Berkeley, at Stanford and, before he assumed his present position, at the University of Alberta, where he served for three years as Chairman of the Department of Political Science. He is the author of *The Structure of Freedom* (Stanford, 1958, 1970) and numerous papers in professional journals and contributions to scholarly books; his main concerns have been with the 'great issues' of citizenship, political education, human emancipation and the democratization of professions and universities.

**Hiram Caton** has published articles on a wide variety of subjects and *The Origin of Subjectivity: An Essay on Descartes* (Yale University Press, 1973). His first novel, *The Teacup War*, will be published this year. He is presently writing the first of a three-volume study of modern politics. He is professor of philosophy in a Brisbane university.

**David E. Cooper** was born in 1942, and educated at Oxford University where he lectured in philosophy from 1966 to 1969. Since then he has taught at the Universities of Miami (Florida) and London. He has held Visiting Professorships at the Universities of Minnesota and Khartoum. At present he is Reader in Philosophy at the University of Surrey. His books include *Philosophy and the Nature of Language* (Longman, 1973) and *Knowledge of Language* (Prism, 1975). He has written articles in the areas of linguistics, social anthropology and education, as well as philosophy. Among the journals

247

he has contributed to are *The Philosophical Review, Mind, The Notre Dame Journal of Formal Logic, Man, Foundations of Language* and *Lingua*.

**James Chowning Davies** is a professor of political science at the University of Oregon and has taught at the California Institute of Technology and at the Berkeley and Los Angeles campuses of the University of California. He did his undergraduate work at Oberlin College and his graduate work at the University of California at Berkeley. He has held fellowships from the Social Science Research Council, the Carnegie Corporation and the Rockefeller Foundation. His major interests are in political socialization, development and revolution, as these can be analyzed psychologically. He has developed a theory of revolution, called 'the J-curve', which sees revolution as occurring when, after a period of steady progress, the gap between what people want and what they get widens rapidly. He has also developed a theory relating stages of individual development to stages of political development. His best-known books are *Human Nature in Politics* (John Wiley, New York, 1963) and *When Men Revolt and Why* (Free Press, New York, 1971).

**Ross Fitzgerald**, born in Melbourne in 1944, gained his Ph.D. in political science from the University of New South Wales. Dr Fitzgerald now teaches in the School of Humanities, Griffith University, Brisbane, Australia. His particular scholarly interests lie in contemporary social and political philosophy, and in the relation between politics, philosophy and the creative arts. He is the editor of *Human Needs and Politics* (Pergamon Press, Sydney, 1977) and the author of *The Eyes of Angels* and of a number of other poems and stories.

**Richard Gelwick**, B.A., Southern Methodist University; B.D., Yale University; Th.D., Pacific School of Religion; Post-doctoral studies in biological sciences, Clare Hall, Cambridge University. Head, Religion and Philosophy Department, Stephens College, Columbia, Missouri. Student of the thought of Michael Polanyi; studied with him at Center For Advanced Studies in Behavioral Sciences, Stanford. Special interest in problem of knowledge and modern religious thought. Author of *Collected Articles and Papers of Michael Polanyi, Credere Aude* and most recently *The Way of Discovery* (Oxford University Press, New York, 1977).

**Francis Xavier Herbert**, born 1901, Murchison District, north-western Western Australia. Educated State Schools and Christian Bros, Perth Tech. Coll., Diploma Chem., Dip. Pharmacy. Studied Med. short while, Univ. Melb., meantime took to writing, realizing bent for criticism of Aust. society, particularly with respect to the fundamental anomaly, ill-treatment of Aborigines, which very close to during youth. Returned to remote parts for further study of Aboriginal situation. Worked for time as Protector Aborigines,

Northern Territory. First novel *Capricornia*, published 1938, considered first powerful indictment of national callousness towards Aborigines and means of creating sense of guilt. War intervened to check literary career. Served A.I.F. Pacific Zone. After war embarked on work to be indictment of Australian dishonesty and stupidity generally, to be called *True Commonwealth*, but realized that such a work, of necessity huge, would require extraordinary ability for success, and put himself to learning 'perfect novel construction', without involvement in the local social scene. The job took ten years, the result *Soldiers' Women*, 300,000 words, a study of female psychology, hailed as perfectly constructed, established as a classic. Then as preliminary to getting on with the great work, short stories, an autobiography of youth, a small novel dealing with Aboriginal culture under stress of civilization and alienness of the whiteman in the landscape, *Seven Emus*. At last time for *True Commonwealth*, begun in 1964, finished 1973, as *Poor Fellow My Country*, 820,000 words. Published in 1975, is already established as a classic, '*The* Australian classic', according to *Times Lit. Supplement* review.

Now at 77, declares finished with novel-writing, which he dubs 'Neurotic art, either expressing the author's personal neurosis, as it usually does, or communal neurosis, as in the case of the socially-critical novelist. All neurosis must be got rid of if one is to die sane.' Aspires to ending his days inspiring people to Humanism.

Books. Novels: *Capricornia, Seven Emus, Soldiers' Women, Poor Fellow My Country*. Autobiography: *Disturbing Element*. Short Stories: *Larger Than Life*.

Awards: C'wealth Sesqui-Centenary Lit. Prize., Aust. Lit. Soc. Gold Medal, Miles Franklin Award. Hon. Doctorates: D.Litt. Uni. of Newcastle, D. Litt. Uni. of Queensland.

Writer in Residence, U. of Newcastle 1975, ditto U. of Queensland 1976, Visiting Fellow Creative Writing, James Cook University of North Queensland 1977, Fellowship in Creative Arts, Australian National University, 1978.

**David Holbrook** was born in 1923 in Norwich, England. He was educated at the City of Norwich School and Downing College, Cambridge. He served in the tanks in Europe in the War and afterwards worked in publishing, journalism, adult education and school teaching. He was made a Fellow of King's College, Cambridge for 1961-65 and has since been college lecturer in English at two other Cambridge colleges. He was 'writer in residence' at Dartington Hall in 1971-73 and has received research awards from the Leverhulme Trust and the Arts Council. He spent five months in Australia in 1970 and has also lectured in America. He is now an independent author.

His best known work is *English for the Rejected*, a study of creativity in less able children. His other works on the teaching of English include *English for Maturity* and *The Secret Places. English in Australia Now* appeared in 73. He has published two novels, *Flesh Wounds* and *A Play of Passion*; five volumes of poems, of which the last is *Chance of a Lifetime*. He has also published a large number of books on the psychology of culture, including studies of Gustav Mahler, Sylvia Plath and the philosophical problems behind modern art in *Lost Bearings in English Poetry*. Holbrook is married with four children, mostly grown up. His most recent educational work, *Education, Nihilism and Survival*, has been met with heavy indirect censorship in Britain, nearly all journals refusing to review it.

**H.J. McCloskey** was educated in the University of Melbourne at which he has taken out an M.A., Ph.D. and Litt.D. He is presently a professor of philosophy, La Trobe University, Victoria, Australia. He was born in Melbourne, 1925. He has published four books: *Meta-Ethics and Normative Ethics* (Martinus Nijhoff, The Hague, 1969), *John Stuart Mill: A Critical Study* (Macmillan, London, 1971), *God and Evil* (Martinus Nijhoff, The Hague, 1974), and *Derechos Y Sociedad En La Filosfia Analitica* (translated into Spanish by F. Quintana, no English edition: Universidad de Chile, Santiago, 1976). He has also contributed papers, mainly in the areas of political philosophy, ethics, and philosophy of religion, to collections and to learned journals including: *American Philosophical Quarterly, Australasian Journal of Philosophy, Australian Rationalist, Canadian Journal of Philosophy, Ethics, Indian Journal of Philosophy, Inquiry, Journal of Bible and Religion, Journal of Philosophy, Journal of Value Inquiry, Mind, Philosophical Quarterly, Philosophical Review, Philosophical Studies, Philosophy, Philosophy and Phenomenological Research, Question, Ratio, Rationalist Annual, Review of Metaphysics, Sophia, Southern Journal of Philosophy, Teoria.*

**John O'Neill** is Professor of Sociology at York University, Toronto. He is the author of *Perception, Expression and History* (1970), *Sociology as a Skin Trade* (1972) and *Making Sense Together* (1974). He is the editor of the International Library of Phenomenology and Moral Sciences, published by Routledge and Kegan Paul, and an editor of the quarterly *Philosophy of the Social Sciences*. His next book will be *Essaying Montaigne*, a study of the arts of reading and writing.

**Roger Poole** lectures in English Studies at the University of Nottingham. He is the author of *Towards Deep Subjectivity* (Allen Lane, 1972) and *The Unknown Virgina Woolf* (Cambridge University Press, 1977), a study in the inter-relationship of text and the 'lived body' which represents an integration of philosophical and literary studies. He also wrote the introduction to Claude Lévi-Strauss's *Totemism* (Pelican Books, 1969). A paper on embodiment and text, in the case of Swift, appeared in the Proceedings of the International Congress of Psychoanalysis at Milan (1977), and other studies along these lines are nearing completion. *Indirect Communication*, a study of ethical achievement of the embodied communicator, is under consideration for publication. The theoretical background for this may be found in 'Objective Sign and Subjective Meaning' in *The Body as a Medium of Expression* (Allen Lane, 1975). Since 1975 he has been a member of the Editorial Panel of *New Universities Quarterly*.

**M. Brewster Smith** has been Professor of Psychology at the University of California, Santa Cruz, since 1970 and previously taught at the University of Chicago, Berkeley, New York University, Vassar and Harvard, where he earned the Ph.D. in 1947. He is co-author of *The American Soldier* (with S.A. Stouffler, 1949) and *Opinions and Personality* (with J.S. Bruner and R.W. White, 1956), and author of two collections *Social Psychology and Human Values* (1969) and *Humanizing Social Psychology* (1974). His long-term interests in personality and social psychology have recently taken a more metatheoretical or philosophical direction. In 1978 he is President of the American Psychological Association.

**Fay Zwicky** was born in Melbourne in 1933 and now lives in Perth, Western Australia, with two children. Formerly a concert pianist, she is currently a lecturer in English at the University of Western Australia. Poet, short story writer and critic, she is the author of *Isaac Babel's Fiddle* (Maximus, S.A., 1975) and a frequent contributor to Australian literary journals and anthologies. She has lived and worked in Indonesia, the United States and Europe.